Man's Ultimate Challenge

Being A Man of Virtue in a Culture of Vice

Second Edition

PETER P. LACKEY, JR.

(COL 2:8)

ISBN: 1535283513
ISBN-13: 978-1535283519

Col 2:8

DEDICATION

I want to dedicate this book to my wife Cheryl and our three children Jonah, Sarah and Nathan, who daily endure my shortcomings as I, struggle to break the chains of my own vices on my journey to become the man of virtue both God and my family deserve.

REVIEWS

Pete has resurrected a simple truth; "You can't become a Godly man without becoming a man of virtue." I have worked with young men for the last forty-five years. During that time I prayed for a book that would help define what it means to be a man of virtue. This book goes a long way toward filling that void. Every chapter will cause a thinking man to stop and ask himself, "Is this true of me?" Every man seeking to live a Godly life needs to give it a careful read.

Timothy C. Tatum, EdD
Chaplain (Colonel), US Army Retired

Pete Lackey delivers a powerful and convicting story line of unchanging principles that endure every level of scrutiny. His book interviews the soul and either unsettles our conclusions or affirms lifestyle decisions. This book speaks to us like an interactive GPS coaching us to that destination with our true self--our soul-- and equips us to answer the question: Are we connected or disconnected with God? The journey is narrated with the literary voice of Proverbs-the original sound bites of life- and holds the course perfectly.

Mike Hoyt,
Chaplain (Colonel), US Army Retired

CONTENTS

ACKNOWLEDGMENTS

I would first of all like to thank my Lord and Savior Jesus Christ for radically changing my life over 20 years ago. I honestly have no idea where I would be without Him and the critical guidance of the Holy Bible! Thank you Lord Jesus for renewing my mind (Romans 12:2) and restoring my love for learning. Second, I want to thank my truly amazing wife Cheryl for loving me and constantly sowing belief into my heart with everything I do. Her excitement about this idea when I first dreamed it up and support for my many nights researching and working on my coin designs and writing this book into the wee hours of the morning made all of this possible. Then she lovingly edits this book while enduring the days of me typing, researching, and Summa wrestling with the great mind of Thomas Aquinas on whose shoulders I stand! Thank you Cheryl for your amazing gift of making everyone around you feel special with your many personal touches of grace. Third, I would like to thank my kids Jonah, Sarah, and Nathan for supporting their Dad as I stared at the computer screen researching and writing as I prepared this manuscript.

Thanks to Dr. Tim Tatum, Dave Ramos, Jim Supp and all of the men of McLean Bible Church's First Light community for being the very first men to believe in this project. Thanks to Chaplin Mike Hoyt for taking the time to review this book and provide encouragement and feedback. A Special thanks to Greg Ayers for both discipling and encouraging me as a new Christian. Thanks to MBC Loudoun men who packed out a room for a 10-week series around the book and provided valuable input for this second edition. Thanks to Will Gaines for his thoughts on breaking up the book into bite size chunks and the men of his small group at Park Valley for digging into the book and encouraging me. Thanks to my friend Paul Dillmuth for being a good friend and encouraging me on the impact of the book, it's content, and my passionate teaching style. Finally, I want to thank one of my heroes in the faith Dr. Norman Geisler who has taught me so much about the importance of clear thinking when it comes to thinking about God, life, and defending the Christian Faith. His intellectual and spiritual fortitude to stand up for truth when the cuddly Christians invade the church with compromise inspires me that real men stand up for truth period! Inerrancy is his battleground now, and I join him in the fight for biblical inerrancy and so should you: www.defendinginerrancy.com

.

FORWARD

By design, human beings impact and shape other human beings. More specifically, older human beings imprint younger human beings as the younger move through life. Whether we refer to modeling, mentoring, discipling, training, parenting or even sowing and reaping, the principle of someone further down the path investing in someone who isn't quite as far down the path is evident in all of life.

Unfortunately, due to a lack of clarity about the 'what' and the 'how' in their own lives, most investors fail to be purposeful about what they are investing in those who are not as far along the path. How many times has someone assessed what they 'don't want to be like' regarding their parents, only to observe themselves doing the exact same thing with their own children. Ah, the power of modeling and the lack of purposeful investing.

By God's design, every man is called to embrace the inextricable link between his investment and the growing maturity of those around him – other men and especially his own children. The work of maturity unto Christ likeness is orchestrated and accomplished by God himself, but he has chosen as his primary mechanism the investment of those who are a bit more seasoned. That's you – Dads.

Few men have had a more significant impact on my journey as a man than Pete Lackey. For nearly 18 years Pete has evidenced in deep and practical ways what it means to invest in others – to invest in me. Pete has walked with me through the darkest hours of my life and has been a key instrument in God's hand for shaping, developing and maturing in me. As God has provided children in his home, Pete has taken his years of personal study and experience regarding God's design and has crafted them into a transferrable template for investing. Man's Ultimate Challenge is the result. You are investing something in others whether you know it or not. The challenge for every man is to embrace God's call to invest well in the lives of those around him – especially his children. Man's Ultimate Challenge is a critical resource for your library as you seek to invest well in the lives of those God has entrusted to you.

When you stand before God one day desiring to hear those famous words, "Well done, my good and faithful servant," know that one element of your life that will be assessed is how well you invested in others on their journey toward Christ likeness. May this book be a powerful resource for you as you "lay-up treasure" for yourself in heaven by becoming a proactive investor today.

Reverend Jim Supp

Loudoun Campus Pastor, McLean Bible Church

The Man of Virtue

INTRODUCTION
WHAT IS MAN'S ULTIMATE CHALLENGE?

"There is in us a natural aptitude for virtue" – Aristotle

If you are a man then this book is for you. If you are a man who is considered Silent Generation, Baby Boomer, Generation X, Millennial, or Generation Next then this book is for you! If you would like to pass on what matters most to the next generation, you guessed it, this book is for you. Why? Because the classic virtues, which form the very foundation of biblical masculinity, is weaved into the fabric of every man by the Grand Weaver Himself. The goal of this book is to provide practical, biblical wisdom that you can apply immediately, and pass on meaningfully through discipleship, mentoring, and most importantly, fatherhood.

We are in a battle, a battle for the very identity of what a man looks like in our culture and there is no modern tool available to turn on that internal man switch inside of every man. So what is the result? We have today a culture of boys in the body of men. I know this personally because this certainly was true of me. Think about this question: do you recall a time when your father or another man of significance "flicked the switch" and challenged you to be a man? God gave us body signs during puberty that begins the process of changing our bodies into men; however, there is no spiritual or emotional puberty, a puberty of the soul if you will! We have to be challenged by other men with vision and purpose to make this happen. It has been said that mothers make boys and fathers make men. I believe that this is not only true, but is by design. The primary goal of Man's Ultimate Challenge is to provide a relevant way for fathers, mentors, teachers and coaches to make this happen in the lives of the young men God has placed in their life. Of course, this presupposes that you as a father, mentor, teacher, or coach have embraced this challenge for yourself. This then leads me to chief goal of this book—equipping the equipper, mentoring the mentor, teaching the teacher, and coaching the coach to be men of virtue in a culture of vice. So, grab some other men, and shoulder to shoulder, work together in this process because men are hungering for it, and young men desperately need it.

Man's Ultimate Challenge is a practical real life application instrument like no other in that it is a book and workbook in one. No need to buy yet another book. This book is designed for personal reflection, immediate application, and geared toward discipleship, mentoring, self-study, and most certainly small group study. Immediately after a thought is introduced conceptually and visually, there is a reflective question geared to personalize the truth as you place your own thoughts, notes, reflections, and life application goals. I highly recommend that you do this study together with other men. If you are reading it for the first time by yourself then do it again with a group of men. This is moving from mere knowledge to understanding then eventually wisdom as I will demonstrate in the chapter on being a man of prudence not carelessness. Study the book, don't just read it! Taking in information once is never enough for a man who is serious about learning and growth. In short, the purpose of this book is to equip men to heed the Bible's specific call for us to man-up and live with purpose:

1 Corinthians 16:13-14 – [13]Be on the alert, stand firm in the faith, **act like men**, be strong. [14]Let all that you do be done in love.

I do not say this lightly, but God gave me this idea for the Man's Ultimate Challenge a few weeks before Christmas in 2011 when I had a desire to do a rite-of-passage ceremony for my soon-to-be 13-year-old son. I had been thinking about what I would do to mark this important transition into manhood ever since I participated in a rite-of-passage ceremony that my friend and coworker in Christ Mark Hernandez had for his son. I had never experienced anything like it myself and, like the other men who participated, I got emotional when it was my turn to speak to his son. What a great idea I thought to myself. Why doesn't our culture have anything like this? (see appendix D for my ready-made tool for fathers/mentors)

This book is meant to challenge men to:

1. be men of **Fortitude** and not **Fear**

2. be men of **Prudence** and not **Carelessness**

3. be men of **Temperance** and not **Gluttony**

4. be men of **Justice** and not **Injustice**

5. be men of **Faith** and not **Uncertainty**

6. be men of **Hope** and not **Despair**

7. be men of **Charity** and not **Indifference**

These virtues sit at the core of a man and give a man a meaningful target to shoot at! I want to place a powerful tool in the hands of men who are sick of the sin management approach to their walk with Christ and replace it with a hope filled call to live a virtue-driven life in Christ. I know men want to have Christ impact their lives in a meaningful way and then pass it on by making a significant difference in the lives of other men.

Book Guide For Individual, Discipleship, or Small Group Study

I am an equipper at heart; so my job is to have you dig in as you read this book so that you come away learning things about God and yourself no matter where you are on your journey. Please take

3

note of the footnotes where I will provide additional historical and theological information throughout this book; you will be glad you did. Within each chapter you will find questions that provide an opportunity to personally reflect on what you just learned. At times there will be spaces to put notes as I send you off to do some research on websites of para-church ministries and interact with the text through questions. Each of these places provide some great small group opportunities to dig deeper with other men for a rich learning experience as each man shares how to apply what he just learned. Don't make the mistake of making this another *informational* study when it is designed to be a *transformational* study.

When using this book for discipleship or small group study, follow the mile markers that break down the book into bite-sized chunks. There is a lot of information in this book that is focused around helping men to transform from the inside out. When discipling men with the first edition of the book, to include my son, I found myself breaking the book down into smaller sections to ensure the concepts were understood and transferred into action. Additionally, I discovered men doing the same thing when using the book in small groups, so I decided to provide these mile markers as helpful markers of where to start and stop on your journey. I believe that you will get more out of the book if you use these mile markers as places to stop and reflect on what you just learned.

Man's Ultimate Challenge Virtue Summary Coin

Symbols have always served as powerful tangible reminders to provide a sense of belonging or as a device to point to truths that need remembering. The US military has had a tradition since World War I of carrying 24/7 a small medallion embossed with their unit symbol[1] on it. Decades later this medallion became known by service members as a challenge coin because service members would challenge other service members at local establishments to prove they

---

[1] Fascinating history of the challenge coin can be found on my website: http://www.MansUltimateChallenge.com/backstory

were carrying their unit coin. If a service member were not, then that service member would have to buy a drink for the man who issued the challenge along with his fellow service members.

Following this tradition I designed a Man's Ultimate Challenge coin with symbols for you to carry with you every day 24/7. This challenge coin is for you to carry with you as a continual reminder of where you get your identity and how you are to represent the King of Kings daily. I do prayer walks and use my coin to pray specifically where God would like my to apply His virtues to situations in my life. What I found amazing is that very best of who I am in Christ comes out during the day.

In the picture of the coin below you will notice the Trinity Knot that serves as our unit symbol with the Latin phrase *Spiritus Gladius* and *Veritas* surrounded by a pair of swords. This serves to remind you that your primary battle in life is for truth (*veritas*) and the weapons you fight with is God's truth as revealed in His Word, the sword of the Spirit (*spiritus gladius*). If you are interested, you can purchase this coin, made in the USA by a US Marine, from my website:

www.MansUltimateChallenge.org

Man's Ultimate Challenge Summary Coin

What a nice tangible reminder! I researched the symbols and each one has a long rich history as representing these classic virtues. The Luther Rose represents **charity**, the cross **faith**, the anchor **hope**, the scroll **prudence**, the pillar **fortitude**, the balanced scales **justice,** and the harp **temperance**.[2] There is a summary table at the

---

[2] Interestingly the anchor is the oldest symbol found in archaeology. It is throughout the catacombs representing hope from Hebrews 6:19 "This **hope** we have as an anchor of the

end of each virtue chapter in of the book where you will do a deep dive studying the virtues and vices. This table will include a list of sub-virtues or properties of each virtue that I want you and every member of your group to memorize. This will do two things: (1) place hooks in your mind for you to quickly have access to as you seek to apply the specific virtue to your life, and (2) It will provide a common language for you and the men in your life to use as you talk about victories, struggles, and how the virtues revealed the answer.

---

soul…" The pillar has represented fortitude since the time of the Greeks.

1
IMAGE PROBLEMS

"Every vice leads to cruelty" – *C.S. Lewis*

The fundamental questions at the center of every man are: Who am I? Why am I here? Where am I going? If there is a God who created me, then there is a purpose. If there is a purpose, there must be a map. If God has a map, then by definition His map is the true map I must follow. It is in following this map that I discover who I am and where I am going. First, though I have to find the map! God gives us clues that there is a map, and as we seek we will find not only the map but also God Himself. In fact, finding Him is the first purpose of the map, finding your true self and purpose is the second.

Do you remember in the Movie *National Treasure* when Benjamin Gates, played by Nicolas Cage, discovered the glasses of Benjamin Franklin? When he put on the glasses, he was able to see a mysterious map on the back of the Declaration of Independence that was always there but remained invisible without these special glasses. This reminds me of how we all wander around aimlessly unable to see the map or plan God has for us because we are wearing the wrong glasses. The glasses that I am referring to however are the glasses we wear on our mind's eye.

We all walk around wearing a pair of glasses that distort, discolor, and filter the way we see the world and our own place in it. This way in which we see the world is known as a *worldview* and is the framework through which or by which a person makes sense of the data of life. Everyone has a worldview and the majority of us have no idea what our worldview is and the impact it has on our decision making process. A worldview makes a world of difference in one's view of God, origins, evil, human nature, ethics, and our ultimate destiny. A worldview should be coherent, consistent, and comprehensive for it determines how one makes all of the experiences in reality fit together. When our worldview is distorted and discolored, nothing in life seems to fit together. James Sire defined a worldview this way:

"A worldview is a commitment, a fundamental orientation of the heart, that can be expressed as a story or in a set of presuppositions which we hold about the basic constitution of reality, and that provides the foundation on which we live and move and have our being."[3]

How has your worldview been shaped? More than likely it has been "caught" by the worldview of others in your family, by your friends, in school, and especially through our primary story telling sources of TV, movies, and books. Even an hour-long program on the History Channel and A&E is shaped into an historical narrative that smuggles in a view of reality shared by those who put the show together. In our culture of 24-hour news, a worldview of the producers determines what is considered news, what the news reported means, and opinions of what we should and should not do about it. But out of all of these places, you more than likely received your official pair of worldview glasses from one place in particular— The University. The worldview glasses that you were provided color and distort your vision toward secular humanism, a worldview rooted in the philosophy of naturalism and the presuppositions of sociological Marxism[4]. World-renowned Christian philosophers J.P.

---

[3] James W. Sire, *The Universe Next Door* 4th ed. (Downers Grove IL: InterVarsity Press, 2004), 17.
[4] Check out my series called "The Four Pillars of Secular Fundamentalism" at

Moreland and William Lane Craig explain the importance of the University in shaping our worldview:

"For the single most important institution shaping western culture is the university. It is at the university that our future political leaders, our journalists, our teachers, our business executives, our lawyers, our artists, will be trained. It is at the university that they will formulate or, more likely, *simply absorb the worldview that will shape their lives.*"[5]

What do you think the impact is of your worldview on truth? I can promise you that it is everything! In fact, what this book means to you, and how it impacts you, has everything to do with how much you believe that what you are reading is *really* true. Notice I highlighted the word 'really'. One of the biggest issues with us men today is that we do not really believe the Bible is true. A book like this one that anchors itself to the power of the virtues by using Bible verses as support makes little difference to the man who does not believe the truth of the Bible in the first place. You may be thinking to yourself "Hey, the Bible has to do with faith which is a different kind of truth, so what's the big deal?" Not so! The false view of faith as blind and rooted in feelings alone apart from reason has more to do with the New Age mysticism and eastern thought rather than Christianity. As CS Lewis aptly put it "He [God] wants a child's heart, but a grown-up's head."[6]

I will deal directly with this unchristian view of faith and its impact in the chapter on the theological virtue of faith. What I can say for now is that this false view of faith minus reason is the motivation for the two appendices at the end of this book on "How We Got The Bible" and "Non-Christian Sources That Mention Jesus." As a matter of fact, I suggest you bookmark this page and take the opportunity to read appendix B and C. If you are in a small group or discipleship/mentoring relationship be prepared to discuss

---

www.MansUltimateChallenge.com. What are the four pillars? (1) A Dichotomy Between Faith & Reason; (2) Evolution is a Fact That Accounts For Origins; (3) Miracles Are Impossible; (4) God is Created In The Image of Man.
[5] J.P. Moreland & William Lane Craig, *Philosophical Foundations for a Christian Worldview* (Downers Grove, IL: InterVarsity Press, 2003), 2 [Emphasis mine].
[6] Ibid., 75.

them. A faulty secular worldview that includes this view of faith minus reason no doubt colors how we "see" ourselves, our purpose in life, and where we develop meaning and value.

How have college courses on sociology, psychology, anthropology, gender studies, etc. impacted you? What are some of the messages in the culture on where to find meaning and purpose? How is Christianity portrayed?

_____

_____

_____

What do you assume is true? What do you assume is quote scientific?

_____

_____

_____

Write down some things that you learned from reading Appendix B: "How We Got The Bible" and Appendix C: "Non-Christian Sources That Mention Jesus."

_____

_____

_____

_____

Why The Question of Origins Matters

Men we have an image problem. When I say image problem I do not mean how people see us, how the culture portrays us, or even how we see ourselves. What I am referring to is deeper than that; it is a problem of being. One of the most overlooked and oversimplified doctrines for most of us is the biblical doctrine of the Fall.[7] It is overlooked in that we do not think about it and it is

---

[7]In Christian teaching the 'Fall' refers to the time when we fell into disobedience and all humans since inherit a fallen sin nature. This is a critical part of Christian anthropology. We as Christians believe that man is made in the image of God, has His moral Law written on his heart, but is rebellious to its authority in his life making him particularly rebellious toward our heavenly Father whom placed the law there. In fact, Socialism, Marxism, and Communism speedily swept through the world and failed miserably for one main reason: a failed anthropology, or view of the nature of man. Karl Marx built his entire system on two pillars that both crumbled: (1) God does not exist, and (2) Man is naturally good. Why did

oversimplified in that when we do think about it we state the Fall as a rote but distant fact. We rarely think about it and recognize its impact on us and those we love even though it is the most personal doctrine in all of Christianity. Understanding this doctrine is of first importance because it is from here that the story of the redemptive message of Jesus Christ begins. It is why origins are the primary area of attack by the secularists in the educational system. Sociology, psychology, anthropology, and the rest of the humanities all presuppose the origins message of:

Infantile ➔ Reptile ➔ Gentile

If you bought into the culture's "science" message of origins, at this point of the book you are already annoyed and preparing yourself for a nonintellectual chapter that you may choose to skip. I put science in quotes because what is really being taught is the philosophy of naturalism and materialism that is smuggled into science. If you want to learn more check out footnote four. But why put your faith into the message in a textbook as if it is true because the class cost a few thousand dollars? I ask that you take a breath, say a prayer, and be teachable as this is in fact the most important chapter of the book. Why? Because the secular view of origins that we all have learned reverses God's order by placing humans at the bottom of the creative hierarchy of importance while placing the earth at the top. In fact, Peter Singer who used to sit in the chair of ethics at Princeton University and considered the father of the modern animal rights movement states that:

> "It is time for the courts to recognize that the way we treat chimpanzees is indefensible. They are persons and we should end their wrongful imprisonment."[8]

I think that we have a problem when one of our Ivy League schools give a philosopher like Peter Singer an honorable and influential position. He even coined the phrase "specism" which is a form of racism where one believes that his species is better than

---

they crumble? Because both pillars are lies of the enemy; thus, proved to be false!

[8] Peter Singer. "Chimpanzees are people, too: The moral case for protecting their basic rights," *New York Daily News*, accessed October 27, 2014, http://www.nydailynews.com/opinion/peter-singer-chimpanzees-people-article-1.1982262.

another. This represents a serious image problem.

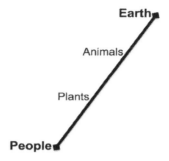

Secular View of Origins: Earth on Top

In Genesis Chapter One God gives us an orderly account of creation whereas Genesis Chapter Two gives us the details of the crown of His creation—man and woman. God created the world out of nothing by merely using His words as He spoke and the universe came into being. Sorry faith movement and the "Secret," only God has the power to create with His words. Only God can create something out of nothing, whereas we create something out of something. God has an idea, makes a choice, speaks, then creation moves in response. We have an idea, make a choice, and then we have to move creation with our hands. From a biblical perspective, then, creation is apart from God like an artist is apart from his art or a carpenter is apart from his house. God is not **in** creation as taught in Animism, New Age, Wiccan, or pantheistic religions such as Buddhism and Hinduism. God is both transcendent (He is over creation) and He is immanent (He is within creation) as the sustaining cause. God is the cause and is wholly apart from His creation—that is the effect, but at the same time He is active within creation and ultimately sovereign over it.

God created in a sequential order as Chapter One of Genesis lists. God dedicated a detailed chapter on the creation of human beings because we are special and unique in all of His creation. I want you to notice God's creative approach while He is creating land, plants, sea creatures, and animals. God keeps Himself once removed and impersonal as He places a material distance between Himself and

His creation. He commanded the land and the sea to do the work at His command.

Genesis 1:11-12 "And God said, let the land produce vegetation…God saw that it was good"

Genesis 1:20-21 "And God said, let the waters teem with living creatures…God saw that it was good"

Genesis 1:24-25 "And God said, let the land produce living creatures… God saw that it was good"

Everything changed when God created the first humans male and female. Unlike the trees, plants, animals, and sea creatures, humans are created with no material distance between Creator and creation. God touches us and brings us into being with a personal Divine touch, breathing new life into us. Why? Because we are different from the rest of creation since God created humans, and only humans, in His image.

Genesis 1:26-28

[26]Then God said, "Let Us make man in Our image, according to Our likeness; and let them rule over the fish of the sea and over the birds of the [ak]sky and over the cattle and over all the earth, and over every creeping thing that creeps on the earth." [27]God created man in His own image, in the image of God He created him; male and female He created them. [28]God blessed them; and God said to them, "Be fruitful and multiply, and fill the earth, and subdue it; and rule over the fish of the sea and over the birds of the [al]sky and over every living thing that [am]moves on the earth."

Men, God created us not just with words, but with His lips and breathed His breath into us in a very personal way.

Genesis 2:7 – "the Lord God formed the man from the dust of the ground and breathed into his nostrils the breath of life, and the man became a living being."

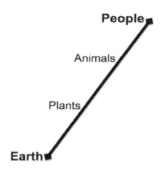

Biblical View of Origins: People on Top

This personal touch continues as God reveals more information about Himself and His relationship to us as the sixty-six books of the Bible are progressively revealed to us through His chosen instruments. For instance, according to the book of Psalms, God continues His personal creative touch and determines the number of our days on earth as He ordains them.

Psalm 139: 13-16

For You formed my [i]inward parts; You wove me in my mother's womb. [14]I will give thanks to You, for [j]I am fearfully and wonderfully made; Wonderful are Your works, And my soul knows it very well. [15]My [k]frame was not hidden from You, When I was made in secret, And skillfully wrought in the depths of the earth; [16]Your eyes have seen my unformed substance; And in Your book were all written. The days that were ordained for me, When as yet there was not one of them.

In the New Testament we are told that the exact places where we will live, and exactly when we will live there is ordained by God. People may have "accidents" in that a couple may have never intended to get pregnant, but God makes no accidents. As Rick Warren notes in his best selling book *The Purpose Driven Life*, "While there are illegitimate parents there are no illegitimate children. Many children are unplanned by parents, but they are not unplanned by God. God's purpose took into account human error, and even sin."[9] The Bible illustrates this fact in Matthew 1:5 where it lists the

---

[9] Rick Warren, *The Purpose Drive Life: What On Earth Am I Here For?* Exp. Ed. (Grand Rapids, MI: Zondervan, 2012), Expanded Edition, 27.

Canaanite prostitute Rahab in the lineage of Jesus. Rahab is the harlot who saved the Jewish spies as recorded in Joshua chapter two. Matthew 1:5 also includes Rahab's grandson Boaz and his wife Ruth in the lineage of Jesus. Ruth is the Moabite woman who saved the Jewish race, and whose life story is told in the Bible's book of Ruth. So, in the lineage of Jesus we have a prostitute and a two gentiles in a family tree that the world would view as shameful, but God, in His foreknowledge, views as providential.

Acts 17:26 – He made from one man every nation of mankind to live on all the face of the earth, having determined their appointed times and the boundaries of their habitation.

What should be our reaction to this difference between the rest of creation and us?

_____

_____

_____

What Does God's Image Include?

Since God made us in His image the natural question that follows is, what exactly does this mean and what does God's image include? In Christianity, unlike many pagan religious systems and ancient Greek philosophy, both the body and the soul[10] are good. We are not a good a soul or spirit trapped like a prisoner inside a bad body. As the diagram on the next page depicts, we are in fact a body/soul unity with interactions between both dimensions of our nature so that the body influences the soul and vice versa. This is why when Jesus came to redeem humanity, he rose from the dead bodily and not "spiritually" as some cults teach. Salvation in Jesus was *in* the body, not *from* the body. As Dr. Norman Geisler summarizes human nature, "In addition to being one in nature (soul/body) and two in dimension (inner and outer), human beings are three in direction: They have self-consciousness, world-consciousness, and God-consciousness."[11]

---

[10] I use soul and spirit interchangeably to refer to the immaterial dimension of a human.
[11] Norman Geisler, *Systematic Theology, Volume three* (Bethany House: Bloomington, MN), 78.

15

God breathed and brought us to life so that we would see ourselves as finite reflections of God's infinite qualities. One such quality of God's image in us is first and foremost the fact that we are relational beings created for relationship. This is what is meant by us being created with relational awareness in the three directions of self-consciousness, world-consciousness, and God-consciousness. God created us for relationship with Himself, our own selves, and with one another as demonstrated by the summary of the entire Bible provided by Jesus in answer to a question as to which is the greatest commandment. In short, Jesus taught that we are to love God and to love one another as we properly love ourselves. Love by its very nature is both relational and multidimensional.

Matthew 22:37-40

[37]And He said to him, "'You shall love the Lord your God with all your heart, and with all your soul, and with all your mind.' [38]This is the great and [o]foremost commandment. [39]The second is like it, 'You shall love your neighbor as yourself.' [40]On these two commandments depend the whole Law and the Prophets."

(1) God's image in us is creative. We have the ability to create things, actually pretty amazing things! Look around you and see what we as humans can create. Now compare this to the animals whose creative ability seems capped while ours seems limitless as we continue to have completely new ideas and ideas that build on other ideas from others or ourselves. There really is no comparison.

God as a gift originally gave work. We are made to work and in the beginning, before sin entered the world, work was good and working reflected God's image. As a matter of fact, God gave man a job before He gave man a woman. God worked in creation and rested. Likewise we are to work in creation and rest. It was so natural that work required no command like, "Hey get to work!" Man as a creation in the image of God was created to work. As a part of God's original design man reflects this part of God's image both when he works and when he rests.

> Genesis 2:2-3, 15 – "By the seventh day God completed His work which He had done, and He rested on the seventh day from all His work which He had done. ³Then God blessed the seventh day and sanctified it, because in it He rested from all His work which God had created [a]and made…¹⁵Then the Lord God took the man and put him into the garden of Eden to cultivate [work] it and keep [protect] it."

When it comes to creativity think about music for a moment. Have you ever wondered why there is such a thing as music? What evolutionary advantage is there with the creation of music? Music serves one purpose and that is to remind us that we are created for worship. Tie this into the greatest commandment and we can quickly see the benefits of two categories of music. One type of music is meant for God and another type of music is made for man. This is why there is a difference between worship music that has its focus upward and country, rock, rap, or Christian music that has its focus outward. Does the music you listen to bring out the best of God's image in you or does it bring out the worst of the fallen nature in you? Secular songs can tug at your heart and pull you toward God or away from Him. In my own life when I was making a big career decision it was the secular song by Kenny Chesney called "Don't Blink" that God used to tug at my heart and decide to make the career move that would give me more time with my family. There can be no doubt that music moves us, the question is, in what direction?

(2) God's image in us is mental. Before we can create we first come up with an idea. God came up with the idea of creation and spoke it into being out of nothing. God's image in us enables us to come up with an idea and take pieces of creation in order to make the idea a physical reality. Additionally, we have the ability to discover truth and draw conclusions. This ability means that we have mental capacities that can reason, discern, and inform a response to the truth we have discovered.

Psalm 51:6 – Surely you desire truth in the inner parts; you teach me wisdom in the inmost place

Isaiah 1:14 – Come let us reason together says the Lord

The Bible reminds us that this ability to reason is an additional capacity that animals do not have. This adds to the evidence that mental properties and the reasoning faculties are unique to humans and thus reflective of the image of God in us. The fact that you are reading this book, weighing the evidence presented, and deciding what choices to make in light of what you learn also point to the reasoning capacity. As the famous Reformation theologian John Calvin noted, "God has provided the soul of man with intellect, by which he might discern good from evil, just from unjust, and might know what to follow or to shun, reason going before with her lamp..."[12]

Jude 10 – "But these men revile the things which they do not understand; and the things which they know by instinct, like **unreasoning animals**, by these things they are [a]destroyed."

(3) God's image in us is moral. There is a moral law written on every human heart, and it is easily discovered. Let's say that you and I were walking down the street after a men's event at our church. As we walk past a dark alley we hear a woman scream "Help! Help!" The first thing that both of us experience is a heightened awareness of danger as the fight or flight response bubbles up within us. Then almost instantaneously another law appears which informs you that you "ought to go help." Both you and I know at that moment that this third law appeared in each of us, but only you respond and run toward the danger to help the woman, while I on the other hand run from the danger. Let's say the Pastor hears about the incident. Who is he going to celebrate at the next men's event, you or me? In other words, who is the hero and who is the zero? How do you know that? Where did that third moral law come from?

Additional evidence of the moral law is the fact that we all make excuses for breaking it, and we experience guilt when we break it. Donald Brown's study *Human Universals* reveals more than 300 patterns of behavior & moral beliefs shared by all cultures. For

---

[12] Ibid., 73.

example, not one culture had cowardice and dishonesty as a virtue.

> Romans 2:15 – since they show that the requirements of the law are written on their hearts, their consciences also bearing witness…

(4) God's image in us is volitional. We have the ability to make choices using our volition or free will. God giving us commands to obey presupposes a choice by us to obey or disobey. In fact, it is this very freedom that made evil possible. God did not create evil, but made evil possible by giving human beings an important aspect of God's image; free will. Think for a moment of God's choices. He could have chosen to not place this part of His image in us. So His choice becomes either create humans with no free will or create humans with free will. In other words, create robots that do as programmed. Would this be a great perfect world of pure obedience and goodness? Well not exactly. It is not obedience if the robot person does as programmed is it? Think about it! No evil but no love either since love requires a choice. What if your wife, kids, and friends all "loved" you because their genes are programmed to "love" you specifically. Honestly, is that really love?

There is a fantastic movie starring Jeff Bridges and Meryl Streep titled *The Giver* that makes this very point. I highly recommend that you see this secular movie due to the interesting implications of the removal of free will that it teases out. In this movie, there is a perfect little world created on top of a mountain where every day people take a shot of medication in their wrists before they leave for the day. The purpose of this medication is to remove free will, emotions, and sense of the moral law. The whole movie is done in black and white in order to demonstrate that a world without free will, emotions, and a moral law is a world without color. The Giver is a man who does not take medication and has memories of a world with free will, emotions, and a sense of the moral law within. His job is to serve the god-like role of remembering this history, and to then pass this gift of memories on to the next "Giver," a teenage boy named Jonas. As Jonas stops taking medication and begins receiving memories he feels for the first time a range of emotions as he receives memories of war and then a wedding at the same time. He experiences pain and suffering but also love and belonging. The first thing that happens to Jonas as he goes back into his community is that he experiences colors. What a powerful illustration that a world without free will, emotions, and a moral law is a world without color.

This world that we live in now is a world of color where free people, according to God's foreknowledge and providence, are choosing to be with God for all eternity or to be without God for all eternity. When the New Heaven and New Earth come it will be the world without suffering and pain that we all long for. At the same time it will be a place with free will, emotion, a moral law, and a restored human nature. All who are there chose to be there! What a clever solution that the Lord made that solves the dilemma. Free people choosing now to be with Him forever in the restored creation.

> Genesis 2:16-17 – And the Lord God commanded the man "You are free to eat from any tree in the garden, [17]But you must not eat from the tree of the knowledge of good and evil…"

(5) God's image in us is emotional. There are ranges of emotions that we as human beings experience that are in addition to instincts. Movies, good books, poetry, and music all have the ability to stir our emotions. God is essentially emotional and we who are made in His image are as well. Emotion is a word that contains the word motion because it is our emotions that move us. I remember the strange array of emotions that I experienced on my wedding day when for the very first time I saw my wife appear in her wedding dress at the end of the church aisle. It was a powerful experience.

> Ecclesiastes 3:4 – A time to weep and a time to laugh; A time to mourn and a time to dance.

(6) God's image in us is eternal. God is eternal in that He has always existed. He is without beginning or end, He is the Alpha and Omega.

> Isaiah 44:6 – "…I am the First and I am the Last, apart from me there is no God"

We have a beginning but are eternal in the present and into the future without end. The rest of creation is temporary. So, when does eternal life begin for you? The answer is it already has.

Therefore, the choices that you make now, especially about Jesus Christ, have eternal consequences.

Ecclesiastes 3:11 – He has made everything [b]appropriate in its time. He has also set eternity in their hearts…

John 3:16 – …whoever believes in Him shall not perish but have eternal life.

God's Image and The Fall

"Free will, though it makes evil possible, is also the only thing that makes possible any love or goodness or joy worth having." – C.S. Lewis

The creation before the Fall included human beings who existed in a close relationship with God and a virtuous relationship toward themselves and one another. However, in the Fall, the first man and woman took God's gift of a free will and chose to disobey God's only negative command. God gave two commands to Adam and Eve, one positive and one negative.

Positive: Genesis 1:28 – "Be fruitful and increase in number…"

Negative: Genesis 2:17 – "You must not eat from the tree of the knowledge of good and evil…"

The result of this willful disobedience is not the removal of the image of God in us, but a tainting that marred the image of God in us. It is very important you understand this point: the result of the Fall is that the image of God is marred or tainted in humans but not removed. As a result, all people, believers and unbelievers, are made in the image of God and have this marred image of God that is passed pass on through humanity.[13]

---

[13] Have you ever wondered: When is the soul created? Is it at the moment of conception? Is there a time when God creates a soul and deposits it into the baby in the womb? The answer is found in a theological view called 'traducianism'. The word 'traducian' comes from the Latin word **tradux**, meaning "branch or vine". This theological view holds that the soul is passed on from the parents just as the body is; thus, God does not "create" a soul independently, but instrumentally through the parents as He intended from the beginning. God rested on the seventh day of creation and has been resting from creating since as noted in Hebrews 4:4. God ordained and placed creation in motion with procreation from the very beginning as He commanded the first husband and wife to "be fruitful and multiply". This is the best biblical explanation of how a fallen nature inherited from our parents; a fallen soul and fallen body, one unity, fallen and corrupt . As Ephesians 2:1-3 notes we are born with a

As the diagram below illustrates, the consequences of this disobedience extended outside of us to include not only a broken relationship with ourselves, but also a broken relationship with God, and a broken relationship with people made in God's image.

Fallen Nature

World Conscious   Self Conscious   God Conscious

The Fall robbed us of our relationship with God and a life of virtue that flowed naturally out of our nature. It was replaced with a broken relationship with God and a life of vice that now naturally flows out of our nature. Augustine noted that, "Vice, too is so contrary to nature that it cannot but damage it."[14] Renowned theologian and personal hero of mine Dr. Norman Geisler explains it this way:

> Not only were Adam and Eve innocent (without evil), they were morally virtuous by nature of their virtuous state, for God endowed them with moral perfection. Solomon wrote "This only I have found: *God made mankind upright*, but men have gone in search of many schemes" (Eccl 7:29). The Hebrew word for "upright" is *yashar*, meaning "straightness," "uprightness," honesty," or "integrity"; it is the same word used in connection with "rightness" (Deut 32:4), "blameless" (Job 1:1, and "pure" (Job 8:6). Consequently, *yashar* does not merely denote absence of evil but also the presence of good—it is not simply a lack of vice but the reality of virtue.[15]

---

sinful flesh including the mind, for a body cannot sin without a soul. In short, from the time the sperm meets the egg and forms a blastocyst a new genetic human being, body and soul, is created. Or to put it in modern computer terms, our hardware and software are created with the virus of a fallen nature. On a side note, notice that the marriage and family is the only institution created before the Fall.

[14] Ibid., 71.
[15] Ibid., 18.

The consequences of the Fall are steep in that the image of God once had a natural tendency toward the virtues, however it was marred to the point where we now have an unnatural tendency toward the vices. The Fall reversed our tendencies that inform our choices making the passions of the flesh unnatural and untrustworthy. Each step in the process of the Fall brought about the tendency toward the vices.

(1) A lie sowed the vice of **uncertainty** where there once was **faith**

Genesis 3:6 – The serpent said to the woman, "Did God really say…"

Uncertainty about God and uncertainty about God's protection and provision was introduced by the great deceiver and embraced by the deceived. Notice the enemy's tactic of twisting God's word when the Bible was but two commands. How much more twisting is there today now that there are sixty-six books? "Did God really say" is the beginning of uncertainty and the end of faith.

(2) A lie sowed the vice of **gluttony** where there once was **temperance**

Genesis 3:6 – When the woman saw that the fruit of the tree was good and *pleasing to the eye*… [emphasis mine]

Gluttony always comes from discontentment with God's provision. Now what other's have, or what you do not have becomes, "pleasing to the eye." God gave them plenty, but the focus shifted to what they didn't have or what they may be missing. This reminds me of the NBA player who after he signed a multimillion-dollar contract was asked, "How much is enough?" His answer, "A dollar more." Doubts about God will always lead to doubts about His provision. Earlier in Genesis, before the Fall, the Bible states that all of creation was perfect and pleasing:

Genesis 2:9 – And the Lord God made all kinds of trees grow out of the ground—trees that were good for food and *pleasing to the eye*... [emphasis mine]

Everything was pleasing to the eye, except the one thing that they did not have. A little twisting of God's word and everything becomes ordinary and the one thing that is not yours to have becomes pleasing to the eye. This is where addiction comes from as it starts in our heart. We are first gluttonous wanting pleasure for pleasures sake thinking, "This is fun. I have been robbed by God's boundaries. What's the big deal?" Then, over time, slowly but surely, we become slaves to pleasure, which, in the end, leaves us feeling empty. This emptiness in addiction leads us to first stop seeing the image of God in us, then we stop seeing the image of God in others by treating them as a means to our selfish ends. Probably the best example of this is pornography where men and women are reduced from persons with value and worth to commodities.

(3) A lie sowed the vice of **indifference** where there once was **charity**

> Genesis 3:6 – ...She also gave some to her husband who was with her...

The husband is shown as indifferent to his headship and servant leadership role in his marriage. The roles in marriage were there from the beginning, before the Fall. He just stood there and left his wife unprotected from the enemy. Do you see how sin begins in the heart and mind before it comes out in action? The Fall was the result. God creates marriage "very good" with submission and leadership. God gave Adam the command *before* he created his wife, Eve, as Genesis 2:16 records, "And the Lord God commanded the man..."

Question: Where did Eve get the command that Satan twisted?[16]

God holds the husband, Adam, accountable for the failure of his leadership. God knew what happened when He came looking for them. Notice that He did not call out for Eve, "Then the Lord God called to the man, and said to him, "Where are you?"[17] As a consequence the husband's sacred duty of protecting and providing became even harder.

> Genesis 3:17 – "...Cursed is the ground because of you; through painful toil you will eat food from it all the days of your life."

---

[16] Answer: Her husband!
[17] Genesis 3:9.

(4) A lie sowed the vice of **carelessness** where there once was **prudence**

> Genesis 3:6 – When the woman saw that the fruit of the tree was good and pleasing to the eye and also for gaining wisdom…

She became wise in her own eyes as carelessness made a lie look like wisdom. The husband is careless in his leadership and became passive leaving his wife unprotected from the enemy. One thing about a passive husband is that he always acts as if he couldn't care less.

(5) The lie sowed the vice of **injustice** where there once was **justice**

> Genesis 3:12 – The man said, "The woman you put here with me—she gave me some fruit from the tree and I ate it"

Justice has to do with how you treat people; it is the practical outworking of loving other people. Injustice began as the husband shifted to blame, slander, and a shirking of his responsibility as the head of the home whose duty is to protect and provide for his family. Where was he? What we have here men is the very first instance of the passive man. He ignored his sacred duty leaving his marriage open to attack.

(6) The lie sowed **fear** where there once was **fortitude**

> Genesis 3:10 –"I heard you [God] and I was afraid…so I hid"

Shame is powerful once it begins to move within a man. It not only feeds on injustice but it ushers in an inappropriate fear of God where a person falsely believes that he is unacceptable and unloved. Jim Supp probably has best summary of shame that I ever heard: "Guilt is feeling bad for what you have done; shame is feeling bad for who you are." This fear runs deep so excuses, blame, and an inability to "man-up" and own his stuff came forth. Now the shame-filled man begins to demand respect from others by sowing fear, but it is an empty respect because it is not based on love. Think of the gangs of fatherless men getting their identity from one another and demanding this empty respect that is based on loveless fear instead of love-filled faith.

(7) The lie sowed **despair** where there once was **hope**

This is the ultimate vice! Sin moves to blame, then to unhealthy fear, then, left unchecked, always makes you question God's love for you. Shame runs so deep that despair takes over a man. When individual people walk in despair it expands into a family filled with despair, then a neighborhood of despair, and into a culture of despair. All without hope of something better because the something better is illusive and seems out of reach. It is here that the need for a Savior becomes apparent. Only the gospel was designed to restore hope by restoring our relationship with the Creator first, then His creation.

The result of the Fall impacts us every day as we live in the chains of the vices instead of the freedom of the virtues. All people matter to God, so all people need to matter to us. Every person may be a creation of God, but only a person who has accepted God's true Son into his life is a child of God by adoption.

John 1:12-13

But as many as received Him, to them He gave the right to become children of God, even to those who believe in His name, [13]who were [i]born, not of [j]blood nor of the will of the flesh nor of the will of man, but of God.

Ephesians 1:4-5 – …In love [5][e]He predestined us to adoption as sons through Jesus Christ to Himself…

First, the man is brought into the family of God through adoption. Then the redeemed by Christ are under an extreme home make over God edition as He, via the Holy Spirit, begins restoring the image of God in him daily. Now these newly born sons of God reflect the image of God to the world around them as men of virtue in a culture of vice. Born into Adam, born again into Christ.

2
WHY THE VIRTUES?

"There is in us a natural aptitude for virtue" - Aristotle

So why care about the virtues as a man? Do
carelessness, fear, gluttony, injustice, uncertainty, despair,
and indifference sound like a summary of what plagues
the modern male? Read that list again, slowly, because
you will see yourself in it I promise. If you didn't then
you may have a bigger problem and no book will help you—lack of
humility and lack of introspection! Every man has felt himself
chained by these vices and frankly I am tired of it! Like me, do you
sometimes feel like Bill Murray in the movie "Ground Hog Day?"
You know the feeling where every day is a new day but the
experience is more like "same day, same battle." I don't know about
you but I find it hard to fight a battle with nothing more than pithy
statements and vague battle plans such as "walk in the Spirit" and
"put on the armor." I find myself answering, "Ok, the armor is on; I
am filled with the Spirit; now what?"

I remember being told many times on my journey as a

Christian, "Pete, walk in the Spirit." However, nobody ever showed me "how" to walk in the Spirit in any meaningful way. It is like being a fully equipped soldier all dressed up ready for battle yet sitting in a foxhole waiting for orders. Maybe some well-meaning brother in the Lord gave you the same advice and you felt like I did. I would consider this more of a vague spiritual sounding statement than sound advice since I could not apply it. I don't mean any harm here brothers, but this is nothing more than fuzzy feel good information with spiritual sprinkles. It is true that in the book of Romans scripture clearly teaches us to walk in the Spirit and not in the flesh. But it is also true that in the same passages the Apostle Paul tells us just how much of a struggle this advice is for him personally as a man. So why would we expect the struggle to be any easier for us?

Discipleship, mentoring, and coaching are not merely one brother sharing deep rich insights on a life in the Spirit from the Scripture. This is information, and maybe at times can be considered knowledge, but this is only half discipleship if the information does not move into a man's life practically. This movement is what the Bible identifies as wisdom. True discipleship and mentoring is not just knowledge on what to do and not to do with the corresponding why—it is *how!* How brings knowledge into reality by practical application which produces a truly meaningful and virtuous life. Incidentally, the Hebrew root for the word wisdom in the Old Testament means "skill," and skills combine the head with the hands for practical living in everyday life. This is why Jesus walked among the disciples and asked them to follow Him, so that He could *show* them how to live this new life with Him. If we cannot apply God's word to our every day life we will end up living by the vices of the flesh chained to our old habits and way of thinking. Sure we will have a few verses memorized, but never actualized. In fact, the vices' power in our life will grow the more they are applied because these become the actions solidified in the brain.

One of the saddest examples of this knowledge only approach occurred with the abolition of slavery. Although it was a fact that the slaves were set free, many of them willingly picked up their old chains and old way of life because they did not know what else to "do." The "don't be a slave" message was not very helpful without the corresponding "do this as a free man" because this is how free men live. Thus the free men remained slaves because nobody taught them practically how to be free. So what was the result of this half message? Free men in chains—willingly! Hmmm, that doesn't sound free to me. In fact, it sounds worse.

In a similar way, the sad reality is that men today are slaves in their Christian walk for the very same reason. The "don't" message that we get at most men events sadly causes us to focus on the flesh which in turn makes us a slave! Romans 8:6 clearly tells us that, "For the mind set on the flesh is death". Why would we leave a men's event encouraged by a message of "don't" that places our mind's focus on the flesh? God calls us to be FREE and in our freedom we are called to be men of action who "do!" "Do" activates the Spirit of God and makes freedom in Christ a reality!

We have unintentionally changed Christianity into a message of "don't" for men and we wonder why we are not growing and men are leaving the church. Christianity is not a religion of "don't" but a redeemed life of "do!" On the other hand, without any tangible target at which to aim, we end up wandering in the dry desert paralyzed by a half message of "don't." As we know all to well, merely a focus on "don't" creates in us a self-fulfilling prophecy of a life of defeat. So, instead of forward progress toward an objective, we settle in place making the chains of slavery more comfortable. We have to move forward away from "don't" in regards to the vices in our life and direct our focus ahead at the virtues of "do." "Do" gives us a real purpose, and having a tangible objective activates that wondrous sense of duty that inspired the greatest men in history. It is the "do" that will reverse the curse. I hope that you are with me so far.

When we at first want to initiate change in our lives the "don't" message makes sense to us because we are fresh off of the consequences of living a life in the flesh. We know that we must throw off anything that hinders us from reaching our new objective of walking in the Spirit of our new identity in Christ where true meaning, purpose, and freedom are found. It is the virtues that are the "do" we need to fill our mind with, focus on, and act on that will get us there. This, my brother, is walking in the Spirit and places us in a state of true change by breaking the chains of the vices that hinder us from reaching our God given potential and calling. We are not called to constantly stare at the chains of our vices (don't), we are called to a vision forward in becoming a man of virtue (do). The "don't" focus is akin to God calling us to go on a journey toward biblical manhood and we readily jump into a car and discover that it has only rearview mirrors. How far forward are you going to travel on this journey? Even if you have the Holy Spirit as a guide telling you where to go, a car with only rearview mirrors will never take you to a destination you cannot see. Men, I don't know if you are on the wrong road but I do know that you are in the wrong vehicle.

Don't misunderstand me. Every good vehicle needs rearview mirrors to give you perspective as a kind of "you are here" marker on the roadmap of life. But your front window must be bigger than the rearview mirror in order to see the road ahead. Placing you in this type of vehicle on a road with a band of brothers who all have the same objective of moving forward and "doing" is the goal of Man's Ultimate Challenge. Get into this new vehicle and start your engines because there is some territory ahead that God wants you to reclaim—yes, **you**! May God reclaim the culture for Him with a few fully equipped imperfectly good men as he has done many times throughout history.

What is the difference between a focus on "don't" verses a focus on "do"?

_____

_____

_____

Discovering True Manliness

"If you are on the wrong road, progress means doing an about-turn and walking back to the right road." –C.S. Lewis

Many men today have very few examples in both their immediate lives and the culture as a whole of what true manliness is. I believe that this is why we truly do not know what to do with vague advice such as "walk in the Spirit." Instead we are in need of specific guidance on what a real man of virtue does in real life situations. The best advice is "caught" on the battlefield of life when we see men who have been there before pick up the right weapon for the fight and move forward "all in" with a contagious sense of duty. Imitation is the best way to learn, but with the success of the enemy's war strategy of taking out the platoon leader first, fatherlessness by absence and addiction, have left boys trying to form a masculine identity out of thin air. On the one hand we do know how to recognize true manliness when we see it in the news, movies, and yes even video games. We know it because of the way our hearts internally explode with an "oh yeah!" We also know when we do not see true manliness displayed as when we experience an internal sense of "oh no" fueled with a hint of anger as we see the failure of a man often combined with unmanly excuses and attempts of blame shifting. Both of these experiences are somewhat helpful because they reveal something wrong since God, the very source of these honorable qualities, writes the virtues of manliness on our hearts.

God's living water within us is meant to be poured out in our lives so that we have new life springing all around us. The Dead Sea and the Sea of Galilee both have the same source but it is only the Sea of Galilee that is full of life. What is the difference? The Dead Sea has no outlet, so its waters are stagnant and non-life producing. Christian Philosopher Peter Kreeft notes that, "The same thing happens to the "living waters" from God as to the fresh waters of the Jordan. When we bottle them up inside ourselves, they become stagnant. Stagnant faith stinks, like stagnant water. And the world has sensitive nostrils."[18] The bottom line is that we have to get up, throw off the chains that grip us, and embrace our calling and duty to be men of action, purpose, and virtue. My goal is to convince you that the virtues are the keys to unlocking the chains that hold each of us in our stagnant position.

Have you ever felt stagnant in your Christian walk or as a man?

_____

_____

_____

When you look at the vices of carelessness, fear, gluttony, injustice,

---

[18] Peter Kreeft, *Back to Virtue*, (San Francisco, CA: Ignatius Press, 1992), 70.

uncertainty, despair, and indifference. Which one stands out? Why?

_____

_____

_____

Reverse The Curse

"Tolerance is the virtue of the man without convictions." – G.K. Chesterton

The Greek word *arête* is the word translated as virtue in the Bible. I love how the NASB unpacks this powerful Greek word even more by rendering it in the English as "moral excellences." *Arête* represents the force and energy of the Holy Spirit that inclines a man's heart toward God's standards. Interestingly enough the Latin word *virtus*, derived from *Arête*, is where we get the word virtue and it literally means "manliness." How cool is that? Peter Kreeft notes that, "In its classical signification, virtue means, the power of anything to accomplish its specific function; a property capable of producing certain effects; strength, force, potency."[19] God has to pull us up toward Jesus Christ, the exemplar of manliness, for true manliness is always found in a virtuous man.

In order to pull a man up we have to first know what is pulling him down. It is the vices from the curse that came with the first man that are not only pulling him down, but also keeping him down. It is the heavy chains of carelessness, fear, gluttony, injustice, uncertainty, despair, and indifference, and with all that they encompass that is constantly keeping him down. So what does God use to pull a man up from reflecting the fallen man toward reflecting the God-man Jesus Christ? The Spirit-filled virtues of prudence, fortitude, temperance, justice, faith, hope, and charity that are considered God's moral excellences! A Spirit-filled man needs to pivot his heart not only away from the vices of "don't," but toward the virtues of "do." This pivot is a refocus, a goal to strive toward that, in time, will begin the restoration of the image of God in him.

There are seven virtues that are key to the success of every man no matter what your cultural background, physical location in

---

[19] Ibid., 5.

the world, or place in the societal structures of the world. Why? Because every man in every place and at every time is plagued with the same vices due to the curse ushered in by the first man at the Fall. Each virtue has a corresponding vice of the flesh that is as comfortable to us men as an old pair of shoes. So walking in the Spirit of the virtues at first is as uncomfortable as putting on a new pair of shoes that have yet to be broken in. The goal for every man is that, in time, the virtues become comfortable and the vices become uncomfortable.

Historically, the first four of the seven virtues are traced back to Plato and Aristotle as well as to both the Old and New Testaments of the Bible. You may be asking yourself, "But how did Plato and Aristotle come to the same conclusion of the truth of the virtues without the Bible?" Because they are made in the image of the Creator and these virtues are seared into their very nature ready to be discovered. These men and many philosophers since have referred to these virtues as a "natural law" or "law of nature." The Bible affirms this law of nature when speaking of the unsaved Gentiles: "…they show that the requirement of the law are written on their hearts, their consciences also bearing witness…" – Romans 2:15. Here are more men who reveal that virtues are part of the image of God and bring out the best in men:

"The moral sense is as much a part of our constitution as that of seeing, feeling, or hearing" – Thomas Jefferson

"I agree that there is a natural aristocracy among men. The grounds of this are virtue" – Thomas Jefferson

"Virtue is a disposition, or habit, involving deliberate purpose or choice" – Aristotle

"Nature has planted in our minds an insatiable longing to see the truth" – Marcus Tulius Cicero

"Fortitude is the guard and support of the other virtues" – John Locke

"Liberty can no more exist without virtue and independence than the body can live without a soul" – John Adams

"If virtue and knowledge be diffused among the people they will never be enslaved. This will be their great security" – Samuel Adams

Why do you think that John Adams and Samuel Adams linked liberty with virtue?

_____

_____

_____

The Power of The Virtues

"The Christian does not think God will love us because we are good, but that God will make us good because He loves us."– C.S. Lewis

In one category we have the four cardinal or natural virtues of prudence, justice, fortitude, and temperance that are part of natural law and infused into the heart of every man; which, of course, is why Plato and Aristotle were able to discover them. Notices that I said discover and not create! The Latin root for the word cardinal is *cardo* or hinge; thus both Aristotle and Aquinas saw the cardinal virtues as the hinges on which the door of the moral life swings. Man is aware of these virtues though he naturally has a rebellious bent away from them because of his sinful nature due to the Fall. C.S. Lewis said it best when speaking of our fallen nature: "Fallen man is not simply an imperfect creature who needs improvement: he is a rebel who must lay down his arms."[20]

Typically when man does respond to the virtues in the means, often times the end becomes to the glory of man, whether it is himself or another man. One thing for sure is that it is not for the glory of God. Without a reconciled relationship with his Creator through Jesus Christ a man is without eternal hope. So a man either does virtuous means for an un-virtuous end or in reverse, he works un-virtuous means toward a virtuous end. But God and people want both a just means and a just end, which brings us to the necessity of the second category of virtues.

Thomas Aquinas went further than Aristotle and Plato by

---

[20] C.S. Lewis, *Mere Christianity*, (New York, NY: HarperCollins, 1952/2001), 56.

adding to the four cardinal virtues another category of virtues highlighted in the New Testament and unique to Christianity. In the second category we have the theological or supernatural virtues of faith, hope, and charity that are infused into the heart of a Christian man as he is filled with the Holy Spirit of God the day he truly received God's redemption plan through Jesus Christ. A true man of virtue knows that God desires a virtuous means toward a truly virtuous end—the glory of God. When the ends are in God Himself it has the added benefit of bringing honor to fellow men whom bear His image. This is why the Holy Spirit who dwells within a Christian man starts to change his true motivations and goals beyond himself. Of course this only occurs when a man hands himself over to the spiritual disciplines and the working of the Holy Spirit through God's word. The aim of this book is to show you exactly how to renew your mind and walk before God as a living sacrifice.[21] As C.S. Lewis affirms in *Mere Christianity*, "Aim at Heaven and you will get earth "thrown in;" aim at earth and you will get neither."

In many ways the natural virtues, though good in themselves, lack power without the Divine infusion of the supernatural virtues of faith, hope and charity. How can a man have life threatening courage (a property of fortitude) to take a stand for truth without the eternal hope in Christ and the assurance of eternal life He promises? It is the know-so-hope that his eternal destiny is reserved by a faith in Christ who calls him toward an *agape* love (charity) to lay down his life for his friends.[22] This Divine infusion impacts our motives and perfects the virtues "to the glory of God" as the end goal because it is God who enables the means through us to accomplish His objectives. When pleasing God is the object of virtue, people made in His image reap the benefits.

The theological virtues are made supernaturally alive by the Holy Spirit and draw us outside of ourselves, question our true intentions, and provide a firm foundation for all of the virtues

---

[21] Romans 12:1-2 – Therefore I urge you, brethren, by the mercies of God, to present your bodies a living and holy sacrifice, [a]acceptable to God, which is your [b]spiritual service of worship. 2 And do not be conformed to this [c]world, but be transformed by the renewing of your mind, so that you may [d]prove what the will of God is, that which is good and [e]acceptable and perfect.

[22] John 15:13 – Greater love has no one than this, that one lay down his life for his friends.

because they are rooted in the very nature of God. For example, we discover truth because God *is* truth, we *agape* love because God *is* *agape* love, and we can know true justice because God *is* just. Moreover, because we are made in His image we have in part what God has in totality. These supernatural virtues are activated in our image-bearing natural body as it became a temple for the living God[23] whom constantly draws us to live for a higher purpose than self. We are empowered because the God who made us in His image stepped down from heaven and took on flesh, perfectly lived out the virtues among us, and offered His life to us as a free gift. God goes one step further when He chooses to infuse this life within us by sending the Holy Spirit to fill us and personally guide us. Now men, being a man of virtue is one thing if we are to live sixty or seventy years, but it is an entirely different matter when we are made to live for eternity! This is why 2 Peter instructs us to live out our faith as men of virtue.

2 Peter 1:2-9

Grace and peace be multiplied to you in the knowledge of God and of Jesus our Lord; [3]seeing that His divine power has granted to us everything pertaining to life and godliness, through the true knowledge of Him who called us [d]by His own glory and [e]excellence. [4][f]For by these He has granted to us His precious and magnificent promises, so that by them you may become partakers of the divine nature, having escaped the corruption that is in the world by lust. [5]Now for this very reason also, applying all diligence, **in your faith supply moral [g]excellence [virtue], and in your moral excellence [virtue]**, knowledge, [6]and in your knowledge [prudence], self-control [temperance], and in your self-control, perseverance [fortitude], and in your perseverance, godliness, [7]and in your godliness, brotherly kindness, and in your brotherly kindness, love [charity]. [8]For if these qualities are yours and are increasing, they render you neither useless nor unfruitful in the true knowledge of our Lord Jesus Christ. [9]For he who lacks these qualities is blind or shortsighted, having forgotten his purification from his former sins.

---

[23] 1 Corinthians 6:19 – Or do you not know that your body is a temple of the Holy Spirit who is in you, whom you have from God, and that you are not your own?

The Battle Within

"The real man smiles in trouble, gathers strength from distress, and grows brave by reflection" – Thomas Paine

I truly believe that the Bible is the field manual for life as demonstrated by the fact that I just finished my 15th year going through the Bible since coming to Christ. Now I am not sharing this to earn some merit badge or for male bragging rights, but to let you know that this author takes God's word seriously. I find that the more I apply God's word to my life the more God's principles prove to be true. The more God's word proves to be true the more that I am drawn to read God's word. The cycle continues as I build a mental library of experiences to look back on and draw faith from as I remember how God's truth proved true in a similar experience in my past. A man having trouble with reading the Bible is directly tied to the fact that the man has experienced a lack of biblical impact in his life. What he fails to realize is the reason it lacks impact is because he lacks application! The reason he lacks biblical application to his life is directly tied to biblical illiteracy due to a vegetarian biblical diet—no meat!

What I have learned, and I pray that you will come to realize, is that the virtues are the "now what" droids you have been looking for (a little Star Wars pun). We are living breathing beings who are always on the move, minute by minute, progressing toward our purpose and high calling as a man of virtue, or minute-by-minute moving away from our purpose and high calling. Satan lost you forever at the cross when you received Christ, so his goal is to make you an impotent soldier whose life feels meaningless to God's purposes on earth, even though God has a unique plan for you.

Time to dig into God's word and do a little Bible study. I am an equipper at heart so you can go as deep as you want with this study and everything you read in this book. For instance, throughout the book I have footnotes that will provide some detailed information for further study and deeper theological and philosophical insights. In fact, you may have already missed some, so turn back the pages and check the footnotes. The choice is yours if you want to read them or not, but I highly encourage you to do so.

Before you start, some of you may have a tendency to read quickly either because you read a lot, or when you see something you have read before you breeze right through it. Please **do not do this** when reading the Bible because you will miss a lot I promise you. God the Holy Spirit who dwells within you wrote these words through His chosen men and He desires to speak to you personally through the Bible. You have to reflectively and quietly listen as you read so that you do not merely see the words on the page but hear God's voice through these words. You can never hear the Spirit of God if you are the one doing all of the talking in your mind or if you skip over His words to you. So read a verse then pause to listen. Yes feels awkward at first, but this is true for any new habit you are trying to develop. To practice, continue this pattern until finished with the entire passage of Romans. Do this throughout the verses supplied in this book and I promise you will notice a difference in your capacity to grasp the deeper things of God, and most importantly understand its direct implications for you as His son.

With this in mind I want you to read the passages on the next page slowly and reflectively so the section that follows will make sense as the Holy Spirit teaches you. Hopefully this approach will radically change how you hear God and live the Christian life! So pause right now and pray for wisdom. Why? A prayer for wisdom is the one prayer that God promises to always say yes to:

James 1:5 – But if any of you lacks wisdom, let him ask God, who gives to all men generously and without reproach and *it will be given to him*. [emphasis mine]

Step 1: Mark the passages with a highlighter or underline with a pen every occurrence of the words 'flesh' and 'Spirit'. It would be preferable to use a different color for each word so that it stands out. If you are reading this book on a Kindle there are different color highlight options available to you. When you are finished just sit back and look at how the highlights will more clearly reveal God's truth. [Remember read *reflectively*]

Romans 7:15-23;8:1-17

[15]For what I am doing, I do not understand; for I am not practicing what I would like to do, but I am doing the very thing I hate. [16]But if I do the very thing I do not want to do, I agree with the Law, confessing that the Law is good. [17]So now, no longer am I the one doing it, but sin which dwells in me. [18]For I know that nothing good dwells in me, that is, in my flesh; for the willing is present in me, but the doing of the good is not. [19]For the good that I want, I do not do, but I practice the very evil that I do not want. [20]But if I am doing the very thing I do not want, I am no longer the one doing it, but sin which dwells in me. [21]I find then the principle that evil is present in me, the one who wants to do good. [22]For I joyfully concur with the law of God in the inner man, [23]but I see a different law in the members of my body, waging war against the law of my mind and making me a prisoner of the law of sin which is in my members. 8:[1]Therefore there is now no condemnation for those who are in Christ Jesus. [2]For the law of the Spirit of life in Christ Jesus has set you free from the law of sin and of death. [3]For what the Law could not do, weak as it was through the flesh, God did: sending His own Son in the likeness of sinful flesh and as an offering for sin, He condemned sin in the flesh, [4]so that the requirement of the Law might be fulfilled in us, who do not walk according to the FLESH but according to the SPIRIT. [5]For those who are according to the flesh set their minds on the things of the flesh, but those who are according to the Spirit, the things of the Spirit. [6]For the mind set on the flesh is death, but the mind set on the Spirit is life and peace, [7]because the mind set on the flesh is hostile toward God; for it does not subject itself to the law of God, for it is not even able to do so, [8]and those who are in the flesh cannot please God. [9]However, you are not in the flesh but in the Spirit, if indeed the Spirit of God dwells in you. But if anyone does not have the Spirit of Christ, he does not belong to Him. [10]If Christ is in you, though the body is dead because of sin, yet the spirit is alive because of righteousness. [11]But if the Spirit of Him who raised Jesus from the dead dwells in you, He who raised Christ Jesus from the dead will also give life to your mortal bodies through His Spirit who dwells in you. [12]So then, brethren, we are under obligation, not to the flesh, to live according to the

flesh —[13]for if you are living according to the flesh, you must die; but if by the Spirit you are putting to death the deeds of the body, you will live. [14] For all who are being led by the Spirit of God, these are sons of God. [15] For you have not received a spirit of slavery leading to fear again, but you have received a spirit of adoption as sons by which we cry out, "Abba! Father!" [16]The Spirit Himself testifies with our spirit that we are children of God.

Step 2: Make a list of what God says about the flesh and the Spirit.

Flesh	Spirit

Step 3: Now transfer the highlights and notes to your personal Bible.

I am a man who appreciates a good weapon and maybe you are too. If not weapons, how about a set of good quality tools? If you are a musician or painter, what about the difference between quality instruments and the cheap imitations? We all know the cheap stuff when we see it. We also know the quality of stuff makes a difference and it usually lasts a long time. With this in mind: why would you go cheap when it comes to the sword of the Spirit—the Bible? It would be wise to make an investment in a good quality study Bible, preferably a New American Standard Bible (NASB), or New King James Version (NKJV)[24]. I highly recommend the Hebrew-Greek Key Word Study Bible by AMG publishers! Please read footnote 19 below where I include deeper insights into Bible translations. I cannot stress enough the fact that the footnotes contain some real nuggets! Yes, this is the third time I have mentioned it!

Finally, when we get to the chapters on the virtues I will begin with a definition of the virtue and all of the sub-virtues or properties that the virtue encompasses. Keep in mind that because of our inclination toward the vice, it will be the vice of the virtue you will find extremely helpful as you seek to understand the importance of the virtue. A vice is our natural tendency, what our sin nature finds "natural" and defaults to. But this is not what God originally intended for us which is why we must be "born again" so that our

---

[24] Ever wonder why there are Bible verse numbers? They are used for translation. Each of the versions listed here are considered 'word for word' translations, or what theologians call a "formal equivalence" translation of the Bible. This means that the translators moved from the source languages of Hebrew, Aramaic, and Greek to the import language of English taking great care to capture the exact translation of each word. The New International Version (NIV) is a thought for thought or "dynamic equivalence" translation of the Bible where the translator attempts to capture the contextual "thought" of each phrase before it is moved into the import language of English. A nice second choice that I use as well and recommend, but some are wondering the direction of the NIV with the introduction of the tNIV and its gender neutral approach. So try and make sure you get the 1984 version of the NIV. The English Standard Version (ESV) attempts to blend readability with a formal equivalence translation philosophy. I suggest that you never use the New Living Translation or Living Bible for study because these are considered paraphrases and end up being to far removed from the original Bible languages. The problem with a paraphrase is that you can easily put words into God's mouth and misunderstand what He requires of you as His son. Imagine believing that "God said _____" when He said no such thing. A dangerous predicament indeed!

new nature, over time, will begin to transform us until the "virtue" becomes natural and the vice feels "unnatural." This transition will never be complete until either Jesus Christ returns or we return to Him.

Vices are like weeds in our yards. Have you ever noticed that no man ever plants weeds in his yard? Weeds just come naturally when the yard is left to its natural devices. All of the work occurs during the process of getting rid of the weeds at their source or roots! Likewise, we must do the hard work training ourselves to be men of virtue by constantly killing our weeds. But as any man with a green thumb will tell you, the only way to kill weeds is to pull them out by their roots.

Virtuous living is contagious. When you begin to live a life of virtue individually it will impact the community corporately. You will see a restoration of the community around you, beginning with your closest relational circles of influence. When the people of God begin to restore the image of God within them there is an aggregate effect. Over time, a whole community will be transformed as people start acting like the Creator as the image of God moves us inward and projects outward. Why hasn't this happened? Well, because according to Barna, only 7% of Christians have a biblical worldview. I hope to change these statistics one man at a time, then and only then:

(1)   You will see more creativity

(2)   You will see more beauty

(3)   You will experience more harmony

All it takes is a few good men. Are you ready?

3
A MAN OF FAITH
NOT UNCERTAINTY

"Faith is not an option to which one is subscribed but a reality to which one is submitted" – J.R.R. Tolkien

We truly are on journey men. We started off by describing who we are as men made in the image of God; an image that was marred by the Fall. Next, we discovered why the virtues are the key to recalibrating the image of God as we continually strive to be a man of virtue, battling our rebellious enemy within. Finally, we unpacked how our primary battle is truth against lies, but many of these lies seem true as we caught and absorbed the secular worldview of the culture. The rest of the chapters will unpack each virtue, its sub-virtues and the corresponding vices that keep us in the chains of slavery to our old self. Key point of this section is the fact that the virtue is the truth that will break the chains of our vices.

The goal of this chapter specifically is to train you to be a man of **faith** and not **uncertainty**. The Greek word *pistis* is translated as faith in the Bible. This word captures a thought of such a deep personal trust in God and His Word that it only leads a man in one obvious direction—toward its object. This direction first begins internally as a deep desire to please God and know His will. This internal movement progresses outward as an expression of faith in a life of obedience and conformity toward God's design and purpose. Thus, true Biblical faith begins as an internal desire informing the motives of a man to move his will toward an expression of obedience as a demonstration of trust.

The practice of true biblical faith will, over time, decrease uncertainty in a man's life as his faith muscle develops to the point in which he knows, by experience, it is reasonable to believe God truly is faithful. When life feels unfair and cruel, uncertainty will creep in only to have the virtue of faith take over in a powerful expression of a deep trust in the providence of God and His purposes. As the Bible makes clear in Romans 8:28, "And we know that [a]God causes all things to work together for good to those who love God, to those who are called according to His purpose."

The properties of faith include obedience, trust, wisdom, zeal, and passion; all of which cannot help but be expressed in worship and praise. We develop the muscle of faith as we look back and remember when God was faithful, so as to enable us to look forward with a faith-filled zeal for God because we know with certainty that He will be faithful once more. Since the output of faith is obedience you should not be surprised that faith includes the property of wisdom. As you will see in the next chapter, wisdom is a shared property between the virtue of faith and the virtue of prudence. It is as if there is a God-made link between the heart and the head. Surprised? Then be prepared to have a possibly shallow view of faith shaken.

An important and far too often overlooked area of breaking the chains of uncertainty and growing in faith is the critical area of Christian evidences. This growing area for addressing your questions is known as apologetics. God wants you to think and He invites you in Isaiah 1:18 to, "Come let us reason together says the Lord." This growth area will provide you a proper passion and zeal to live for the truths you actually believe in your head and God confirms in your heart. This in turn produces more passion and zeal to study these truths in order to grasp them for obedient application in your life. Only this type of true biblical faith can break you free of the chains of uncertainty that hold you down in pride, disobedience, ignorance, and unbelief. It is this lack of true biblical faith that has led to the practical atheism of the modern man; i.e., saying he believes in God while living as God does not exist. That type of "believing" is for Disney not Divinity. In truth it is not believing at all. As the great reformer Martin Luther once said, "Feelings come and feelings go and feelings are deceiving, my warrant the word of God none else is worth believing."

The Most Important Question in This Book

"Faith goes up the stairs that love has built and looks out the windows which hope has opened" – Charles Spurgeon

Before we go any further I would be remiss if I did not start with the foundation and very object of our faith—Jesus Christ and His good news message to the world. I want you to examine yourself and challenge yourself as to whether your belief is for Disney or Divinity. Here is my question: If you were to die today and stand before God and he said to you, "Why should I let you into my Kingdom?" What would you say?

_____

_____

_____

_____

Now let's test your answer above against the 12 truths of the good news about Jesus Christ and why He had to come that has been preached since the time of the Apostles. Remember read *slowly* and *reflectively*, even twice if you have to. Especially if you think to yourself "oh I know this" or, "I have heard this before."

First, pause and pray in your own words asking for God to show Himself and reveal His truth expressed in His word.

Truth #1: Creation Screams Design

God Speaks to us through the light of His creation:

45

Psalm 19:1-3

The heavens declare the glory of God; the skies proclaim the work of his hands. Day after day they pour forth speech; night after night they display knowledge. There is no speech or language where their voice is not heard.

Truth #2: Our Heart Searches for Meaning & Purpose:

God uniquely created us in the womb with meaning and purpose:

Psalm 139:13-16

For you created my inmost being; you knit me together in my mother's womb. I praise you because I am fearfully and wonderfully made; your works are wonderful, I know that full well. My frame was not hidden from you when I was made in the secret place. When I was woven together in the depths of the earth, your eyes saw my unformed body. All the days ordained for me were written in your book before one of them came to be.

Truth #3: Three Aspects Of Our "Sixth" Sense:

a. When God created us He created us with a spirit:

Zechariah 12:1 – The LORD, who stretches out the heavens, who lays the foundation of the earth, and who forms the spirit of man within him…

b. The moral law of God is written on our hearts:

Jeremiah 31:33 – "I will put my law in their minds and write it on their hearts. I will be their God, and they will be my people."

c. A sense of eternity is placed in our hearts:

Ecclesiastes 3:11 – He has made everything beautiful in its time. He has also set eternity in the hearts of men...

Funerals really reveal this truth! Have you ever been to a funeral and never thought about eternity?

Truth #4: Everyone Has Always Had Access to Truths 1-3

God even determined when and where we would live for one

reason: So that we could find Him!

Acts 17:26-27

From one man he made every nation of men, that they should inhabit the whole earth; and he determined the times set for them and the exact places where they should live. God did this so that men would seek him and perhaps reach out for him and find him, though he is not far from each one of us.

Truth #5: The Eternal Promise

God is discoverable by everyone who truly seeks Him. But, how do we find God? By responding to all of the above with a heart of discovery:

Jeremiah 29:13-14 – You will seek me and find me when you seek me with all your heart. I will be found by you," declares the LORD, "

Truth #6: Do You Recognize God's Providence?

God will reveal Himself fully to you by getting His message of reconciliation, love, and forgiveness through Jesus Christ specifically to you. He will do it through missionaries who have an amazing call to go to some of the most remote places in the world, or by sending one of His followers in your life as a co-worker, neighbor, family member or friend. He will at times do it by media, or books provided to you by these same people. As a matter of fact, He may be doing it right now.

Romans 10:14-15

How, then, can they call on the one they have not believed in? And how can they believe in the one of whom they have not heard? And how can they hear without someone preaching to them?

What is this Message that God wants you and me to hear?

God loves you right where you are, but He loves you too much to keep you there. God stepped down into His creation through His Son to save the world. Love always initiates:

John 3:16-18

For God so loved the world that he gave his one and only Son, that whoever believes in him shall not perish but have eternal life. For God did not send his Son into the world to condemn the world, but to save the world through him.

Truth #7: We All Fall Short Of God's Standards

God sent Hs Son to forgive you of your sins as a result of your fallen nature. You and I are not rebellious sinners because we sin, we sin because we have a fallen nature bent toward rebellion and we act on it:

Romans 3:23 – for all have sinned and fall short of the glory of God,

Sin is an old archery term that means missing the mark. In archery sin is the distance from where a shot arrow landed and the center of the bull's eye or target. What God is telling us is that perfection is the target and no matter how close we get to the mark, we all miss it. There is a price for sin that places us in debt to God. We all miss the mark of perfection so we all need a cure:

Romans 6:23 – For the wages of sin is death…

Jesus paid the sin debt for you and me as a love gift:

Romans 6:23 – …but the gift of God is eternal life in Christ Jesus our Lord.

Truth #8: Jesus Illustrates What UNCONDITIONAL Love and Acceptance Looks Like:

Jesus died for us to pay this debt when we did not deserve it:

Romans 5:8 – But God demonstrates his own love for us in this: While we were still sinners, Christ died for us.

Truth #9: Debt Free Living!

How do we access this account to pay for our debt to God? A transaction has to take place. When we make financial transactions to pay debt we use money, but for spiritual transactions we use prayer. We give God our sins and He gives us credit because of Jesus Christ's payment on the cross. To believe in Jesus means that one receives payment for his or her sins and believes that Jesus made that payment on the cross. For those who believe in Jesus Christ God says this:

> Romans 4:7-8 – Blessed are they whose transgressions are forgiven, whose sins are covered. Blessed is the man whose sin the Lord will never count against him.

What does this spiritual transaction have to do with heaven?

> Acts 4:12 - **Salvation is found in no one else**, for there is no other name under heaven given to men by which we must be saved."

I have often heard people complain how narrow this is. I mean one way! There are a few problems with this objection. The first one is that it is really disingenuous. If God provided two ways, people would want three; If He provided ten ways they would want eleven. In short, what people really want is their way, which of course proves Genesis three and the Fall into rebellion. The second is something that all good leaders know—clarity. Vision requires clarity, and good leaders are always clear in what they expect. God makes it clear the way to heaven. God is the best leader of all providing clarity in His written Word, and physically through His living Word, Jesus Christ. In addition, Jesus met all of the requirements, and our only requirement is to follow the Leader by belief:

> John 6:28-29
>
> [28] Therefore they said to Him, "What shall we do, so that we may work the works of God?" [29] Jesus answered and said to them, "This is the work of God, that you believe in Him whom He has sent."

Here are some more verses providing clarity. Jesus is not a bridge to nowhere, but the bridge to eternity.

> John 14:6 - Jesus answered, "I am the way and the truth and the

life. **No one comes to the Father except through me**.

John 3:3-7 - In reply Jesus declared, "I tell you the truth, **no one can see the kingdom of God unless he is born again**." "How can a man be born when he is old?" Nicodemus asked. "Surely he cannot enter a second time into his mother's womb to be born!" Jesus answered, "I tell you the truth, no one can enter the kingdom of God unless he is born of water and the Spirit. Flesh gives birth to flesh, but the Spirit gives birth to spirit. You should not be surprised at my saying, 'You must be born again.'"

Truth #10: A New Beginning Requires a New Birth:

How is a person born again? He must repent. Repent means a change in direction from going our own way to moving toward God and choosing to follow His way. By doing this, the guilt accumulated from going our own way is removed and our hearts and conscience is refreshed:

Acts 3:19 – Repent, then, and turn to God, so that your sins may be wiped out, that times of refreshing may come from the Lord,

Repent literally means doing a 180-degree turn around from going your own way away from the cross to going toward the cross. You must make this transaction and receive Christ's payment by calling on God in prayer in order to be saved from the consequence of eternal separation from God and His love. This is a free will choice that you must make.

Romans 10:9-13

That if you confess with your mouth, "Jesus is Lord," and believe in your heart that God raised him from the dead, you will be saved. For it is with your heart that you believe and are justified, and it is with your mouth that you confess and are saved -- the same Lord is Lord of all and richly blesses all who call on him, for, "Everyone who calls on the name of the Lord will be saved."

Truth #11: Do you want to make this transaction with God and have a guaranteed eternal home in heaven?

In order to open a spiritual gift you have to use a spiritual means, and that means is prayer. The words you speak do not matter as much as the sincerity of your heart when you pray. Picture Jesus Christ holding out His nail pierced hands with a gift box filled with an irrevocable certificate of eternal life, an irrevocable adoption certificate, and a copy of your name written in the Lamb's book of life at the entrance gate of Heaven.

Pray:

Dear Lord Jesus, thank you for loving me. I admit that I am a sinner and in debt to you so I need your forgiveness. Thank you for dying on the cross for me and I receive your gift of eternal life now by accepting in faith your offer to cancel my sin debt. Please make me the person that you created me to be....AMEN

Truth #12: Will I say "Goodbye" or "I'll See You Later?"

If I were to attend your funeral, depending how you responded to truths 1-11 I will either say "goodbye" or "I will see you later." If you made this eternal transaction with God by praying this prayer with all of your heart, look at the four things that happened at that very moment:

1. You became a new creation!

2 Corinthians 5:17-19

Therefore, if anyone is in Christ, he is a new creation; the old has gone, the new has come! All this is from God, who reconciled us to himself through Christ and gave us the ministry of reconciliation: that God was reconciling the world to himself in Christ, not counting men's sins against them. And he has committed to us the message of reconciliation.

2. You were adopted and became a child of God!

This is important because not everyone is a child of God. It is true that everyone is a creation of God and made in His image, but only those who accept God's only son Jesus Christ will become adopted into His family. You see, brother, adoption was God's idea and this is why Christians adopt children more than any other group of people in the world.

John 1:12-13 – Yet to all who received him, to those who

51

believed in his name, he gave the right to become children of God- children born not of natural descent, nor of human decision or a husband's will, but born of God.

Romans 8:16 – The Spirit himself testifies with our spirit that we are God's children.

3. The Holy Spirit of God dwells in you!

Romans 8:9 – You, however, are controlled not by the sinful nature but by the Spirit, if the Spirit of God lives in you. And if anyone does not have the Spirit of Christ, he does not belong to Christ.

4. The Lord Jesus Himself prepares a place for you to dwell in eternity!

John 14:1-3 - Do not let your hearts be troubled. Trust in God; trust also in me. In my Father's house are many rooms; if it were not so, I would have told you. I am going there to prepare a place for you. And if I go and prepare a place for you, I will come back and take you to be with me that you also may be where I am.

Take note of the date you accepted Christ so that you can celebrate your spiritual birthday every year.

Your Name:_____

Your Spiritual Birthday:_____

Well Now What?

1. Tell someone!

Now, as with all good news, please tell someone!!! Share this good news with someone who you know will celebrate with you and help you grow in your faith.

2. Find a Bible believing church!

One of the primary ways to grow is by getting connected to a good Bible believing church.

Hebrews 10:25 – Let us not give up meeting together, as some are in the habit of doing, but let us encourage one another — and all the more as you see the Day approaching.

While you are looking for a local church, please feel free to join me at our Internet Church campus at: www.McleanBible.org/internetcampus

3. Answer the question about heaven accurately!

Ephesians 2:8-10

[8]For by grace you have been saved through faith; and [h]that not of yourselves, it is the gift of God; [9]not as a result of works, so that no one may boast. [10]For we are His workmanship, created in Christ Jesus for good works, which God prepared beforehand so that we would walk in them.

Verse 8: According to this verse how are you saved?

_____

_____

_____

Verse 9: According to this verse why is it not by works?

_____

_____

_____

Verse 10: According to this verse what is the purpose of works?

_____

_____

_____

Now back to the original question: If you were to die today and stand before God and he said to you, "Why should I let you into my Kingdom?" What would you say?

_____

_____

_____

I would say, "Because I am saved by grace through faith because I believed in Jesus Christ, and accepted His payment for my sins. You can check the Book of Life, and you will find my name with the inscription: "Paid in Full"

As Ephesians 2:8-10 make clear, we work from our faith not for it! Most people say in their own words, "I am a good person" or, "My good deeds will outweigh my bad deeds." The problem is that they never really considered the implications of this answer. What is your measure? Sitting in a hen house won't make you a chicken and sitting in a church house will not make you a Christian. God cares about **why** you are sitting there.

4. Get Baptized!

I came to Christ at the age of twenty-five. A couple of years after coming to Christ, I began to wonder if I should get "re-baptized." I grew up Catholic and was "baptized" as a baby. In seventh grade I made my Confirmation where, according to the process, I was "renewing my baptismal promises." The problem in my case is that this was all rote religious activity that followed a process my parents put me through. A lot of churches have a similar process, so whether Catholic or Protestant in your upbringing, the real question to ponder is, "Was I baptized already?" Remember, baptism is a symbol, and symbols by definition point beyond themselves to a substance. In this particular instance, if there was no substance of spiritual birth when you were "baptized," then no actual baptism occurred. You were at an event called a baptism that included water, but in the end the event was a meaningless activity.

So what did I do? First I realized there is no such thing as a re-baptism so I had to correct my thinking and humbly realize that I am in a state of disobedience. I would remain in this state if I do not obey this first and basic command from our Lord. So, in response to my new spiritual rebirth, I got baptized in a church member's swimming pool in Manassas, Virginia. I invited the guy who witnessed to me, a man who was discipling me, and some unbelieving friends as a witness to them. This was my first actual baptism following the biblical model of belief then baptism.

Jesus gave us the great commission in Matthew 28 which

includes: (1) sharing the gospel, (2) baptizing those who believe by faith, and (3) teaching them what it looks like to obey God; i.e., function as you are designed to function.

Matthew 28:18-20

And Jesus came up and spoke to them, saying, "All authority has been given to Me in heaven and on earth. [19][a]Go therefore and make disciples of all the nations, <u>baptizing them</u> in the name of the Father and the Son and the Holy Spirit, [20]teaching them to observe all that I commanded you; and lo, I am with you [b]always, even to the end of the age."

If you believed then you should be baptized in response to that belief so as to symbolize the fact that you are putting on this new identity in Christ as the old man is buried in the water and the new man rises from the water. It is truly a powerful moment. Every person who has believed in Christ should be baptized in obedience to the great commission. Here are some examples of the great commission being carried out in the early church:

Acts 8:35-38

Then Philip began with the Scripture and told him the good news about Jesus. As they traveled along the road, they came to some water and the eunuch said, "<u>Look, here is water! Why shouldn't I be baptized?</u>...Then both Philip and the eunuch went down into the water and Philip baptized him."

Acts 2:41 – Those who accepted his message <u>were baptized</u>.

Acts 8:12 – But when they believed Philip as he preached the good news of the kingdom of God and the name of Jesus Christ, they <u>were baptized</u>, both men and women.

The Four Types of People who Hear the Gospel
"Faith is trust or commitment to what you think is true" – William Lane Craig

Test yourself: when you prayed to receive Christ, were they empty words or were they a fruitful expression of a seed that took root in your heart? There are four types of people who hear and respond to the word of God, and according to this parable, only one of them is saved; i.e., really a Christian. Which one are you?

Matthew 13:3-8; 18-23

[3] And He spoke many things to them in parables, saying, "Behold, the sower went out to sow; [4] and as he sowed, some *seeds* fell beside the road, and the birds came and ate them up. [5] Others fell on the rocky places, where they did not have much soil; and immediately they sprang up, because they had no depth of soil. [6] But when the sun had risen, they were scorched; and because they had no root, they withered away. [7] Others fell [a]among the thorns, and the thorns came up and choked them out. [8] And others fell on the good soil and *yielded a crop, some a hundredfold, some sixty, and some thirty....[18] "Hear then the parable of the sower. [19] When anyone hears the [i]word of the kingdom and does not understand it, the evil *one* comes and snatches away what has been sown in his heart. This is the one on whom seed was sown beside the road. [20] The one on whom seed was sown on the rocky places, this is the man who hears the word and immediately receives it with joy; [21] yet he has no *firm* root in himself, but is *only* temporary, and when affliction or persecution arises because of the [j]word, immediately he [k]falls away. [22] And the one on whom seed was sown among the thorns, this is the man who hears the word, and the worry of the [l]world and the deceitfulness of wealth choke the word, and it becomes unfruitful. [23] And the one on whom seed was sown on the good soil, this is the man who hears the word and understands it; who indeed bears fruit and brings forth, some a hundredfold, some sixty, and some thirty."

Using your own words, fill in the four types of people who hear the gospel and their response.

Verse 19: The Hearer

_____
_____
_____

Verse 20: The Stoner

_____
_____
_____

Verse 22: The Thorny

_____

_____

_____

Verse 23: The Christian

_____

_____

_____

Doesn't this explain why people "say the prayer" then in time fade away? My question is which one are you?

_____

Faith and Reason

"Faith is a firm and certain knowledge of God's benevolence toward us" – John Calvin

It should by now be clear why I wanted to start with the virtue of faith. First, I wanted to begin by clearing away any idea that biblical faith is rooted in feelings alone, and second, I wanted to make sure that you had faith to begin with. The way in which the term faith is carelessly used in our culture as a whole, and more importantly in the church at large, is not even close to the biblical definition I provided at the beginning of the chapter. Furthermore, you can see by the twelve biblical truths that God has left us enough forensic evidence to find him with our reason, but not too much evidence that we would be devoid of faith. So then, true faith in the Christian sense of the word, has never meant and it never will mean, "blind faith." Blind faith is a New Age idea today that is a product of the faulty idea we must place faith in a separate category from reason. It is unfortunate, but this false view of faith has become popular in many Christian circles. This is a false dichotomy started during the period in history known as the Enlightenment, and continues today due to the dominant philosophy of naturalism and materialism our modern secular society is built upon.[25] The Bible warns us not to make this mistake of taking the philosophy of the culture and importing it into our lives as followers of Christ.

Colossians 2:8 – See to it that no one takes you captive through philosophy and empty deception, according to the tradition of men, according to the elementary principles of the world, [a]rather than according to Christ.

False Dichotomy: Faith & Reason never touch

The Secular view of Faith and Reason

A lot of Christian's hold the false new age and secular view of a separation between faith and reason or the intellectual and the spiritual without really understanding the implications of it.

Be honest, do you in some way hold this view? Explain.

_____

_____

_____

_____

When faith is blind it is no wonder so many men are bound by the chains of the vice of uncertainty. Spiritually blind men will always be uncertain! It is worth repeating, Christianity does not, never did, and never will, support blind faith! I agree with Chuck Colson and Nancy Pearcy who observed:

Today we must break down this false dichotomy between the

---

[25] Naturalism and materialism are technically different but practically the same in its understanding of reality. These views assert that matter is all that matters because the material world is all that there is and ever will be. This very view is itself a faith statement that cannot be falsified, proven or disproven using 100% reason. As a matter of fact faith always comes first for there has to be a faith in the power of reason so as to trust what reason produces. If you are interested in a deep dive I have an entire series dedicated to this topic and its implications on the blog portion of my website www.mansultimatechallenge.com. The title of the series is "The Four Pillars of Secular Fundamentalism."

spiritual and the intellectual and recover the calling to save minds—especially in our highly educated society. Unlike a generation ago, churches today are filled with college graduates; in fact, polls show that evangelicals are better educated than the general populace, a striking change from forty years ago.[26]

They are certainly correct and the Bible agrees! The Biblical definition of faith can be found in the book of Hebrews chapter eleven right before the chapter provides us with 34 verses of examples of true biblical faith.

Hebrews 11:1-3, 6

Now **faith** is **being sure** of what we hope for and certain of what we do not see. This is what the ancients were commended for. By faith we understand that the universe was formed at God's command, so that what is seen was not made out of what was visible….And without faith it is impossible to please God because anyone who comes to Him must believe that He exists.

The Greek words used in these verses are very interesting:

#1 "being sure" Gk: *hupostasis* = A mental assurance

#2 "faith" Gk: *pistis* = Has 3 basic elements:

The first element of faith involves the mind and entails more than knowledge but an understanding as to what this knowledge properly means to the person. The second element of faith moves into the person's will and involves an internal agreement the information is true. Both of these elements make biblical faith incomplete and meaningless without the third element of trust. Trust here involves more than trusting in the truth of the information, but is a trust in God who is the very source of the information. In short, this trust is not merely informational but relational.

---

[26] Charles Colson & Nancy Pearcy, *How Now Shall We Live* (Wheaton, IL: Tyndale House Publishers, Inc., 1999), 34.

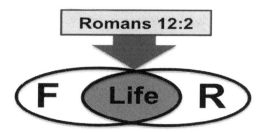

The Biblical view of Faith & Reason

The two gloves both the Christian and the non-Christian have in order to grasp reality are faith on the one hand and reason one the other. Like Michael Jackson wearing just one glove, a person will never get a full grasp of reality with only faith or only reason–"he he." You heard his voice didn't you?–Sorry! Now we will apply these verses from the book of Hebrews in order to demonstrate the truth of the partial overlap view of faith and reason. I am going to provide three examples of different types of truth that will be located in three different places in the diagram above. One truth will be located in reason, another in faith, and another in the overlap requiring both faith and reason to understand. What should become obvious to you is the fact that the Christian will spend the vast majority of his Christian experience inside the space where faith and reason overlap.

A truth of reason and not of faith is not revealed by God personally but is provable by reason alone; for example, 2+2=4 or "you are reading a book right now." The fact that you are reading a book right now is proven by reason to you now and anyone else who is watching you because they can see you. This very same fact is proved by both faith and reason tomorrow as you tell a friend that you read a book called "Man's Ultimate Challenge" yesterday. He may ask to see the book and check for its existence and a bookmark or folds showing use. He may further ask for an eyewitness to testify that he saw you reading this book. This fact can be proved by faith alone because your friend trusts you so he merely asks "how is the book" and listens to your response. Based on the fact he trusts you already demonstrate that his faith in you is not blind.

Another example in reverse are truths of faith and not of reason such as things revealed by God but not provable by reason such as the Trinity. Now though a truth such as the Trinity is not provable by reason, it must not contradict reason in order to be true. God is pure Reason and God does not have any contradictions in Himself or His revelation. For instance, it would be a contradiction to say that there is one God and three persons who are God and use the mathematical equation of 1+1+1 that equals 3. The error would be in your reasoning, not God's revelation. On the other hand, it is not a contradiction and makes sense to say that there is one God and three persons who are God by using the mathematical equation of 1x1x1 that equals 1.

Finally there are truths of both faith and reason which is where most of what we believe is located. These may be revealed by God but are provable by reason; for example, the existence of God. This is what we call "Natural Theology." Christian philosopher Dr. William Lane Craig explains the relationship of faith and reason to natural theology this way:

Natural theology is what faith proposes and reason recovers. That is to say, natural theology concerns those truths which God reveals to us but which are also provable by human reason apart from divine revelation. Natural theology preoccupies itself with arguments for God's existence and nature. Revealed theology is what faith proposes, but reason does not recover. That is to say, revealed theology concerns those truths which God reveals to us but which human reason alone cannot prove.[27]

This view is beautifully articulated in the New Testament, "For since the creation of the world His invisible attributes, His eternal power and divine nature, have been clearly seen, being understood through what has been made, so that they are without excuse." – Romans 1:20

In fact, this whole book assumes that you as a man of God will see that these virtues are true because, by using faith and reason, you can see that these virtues are written on your heart and written in God's word. After a self-realization of these facts your reason confirms, you will, in faith, choose to apply these truths to your life. As you can see, obedience demonstrates that you have faith in God

---

[27] William Lane Craig, *Does the Holy Spirit Exist* http://www.reasonablefaith.org/does-the-holy-spirit-exist; Internet [accessed October 24, 2014.]

and truly believe what He says is true. Similarly, disobedience demonstrates a lack of faith in what God says is true.

What are the implications of a proper view of faith and of reason? Did you learn anything new? If so, what?

_____

_____

_____

In *Mere Christianity* C.S. Lewis states that "God is no fonder of intellectual slackers than of any other slackers." With this in mind read the verse below and write it down in your own words what this means.

Romans 12:1-2

Therefore I urge you, brethren, by the mercies of God, to present your bodies a living and holy sacrifice, [a]acceptable to God, *which is* your [b]spiritual service of worship. [2]And do not be conformed to this [c]world, but be transformed by the renewing of your mind, so that you may [d]prove what the will of God is, that which is good and [e]acceptable and perfect.

_____

_____

_____

Can the virtues and their truth transforms your life without involving your mind; i.e., reason? Why or why not?

_____

_____

_____

Now that you have a proper understanding of where you are in relation to biblical faith and its link to your mind via your reasoning faculties, it should become abundantly clear that embracing blind faith is dangerous to both yourself and to others. Biblical faith enables you to see whereas blind faith is impotent and makes little to no impact in a man's life. I like how C.S. Lewis describes the role of biblical faith in a man's life, "I believe in Christianity as I believe that the sun has risen. Not only because I see it, but because by it I see everything else."

This reminds me of the first time I realized I needed glasses. I was driving home from a Comedy club with my friend Dave Weaver and his girlfriend at the time, Pam. Dave was sitting in the passenger seat as I was driving home on route 66 in Virginia. In classic 80's fashion Dave dude bombed me with a, "dude do you need glasses?" I looked at him a little startled and said "uh, no, why?" He noted how I was squinting at road signs and offered me his glasses with the comment, "Try these. It is a light prescription for distance." When I put the glasses on, I was stunned! I had no idea how blind I was until I had this moment of vision correction. I had gotten so used to my gradual loss of vision that it became my new normal. In a similar way, life was blurry and out of focus until Christ, through deep Bible study challenging all of my beliefs, put glasses over my mind's eye enabling me to see the world and my place in it clearly. With Christian George Barna's surveys showing that 93% of Christians do not have a biblical worldview, you would be wise to assume that you are the 93% until God proves otherwise. Ready to do the necessary work of "renewing your mind" and put on a new pair of worldview glasses?

Three Levels of Faith in a Believer

"Faith never knows where it is being led, but it loves the one who is leading"

– Oswald Chambers

Just like any muscle, faith can be either weak by little exercise or strong with a lot of exercise. It all depends on how you train and the type of training program you use. 2 Timothy 3:16-17 teaches that, "All Scripture is [a]inspired by God and profitable for teaching, for reproof, for correction, for [b]training in righteousness; [17]so that the man of God may be adequate, equipped for every good work." So it is clear that the Bible does not simply contain God's training program, it *is* God's training program. This leads us to the three levels of faith.[28]

First, there is the *content of faith.* This is the input of God's word as a man of God asks questions and seeks God's answers to

---

[28] I first got the idea of these three levels of faith from JP Moreland's wonderful work *The Lost Virtue of Happiness.* He labeled them: content, strength, and centrality.

those questions. Similar to going into any type of training a man usually starts strong with a belief he will accomplish his goals. The level of commitment in the coming weeks will determine if he truly is "all in." In this case, a man who starts off with once a week Sunday feedings is getting a little content but not enough, so his commitment is weak and will remain so for some time. On the other hand, the man who feeds daily and has biblical training as a part of his daily routine will gain more content because he has more commitment. The times of testing are coming, and God will smoke out the first man more easily than the second. Beware men, for when God tests Satan also tempts.

Second, there is the *conviction of faith.* At this level of faith when the morsels of truth begin to break down and nourish your body you will find your former beliefs challenged. A conviction differs significantly from an opinion as Christian Apologist Ravi Zacharias notes, "An opinion you carry, but a conviction carries you." How a man responds to the conviction of faith will determine if this man is really ready to believe God or play god. The godly man who wants to believe God will begin to distrust his former beliefs and seek answers to why God says what He says while discerning what God requires him to do in response. The man who wants to still play god will blow right past what God says because he falsely believes he knows best. This is where apologetics comes in.

The term apologetics comes from 1Peter 3:15, "but [i]sanctify Christ as Lord in your hearts, always being ready to make a [j]defense [apologetic] to everyone who asks you to give an account for the hope that is in you, yet with gentleness and [k]reverence." The type of apologetic defense in this verse is a legal defense. So is God guilty of an error or are you and whoever is the source of your contradictory information? Do you really believe God? At this very point you are in the partial overlap of faith and reason wrestling with God. Notice this verse begins with "but [i]sanctify Christ as Lord in your hearts…" The meaning is clear that you have to be the first person convinced before you try to convince another. Here the biblical view of faith and reason becomes vitally clear. If you punt to "in my faith I believe ____ but in my head I believe ___" then you do not believe God at all. You my friend, are a modern day Gnostic. Whatever little faith you have will either be taken away from you, showing that you are not truly saved, or it will stay but make you irrelevant for the Kingdom.

1Corinthians 3:13-15

Each man's work will become evident; for the day will show it because it is to be revealed with fire, and the fire itself will test [e]the quality of each man's work. [14]If any man's work which he has built on it remains, he will receive a reward. [15]If any man's work is burned up, he will suffer loss; but he himself will be saved, yet so as through fire.

Third, there is the *centrality of faith.* At this level your worldview is absolutely driven from a biblical perspective. If there are no convictions about God's truth, then God will never be the center of your life. The result is that your ability to find His path will be nearly impossible. The more central a belief is, the more your desires will be moved toward obedience. The output of faith, as a product of obedience, will be natural for you because God's answers (content) plus your trust that God knows best (conviction) will, as a result, both move you toward God's path and help to keep you there (centrality). Moreover, sharing the truth of God in whatever area God is central will naturally follow. This is evidence you truly believe it and have been trained "so that the man of God may be adequate, equipped for every good work."

There is a process to making Christianity truly central to your outlook on life, and central as far as its impact in your life. There is a desire for obedience, which occurs when there is an internal movement of the content of a belief within your soul. Hebrews 4:12 instructs us that "the word of God is living and active and sharper than any two-edged sword, and piercing as far as the division of soul and spirit, of both joints and marrow, and able to judge the *thoughts* and *intentions* of the heart." Are your thoughts about how to obey or how to avoid obeying? As the desire moves toward your free will, do you intend to obey or intend to ignore God's word? The conviction produced by the content of faith will move from desire toward action as you choose to believe God, as the Holy Spirit of truth speaks to your soul. Acts in obedience occur as you internally respond to his desires in order to please God. The gift of free will submits as you choose to obey as a demonstration of faith. The more frequency by which this movement occurs the more God's truth changes your convictions. Over time this faithful discipline will make these beliefs more central to your identity in Christ.

God's strategy for growing your faith to level three can be summarized in four steps: erase, replace, embrace, and grace. The man of God is to partner in response to God in each step or he will never grow. In the first step, God uses His word and the Holy Spirit to motivate you to erase the bad data. Second, God wants you to replace the bad data with good data (content of faith). The third step is a turning point where God moves and you respond, in faith, and embrace the truth revealed as your own. Finally, at the forth step God loves you like a good Father, lovingly encouraging you as you stumble along in obedience, imperfectly attempting to apply God's truth to your life daily. Growth takes time! The more you move through the process, the chains of uncertainty will begin to break. Christian counselor Dr. Henry Cloud has a great formula for growth in his influential book *Changes That Heal*.[29]

Grace + Truth + Time

Not sure where you are? Are you level 1, 2, or 3? Let me ask you a diagnostic question. If I removed Christianity from your life, how much impact to the way you live daily will it make? Will anyone notice? Will you notice?

_____

_____

_____

How To Become a Level Three Believer

"It is inbred in us that we have to do exceptional things for God: but we have not. We have to be exceptional in the ordinary things…this is not learned in five minutes" – *Oswald Chambers*

Faith needs to be tested so that you know what you really

---

[29] Next to the Bible, this book had the biggest impact on me. I highly recommend it.

believe. When God tests, Satan tempts, so be ready. When I think of the type of faith testing described in the book of James, I think of the birth of my son Jonah. Cheryl and I had been trying to get pregnant for over a year with no success. Then finally it happened and we were so excited. When Cheryl got her initial blood work back her platelets were dangerously low. She had a pregnancy induced autoimmune disorder called ITP that caused her lymphatic system to flag her platelets with an antigen as foreign and remove them like the game of Pacman. Nothing could be done so all of this had to be managed with medication until Jonah was born.

Here came the big day and Jonah was born a few weeks early and full of complications. As happy parents were leaving the hospital with their child, we left with a brand new baby carrier, empty, though not as empty as our hearts. Jonah had an infection that led to antibiotics being pumped around his heart, jaundice, was holding in water, pneumonia on his right side, and needed a red blood cell transfusion. There was a scary window of time there where it could have gone either way.

Here we are ten months after celebrating our answered prayer of getting pregnant and my wife gets an autoimmune disorder and my son that we prayed for is laying in NICU. What! I remember praying with tears in the hospital Chapel, "Lord, I love that boy please don't take him. If you do I will still love and trust you but I really don't want you to take him." Hardest prayer I ever prayed. From that afternoon on, we got good news instead of every time we saw the doctor it was more bad news. Besides, the pic line to Jonah's heart being successful a big one for me was that Jonah got to use my blood for the transfusion. I did not want him using a stranger's blood after everything else. I had to go to another county to get my blood taken, and they had to separate the red blood cells, get it ready, and ship it to the hospital. Added to this was the fact that only 40% of kids can use their parent's red blood cells. I was so thankful that it made it to be used the next day. I couldn't help but think of the analogy of my blood saving Jonah like Christ's blood saved me.

Jonah made it and we are grateful. The following year it was all about getting my wife's ITP into remission, after initial hopes that it was pregnancy induced so it would end after the pregnancy. Cheryl had to have her spleen removed so that her lymphatic system would not be able to keep up and her platelet level would rise. It worked and she has been in remission ever since.

After two years of all of this, I remember saying to my small group, "I miss God." Isn't that the strangest thing? It is only when you look back on the trials and persevere in your faith that you realize just how close God is. I wish that trials were not the primary means for this, but no doubt they are. The book of James provides a process God uses in order to get us to a level three faith.

James 1:2-7

Consider it all joy, my brethren, when you encounter various [c]trials, [3]knowing that the testing of your faith produces [d]endurance. [4]And let [e]endurance have its perfect [f]result, so that you may be [g]perfect and complete, lacking in nothing. [5]But if any of you lacks wisdom, let him ask of God, who gives to all generously and [h]without reproach, and it will be given to him. [6]But he must ask in faith without any doubting, for the one who doubts is like the surf of the sea, driven and tossed by the wind. [7]For that man ought not to expect that he will receive anything from the Lord, being a [i]double-minded man, unstable in all his ways.

There are a few insights I would like to share regarding this passage of scripture. First, the word for perfect here is not referring to being sinless, but being spiritually mature. Second, wisdom is a promise! This is a guaranteed yes prayer if you do not doubt that God will provide it. This is a specific promise for wisdom and nothing else, so wise living must be extremely important to God. I pray this wisdom prayer over every book I read, test I take, article for work, etc. You name it I cover it in a wisdom prayer! Uncertainty grows with doubting God will provide wisdom, while faith grows believing that God is a God who keeps His word. Asking God for wisdom in prayer is a demonstration of dependence on Him and not yourself for the answers. This is living in the partial overlap of faith and reason where biblical faith resides.

Have you ever experienced a testing of your faith? What did you learn about yourself? About God?

_____

_____

_____

Memorize James 1:5-6 and add it to your prayers for wisdom and watch God increase your wisdom as you pray in faith. When your wisdom grows, uncertainty diminishes and faith grows in its place, for faith grows in the soil fertilized by God's word and watered with prayer.

A Final Call to Duty

"The unexamined life is not worth living" – Socrates

When I play Call of Duty with my kids I love it when I level up. I not only get more weapons to fight the next battle, I get better defense as well. Men, we need to level up and stop fighting the same battles with a small arsenal and no forward progress. It is time to level up and move on. JP Moreland's analysis is that we have become lazy empty selves who expect others to do the work for us, and I agree:

"The empty self is passive. The couch potato is the role model for the empty self, and there can be no doubt that Americans are becoming increasingly passive in their approach to life. We let other people do our living and thinking for us: The pastor studies the Bible for us, the news media does our political thinking for us, and we let our favorite sports team exercise, struggle, and win for us. From watching television to listening to sermons, our primary agenda is to be amused and entertained."[30]

Are you ready to level up? Then take the self-examination from this study and pray that God stirs you with a Holy discontent, then in response make the first move. The next chapter on the virtue of prudence goes hand in hand with this chapter on faith. Write down how you feel challenged about your current level of faith. Pray

---

[30] J.P. Moreland, *The Lost Virtue of Happiness: Discovering the Disciplines of the Good Life* (Colorado Springs, CO: NavPress:, 2006), 21.

about this challenge as you move to the next chapter. It is time to get out of the stands and onto the field.

Memory Table: Commit the properties of faith to memory

Be a man of FAITH and not UNCERTAINTY	
Obedience	Trust
Zeal	Passion
Wisdom	

4
A MAN OF PRUDENCE
NOT CARELESSNESS
"Prudence is the science of what to seek and avoid" —*Augustine*

The goal of this chapter is to train you on how to be a man of **prudence** and not **carelessness**. This rich word prudence is not a word that we hear or use often today, but this virtue encompasses many properties or sub-virtues that we are very familiar with. Both Thomas Aquinas and Aristotle taught that prudence includes the properties of knowledge, understanding, wisdom, intelligence, foresight, reasoning, discernment, shrewdness, circumspection, teachability, memory, and caution. The vice of carelessness has an enormous impact on a man's life given all that prudence encompasses. First and foremost prudence deals with what you think, how you think, where you seek advice and counsel, how you reach conclusions, decision-making, and, most of all, seeing ahead to the long term impact of those decisions made in the moment. Immediately we can see the link to faith because knowledge leads to content, understanding leads to conviction, and wisdom leads to the centrality of a belief that forms the worldview that shapes your decisions.

Prudence is taken from the Latin word *prudentia*, contracted from the Latin word *providentia* meaning "seeing ahead." A prudent man has the ability to apply God's universals to life's particulars in a skillful way so as to competently separate good from evil and right from wrong. On the other hand, a careless man pays no attention to God's word, is clumsy, and foolishly clamors about with a "follow your heart" and "what's the big deal" attitude. The Hebrew word for prudence is *hhakham*, which means a skill to separate between right and wrong. This word is practical and was used to describe a person skilled in his work. Furthermore, prudence includes the ability to receive proper counsel and the discernment necessary to distinguish between good counsel and bad counsel.

A prudent man is not easily angered by another's careless words as he chooses to look beyond an insult and into the heart of the person searching for the hurt or root cause of the issue. He does right actions with the right motives for truth in itself, no matter what the cost, because it is what he senses a godly man *ought* to do for truth's sake and not merely for appearances. A prudent man never carelessly sins in continual willful disobedience to God but struggles to overcome sinful tendencies because he "sees ahead" to the long-term consequences and the slavery of fleeting pleasures. A prudent man shows sharp powers of judgment which enable him to judge between what actions are appropriate with regard to the circumstances as a whole including the timing in carrying out actions.

In summary, prudence as a virtue is always alert and is both offensive and defensive in its application. Prudence is offensive in that it moves one toward right persons, right actions, and right motives. Prudence is defensive in that it moves one away from wrong persons, wrong actions, and wrong motives. Augustine provided a nice one-sentence description of prudence as, "the science of what to seek and avoid." A prudent man is seeking what is right and avoiding anything that hinders him reaching his goal of becoming a man of virtue in a culture of vice. Nothing is done rashly or carelessly in the life of a prudent man.

Prudence is considered both an intellectual and a practical

virtue because prudence has to first get into your head before it comes out in your life. Its associated action(s) are thoughtful and deliberate, so prudence is functionally located in a mans' head, it moves through his heart, then toward practical action in the mouth, hands, and/or feet. It has to do with how you think and what you think about everything in life; especially God, yourself, and others. Prudence begins to function within us similar to the way a GPS system functions in a car. God gave us the GPS when we embraced Him in faith. And, in faith, we have to discover His true path and how He wants us to get from our current position to our final destination. Philosopher Peter Kreeft provides a powerful insight noting that, "Without a road map of the virtues and vices, how likely is it that we will find our way home, especially if we are lost? And the one thing nearly everyone knows is that modern man is lost."[31] A GPS provides you a map with directions on how to get from where you are now to where you want to be. There are usually a few paths to the same destination, but you have to choose to stay the course at every turn, choice by choice, deciding and taking action toward your destination as the Holy Spirit guides you.

In a related way prudence is a governing virtue that guides you toward where to go and the best route to get to the destination in life that God has planned for you. Often times it is not the shortest route either. But a prudent man is patient on his journey, growing in virtue knowing that God cares about the type of person you are when you finally arrive. A prudent man knows that God has a plan and a purpose for him and his job is to discover the path that God wants him to take to get there. I guess that you could say prudence is "God's Positioning System." Unlike a GPS in a car that comes preloaded with the map and a place where you just type in the address of your destination, you have to discover the address by "loading" the data into your mind through God's word (knowledge), processing it through life experience, godly counsel, godly friends, (understanding), then choosing to implement the virtues into your life as you drive (wisdom). The road is your path and the steering wheel reflects your choices. Your destination, however, is not just where you are going, it is who you are as a man when you get there.

---

[31] Kreeft, *Virtue*, p.30.

Prudence The Governing Virtue

"One machine can do the work of fifty ordinary men. No machine can do the work of one extraordinary man" – *Elbert Hubbard*

I would agree with Thomas Aquinas and King Solomon who both list prudence as first in importance when it comes to the four cardinal virtues. Prudence is the governing virtue and acts as an internal GPS in discerning which decision or path to take by properly applying the properties of prudence to the situation. What good is justice without knowing what one ought to do in order to be just? And what good is justice if one does not know how to be just? Moreover, what good is fortitude if we are courageous in standing up for error or immoral behavior and not truth and moral behavior?

Prudence is called for in the theological virtues as well, for what good is zeal in faith without knowledge? The Apostle Paul accuses some of the religious leaders of his day of this very thing as they rejected their Messiah: "For I testify about them that they have a zeal for God, but not in accordance with knowledge."[32] This is why the virtue of prudence is often called "practical wisdom," for prudence is meant for real life application. It is prudence that informs you on what is just and unjust. It is prudence that informs you when and how to show fortitude. It is prudence in your head that must tell you to stop and demonstrate temperance when the passions in the flesh cry out for gluttony. It is prudence that reminds you of hope when you experience despair, it is prudence that reminds you of God's faithfulness when you experience uncertainty. And finally it is prudence that informs your heart of a call to charity and not indifference when actions are needed for the least of these.

Prudence is so important that the wisest man who ever lived listed prudence and all of its sub-virtues as the purpose statement for the book of Proverbs. Circle each property of prudence in the verses below:

Proverbs 1:1-7

¹ The proverbs of Solomon the son of David, king of Israel:

² To know wisdom and instruction,

---

[32] Romans 10:3.

To discern the sayings of understanding,

[3] To receive instruction in wise behavior,

Righteousness, justice and equity;

[4] To give prudence to the naive,

To the youth knowledge and discretion,

[5] A wise man will hear and increase in learning,

And a man of understanding will acquire wise counsel,

[6] To understand a proverb and a figure,

The words of the wise and their riddles.

[7] The fear of the Lord is the beginning of knowledge;

Fools despise wisdom and instruction.

I think God is telling us something men! In these seven verses the properties of prudence and prudence itself is mentioned 17 times. In modern business lingo, **a prudent man** is the goal or desired output of the book of Proverbs, which is why these seven verses sound like goals or purpose statements. Prudence is practical wisdom for everyday use.

The Art of Making A Decision

"The hardest struggle of all is to be something different from what the average man is" – Robert H. Schuller

A prudent man takes knowledge, processes it, makes a decision, and chooses to act on that decision! We will learn that the virtue of fortitude gives a man the courage to act, but it is prudence that directs those actions toward a virtuous end and by a virtuous means. We need to be doers, but we must think before we act. On the other hand, we cannot just sit there in a state of paralysis by analysis either. Prudence is the practical application or outworking of knowledge and truth into a decision. This decision is to be carried out with memory of the past and foresight into the future so as to move forward with proper caution, skill, and faith. This combination of memory and foresight enable a prudent man to anticipate uncertainties that either help or hinder the action that must be done at the present moment. The vice of carelessness here can lead to either the sin of omission where no decision is made, or a very late decision as one is caught in the paralysis of analysis. On the other hand, this vice can lead to a thoughtless; i.e., careless, quick decision with very little counsel, insight, or anticipation of unintended consequences.

As a man you have a natural bent toward one of these extremes, so you must first be prudent in self-reflection knowing your tendency where the vice of carelessness is likely to hinder your growth in becoming a prudent man of God.

Reflect:

When faced with decisions I tend toward: <not always of course, but a bent or internal inclination>

_____ Too much analysis before a decision

_____ Too little analysis before making a decision

If you are not sure what your tendency is in decision making then you can find out really easy—ask someone who relies on you to make decisions and has to live with the outcome!

Whether your tendency is to make a rash decision with very few data points or get bogged down in a state of "paralysis by analysis" you must grow in prudence. Now every complex decision whether personal, on the job, or in your family will necessarily have unknown variables. This tension between having very little information and too much information can only be overcome through the virtue of prudence. The rest of this section is going to equip you to move your process of decision-making into the spectrum of prudence as depicted in the diagram below.

| -----------------[The Spectrum of a Prudent Decision]---------------- |

under analyze | ----------------The Window of Wisdom-------------| over analyze

Treat the virtue of prudence like a muscle that must be trained. At first the muscle hurts and the training feels awkward and painful. But as with other muscles "no pain, no gain!" As the Scriptures teach us: "…discipline yourself for the purpose of godliness; for bodily discipline is only of little profit, but godliness is profitable for all things…"[33]

In the sections that follow we are going to learn that a prudent man knows both his strengths and his weaknesses. He always seeks wise counsel from those who fill his weaknesses and compliments his strengths. He knows the value of having someone outside of himself to see what he cannot see, especially when he is close to personal situations. He further knows how to discern either inordinate fear or evil motives behind bad counsel. Finally, at times a prudent man needs the courage to follow his instinct when he sees things that others do not see.

The Three Chains of Carelessness

"Every vice leads to cruelty" – C.S. Lewis

Since a prudent man is the desired goal God has for us, we need to pursue prudence while at the same time determining how the vice of carelessness manifests itself in our lives, keeping us in chains. Men in chains are not going to get very far. It takes time and humility to peel back the veil and see ourselves as we are right now, while a desire to be a man of virtue allows us to press on and persevere in order to break the chains of carelessness! How the vice manifests itself in your life is a critical data point, but it is important that you do not make this a focal point. So, on the one hand you need the data point so you understand the chains that keep you from moving forward, but if you make the vice a focal point then you will create a self-fulfilled prophecy walking in the flesh and not the Spirit. A man of prudence sees ahead and moves toward the goal before him. No man gets very far when he has his head down staring at where he is instead of where he knows God wants him to be.

The book of Proverbs gives us three different types of people who are in the chains of carelessness: (1) the naïve (simple); (2) the

---

[33] 1Timothy 4:7-8.

fool; (3) the scoffer.

Proverbs 1:22 – How long, O naive ones, will you love being simple-minded? And scoffers delight themselves in scoffing, And fools hate knowledge?

All of us will fall into these categories in different areas of life, while some of us will be defined by one category based upon a stage of life or a lifestyle of walking in the flesh for decades. While it may not be prudent to stare at where you are, it would be foolish to try and move forward on God's map without first finding the contextual red dot of: "You are here." There are certain areas of life where you will be naïve because either you do not have any life experience or very little life experience. For example, you may be single and dating and know a bit about relationships but you are naïve regarding marriage. On the other hand, a young man (high school through college) will fall into the category of naïve out of no fault of his own, but by the fact that he does not have enough life experience. He may have gained some knowledge through observing others with some experience on his own, but not nearly enough life experience. This is especially the case for the young man who has been blessed with only first-world problems due to an upper middle-class and above average financial backdrop. Many of you reading this book may have had the experience of being forced to grow up fast when burdens rested on you and you alone with no chance of a helicopter parent flying in to the rescue. As for the other categories of fool and scoffer both young and old would do well not to be defined in this way by continuing to remain naïve. Here is the natural progression of the careless man who does not desire prudence.

Naïve ⟹ Fool ⟹ Scoffer

Category#1: The naïve

"The younger you are, the more you think you can manage it all on your own...the older you get, the more you realize that without Christ, you would never have made it." - Ravi Zacharias

There are different groups of people who fall into this category such as teenagers, college students, new believers, and addicts who stopped participating in life the moment the energy needed to solve his problems went toward medicating them. For the naïve there are a few things required if you are going to be a man of prudence and not carelessness. If you are a teenager or a recent college graduate you are, by definition and of no fault of your own, naïve. This is simply because you do not have enough life experience and that is something that cannot be helped. The cure for you is true biblical knowledge and not supposed knowledge from college textbook, or worse, relying on the aggregate knowledge of your naïve peers. If you are a new believer then you are naïve in the sense that you more than likely have made many bad decisions and have fully trained yourself on how to make wrong decisions. I remember when I came to Christ at 25 and made it a point to throw everything that I believe on the table. I picked it up again with a biblical perspective, and reprocessed it. I was flabbergasted at how many things I believed but actually had no clue as to why I believed them. At the time I considered myself a pretty smart guy!

No matter what your age is, when you are young in Christ you more than likely have a wealth of bad experience that shaped your thinking and needs renewed as Romans 12:1-3 points out. The final person is the addict who stopped participating in life and literally stopped growing the moment he subconsciously chose to medicate his problems through a bottle, drugs, sexual pleasures, etc. When the same or similar problems faced earlier in life appear this man does a canon ball into his brain's limbic system where his old memories are stored and he ends up making the exact same mistake over and over and over again because it "feels right."

We are all naïve in some area of life. For example, you may be naïve regarding a particular life stage. For example, you may be newly married so you are naïve in this area because the husband role is brand new to you. Or you may be a new parent and are naïve in this area because the father part of your nature is awakened for the first time. I remember how much of an "expert" I was on parenting when I had one child at two years old. Boy, I was not only naïve, but I was an arrogant fool! It is critical that you embrace this reality if you fall into any of these categories, because if you do not, you will end up making a ton of bad decisions and blaming God for the results. Proverbs 19:3 drives this point home teaching us that, "The foolishness of man ruins his way, and his heart rages against the Lord." In short, the first step for you is a realization of the fact that you are naïve and older and wiser men just may have something to offer you. This wise view, requires a teachable spirit and a humble heart.

1Peter 5:5 – "You younger men, likewise, be subject to your elders; and all of you, clothe yourselves with humility toward one another, for God is opposed to the proud, but gives grace to the humble."

If you are a teenager or young man in college, I have some really easy advice for you. Please talk with your father, or mentor! He eagerly wants to hear from you and help you along life's journey. One of the problems the young and naïve have is how information from a parent or mentor is processed. As a young man there is a tendency to interpret advice (knowledge) from a parent or mentor as an overreaction. In this way, what is required is faith. Faith in your earthly father whom you do see and his wisdom is the necessary practice of building your faith muscle when faith in your heavenly Father whom you do not see is required. So try to take advice from this author who may just know a few things about being naïve.

For the adult new believer in his mid 20's – 50's it is critical that you rethink everything! Like myself, you will be surprised at how naïve you are in some areas. For the rest of us, we are all naïve in some area of life because we simply have no experience. This is what makes life exciting and keeps God's word fresh and real because there is always something new to learn and apply as life places you in new roles. As a pastor teaching large Preparing for Marriage classes of 30 -70 couples twice a year, I can tell you that the older the couple getting married, the more unteachable they are and the more problems they will have due to being set in their ways. I repeat, humility is the first step.

Truth time: In what area or areas are you naïve and want to grow in? List and explain below.

_____

_____

_____

What are the steps needed to grow in prudence in order to

break the chains of carelessness in the life of the naïve? The solution lies in the simple definition of prudence provided by Augustine: "Knowledge of what to seek and avoid." I will break this quote from Augustine into two complementary steps. Like a good football team you need a good offense and a good defense.

Step #1: Offence: Acquire knowledge of what to seek.

I want to focus on knowledge because this is what you need to gain *now*, because without knowledge, rooted in truth, you can never truly begin the growth process. The danger with knowledge is that you are faced with a choice: be wise or be clever. Satan took all that he knew and made the decision to be clever. With this in mind, here is the growth process as laid out in the Bible, the primary source of what is true.

Knowledge ⇒ Understanding ⇒ Wisdom

Proverbs 19:2-3 – it is not good for a person to be without knowledge, And he who hurries [b]his footsteps [c]errs. [3]The foolishness of man ruins his way, And his heart rages against the LORD.

Knowledge is when a person has true information his mind acquired, while understanding is an insight into how things fit together when new knowledge is processed in the heart along with other truths so as to gain a complete picture. There are two primary ways in which we gain knowledge. First, by reading and studying information and second, through acquaintance; i.e., by a direct awareness of information through experience. True knowledge is an important first step if you are going to grow. Notice I said "true knowledge." I say this because we have an amazing tendency to believe a lot of things that simply are not true, and false knowledge that is thought to be true can actually be more dangerous than no knowledge at all. Why? Because you have to choose to first distrust the false information, erase it, then replace it with true information. True knowledge is incredibly important as the Bible makes clear in Hosea 4:6, "My people are destroyed for lack of knowledge…"

A sure sign of a movement from knowledge alone to understanding is when you can communicate what something means, and describe its implications along with the causal relationships. A movement from understanding to wisdom is properly applying these truths to your life in a meaningful way. In short, you have to know before you can grow to the point of having something to apply. Take the areas above where you acknowledged that you are naïve, and study them. You can go to www.biblegateway.com and search the Bible for topics in this area and get as much truth into your mind by memorize verses. Here is a small list of websites where you can register for podcasts or search and download deep messages on numerous topics:

www.gotquestions.org - an amazing resource of short essays rich in Bible verses on every topic you can imagine!

www.rzim.org - a ministry of Christian apologist Ravi Zacharias

www.gty.org - a ministry of Bible scholar John MacArthur

www.reasonablefaith.org - a ministry of Dr. William Lane Craig who is a Christian philosopher and one of the best debaters in the world defending the Christian faith.

www.evolutionnews.org - an amazing blog by ID scientists who blog on the latest science news. Also these ID scientists debate atheist scientists on-line.

I want you to notice how this growth process maps to the three levels of faith discussed in the previous chapter. Prudence and faith are linked in a very significant way. It is wisdom that is both a property of faith and prudence, not knowledge or understanding. Faith equals trust, and it is trust that leads to action when a man actually believes something is true..

Knowledge ⇒ Content of faith

Understanding ⇒ Conviction of faith

Wisdom ⇒ Centrality of faith

Growth in Prudence Equals Growth in Faith

Remember in the faith chapter where I said the Christian

would spend most of his life as the Romans 12:2 process is lived out. It was in the partial overlap of faith and reason where prudence informs you as you grow in faith and apply God's truth to your life. As you acquire knowledge in the specific areas you listed, begin the discipline of daily reading God's word. I recommend that you start your Bible reading with the book of Proverbs then jump to John and read all the way through the New Testament. Why? Remember the purpose statement of proverbs?

Proverbs 1:4 – To give prudence to the naïve, to the youth **knowledge** and discretion…

If you are a young man then carelessness here may be expressed as not even bothering to consider God's word as relevant, or even worse—boring! The enemy will do his best to keep you from God's word and will try to have your doubt that it actually is God's word. Now I admit that the Bible at times may seem boring and irrelevant now, but when you are faced with key decisions you will be impressed at how you consider what you memorized from God's word. Again as you gain experience, God's word proves to be both true and relevant. So memorize the proverbs that stand out to you, at least one a week. To really grow, find a good friend or mentor to partner with and hold you accountable.

There is no shortage of websites that supposedly found "the 700 contradictions in the Bible" or "The real gospels that lost the battle". Again, this is one reason for the Appendix on the Bible. Nothing is worse than someone who never read the Bible and all of the sudden share sloppy "cut and paste" articles from skeptic rant sites as if they discovered it as a Bible scholar. Nothing is new under the sun. Read them and see for yourself how foolish and childish they are, or you can read actual scholars. Dr. Norman Geisler has a book that I love called "The Big Book of Bible Difficulties" that is ordered from Genesis to Revelation and addresses actual difficulties in a scholarly way.

When you read God's word, the Holy Spirit who wrote it and dwells within you immediately activates it within you. As you gain knowledge it is easy to mistake the Bible as simply a list of "do's and don'ts", but that is not God's goal. C.S. Lewis said it this way: "We might think that God wanted simply obedience to a set of rules:

whereas He really wants a people of a particular sort." The Bible is much more than that so try to take the "do and don't" commands as nuggets of knowledge from your heavenly Father who created you to function in a certain way. So when you find yourself thinking "what's the big deal?"-pause- and replace that thought with, "God I honestly don't get it but I trust you." This is the virtue of faith in action! See how faith is linked to prudence in a real and practical way? In fact all of the virtues are linked to prudence, because without prudence you can never know what is necessary to be a man of virtue. In fact, if you made it this far in this book, you are already moving toward being a man of virtue in a culture of vice.

How has the vice of carelessness revealed itself in your life? Explain.

_____

_____

_____

Step #2: Acquire knowledge of what to avoid.

The second part of the definition of prudence provided by Augustine concerns what to avoid while you are seeking. Everybody knows that a football team has to have a good offense to make it to the Super Bowl, but it is defense that wins and brings home the ring. The defensive posture of prudence is to understand the second healthy side of fear. Proverbs 8:13 defines the fear of the Lord in very practical terms: "The fear of the Lord is to hate evil..." Why? Because that is what God hates. He hates the sin but loves the person and He never mistakes the sin as the person. God hates evil because it hurts the people He loves and created in His image.

This is very useful and practical given that according to Proverbs 1:7 "The fear of the Lord is the beginning of knowledge." Hating what God hates will help you to protect yourself from the lure of evil that draws all of us in. When one is naïve, what is evil seems like no big deal and where all of the fun is. In fact, the naïve may even find the word "evil" harsh. I promise you that there are several key areas in your life where, if you get careless and choose not to believe God and resist, avoid, and in some cases flee, you will be sorry. Ask any addict and he will tell you that his addictions began in the teenage years when he believed that binge drinking and pornography was no big deal and a big laugh. Don't believe me then please, put down the book and ask any adult addict! Here are a few areas where you can build your defense and choose prudence over carelessness right now that will make a big difference in your life no matter how old you are.

Defense Playbook: *A prudent man is not careless with electronics*

"Extreme standards or extreme regrets" – Andy Stanley

Proverbs 27:12 – A prudent man sees evil and hides himself, the naive proceed and pay the penalty

Being careless with electronics that connect to the Internet can ruin your life because there are traps everywhere! If you are a father with young kids then you would do well to turn off Internet access on these devices. If you have pre-teens or young teenagers then you should lock Internet access with a code. For older teens through adults we need to be vigilant in this area and add monitoring software that will block sexual content. If this area has gripped your life then you need an accountability partner and software that will send your accountability partner reports. The goal here men is to protect the heart while you prepare the heart. If it is a constant battle, then it is time for a radical move, unless you are too soft to do it. Yes, that is a challenge! Go cold turkey! No smart phones and no personal Internet access period. Thinking, "yea right." Then I have a question for you. How is your current plan working out for you? I will provide some tips in the chapter on the virtue of temperance. For now here are a few resources that I have used in the past or currently use.

www.covenanteyes.com - Sends accountability reports to selected accountability partners. Has an install for computers and smart phones.

www.addblockplus - FREE browser plugin that blocks ads.

Ghostery – is a free add block plug-in for Chrome and Firefox.

www.XXXChurch.com - Same as covenant eyes but includes online help for recovery.

Defense Playbook: *A prudent man is not careless in friendship*

We all have heard the sayings before "show me your friends and I will show you your future" or, how about "birds of a feather flock together." Friends are incredibly influential and there is a reason for it. One of the marks of God's image in us is the fact that, like God, we are relational beings. In fact God created us for relationships! Here is the only Bible verse that begins with the phrase "Do not be deceived"

1Corinthians 15:33 - **Do not be deceived**, bad company corrupts good morals"

Why do you think this verse begins this way? How have you seen its truth?

_____

_____

_____

_____

Here are two truths that you can begin to apply right now:

(1) Choose your friends wisely

(2) Be a friend worth choosing

No matter what your age, every one of us tends to be careless in this area. God made us for relationship, and these relationships should be mutually beneficial in that we each sharpen one another and pull one another up. How can you be a band of brothers when you invite the enemy into your foxhole? Of course you will have friends that are not believers, but these friends should not be your most intimate friends. I would add that neither should the soft Christians with a "said faith" and not a "real faith" be your close personal friends. I love how Psalm 26:4 puts it, "I do not sit with deceitful men, nor will I go with pretenders." You need some strong men who love you and are not afraid to say hard things to you. As Proverbs 27:6 reminds us, "Faithful are the wounds of a friend, but deceitful are the kisses of an enemy."

We all have friends that we are close to and not so close to for various reasons. I find it helpful to break your relationships into four relational circles where you would have public, social, personal, and intimate relationships. The public space is where you meet people and connect over a common interest or connect point such as college, hometown, or work. The social space would be where you place your casual friends that you only see at events or due to mutual friends. As you get to know someone better from the outer spaces, you hang out more and over time begin to decide to keep them in the social space or move them closer into your personal space. This experience of friendship development is best stated by C.S. Lewis, "Friendship is born at that moment when one person says to another: "What! You too? I thought I was the only one." Most really close friends stay here unless you are truly blessed to have that intimate friend that truly knows you, dirt and all, but loves you, encourages you, and challenges you like a true brother.

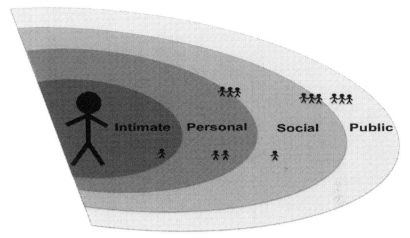

As you can see, these circles represent closeness or distance from your heart where your true self resides and not the false self you put forth. In summary, the further out from you the more acquaintance-friends you have, the closer in toward your personal space a handful of true friends. As men, very few of us have an intimate friend who knows all of our good parts and bad parts, but loves us as a brother. The intimate friend is a man who sows belief in you, celebrates you, challenges you, and sees the best in you because he knows the real you. He is not jealous of your success, but truly happy, proud, and considers himself blessed to call you a friend.

There are many reasons why a man may choose to not allow anyone that close. Most of it has to do with either pride or our trust being violated by someone in our past such as a parent, family member, or our first real friend. This has happened to everyone including Jesus. King David prophetically wrote about Judas betraying Jesus in 1,000BC, "Even my close friend in whom I trusted, who ate my bread has lifted up his heel against me."[34] Putting down that trust bridge which leads to your true self just seems too vulnerable, so we have "many friends" on Facebook, but no real friends in life.

I think of myself and how I spent most of my life with "many friends" but no true friends. Don't get me wrong; I have had what I consider good friends at different seasons of my life who were in my personal space. But a true intimate friend? No, not really. From my experience mentoring and talking to other men I know my experience is not unique.

Proverbs 18:24 – A man of too many friends comes to ruin, but there is a friend who sticks closer than a brother.

Time is an investment, and time is the only resource we use that we can never get back. The relational investments you make pay dividends of good or bad; the choice is yours so be prudent. I had to up my defensive playbook and do some serious pruning in my life after I came to Christ by moving my friendship circles around. I was so serious about this that my wife and I made a commitment early in our marriage to keep negative couples in the social, public space and never the personal or intimate space. Each of us had friends who were our personal friends who also got married. I may love my friend, but honestly him and his wife as a couple not so much. With both Cheryl and me from broken families, our marriage is too precious and must be protected at all costs. My wife must be in my intimate space, and I do not need another woman pulling her out of it. Likewise, I am in my wife's intimate space and she does not need another man pulling me out. Invest in people who matter, and cut the past investments that are not helpful or directly hurtful.

I live in the crazy busy Washington, DC area with long commutes to work, and a wife and three kids who need my time. The resource of time has shrunk significantly over the years. I have a small handful of personal friends that I do not spend nearly enough

---

[34] Psalm 41:9.

time with and one intimate friend that I really do not see enough. Do you think I have time to waste on shallow friendships? No. I have recently decided to try and make more time with my close friends and so should you.

Ephesians 5:15-17 – Therefore [a]be careful how you walk, not as unwise men but as wise, 16[b]making the most of your time, because the days are evil. 17So then do not be foolish, but understand what the will of the Lord is.

Who do you need to prune from your life that is pulling you down? Write down the name(s) below and explain.

_____

_____

_____

If one of your friends were to do this study, how would he say that you are pulling him down? Be honest. Explain.

_____

_____

_____

Category #2: The fool

There is a classic story I heard from my seminary professor and hero in the faith Dr. Norman Geisler that I think pretty well sums up the fool. There was a professor who asked his class "what is the biggest problem in America?" A young man in the back of the room raised his hand and was called on to provide his answer. The young man quipped "I don't know and I don't care!" Friends, that is the biggest problem in America; namely, ignorance and apathy.

In the Bible the fool is a person who lacks mental acumen. In short, a fool does not think! He is careless in the sense that he couldn't "care less" about thinking, to include the consequences of decisions or its impact on himself or anyone else. He is the consummate "eat, drink, and be merry for tomorrow we die."[35]

---

[35] 1 Corinthians 15:32.

Name a time in your life when you were a fool. Explain.

_____

_____

_____

Proverbs 10:8 – The wise of heart will receive commands, but a babbling fool will be ruined.

Proverbs 18:2 – A fool does not delight in understanding, but only in revealing his own mind.

A fool not only doesn't think, he doesn't learn because he doesn't listen. I have heard it said that God gave us two ears and one mouth because we are created to listen twice as much as we speak. Sometimes, the fool doesn't listen because he doesn't care, while at other times he doesn't listen because he is attempting to listen with his mouth open. In short, fools become fools and stay fools because they are unteachable. And when you are unteachable you are unreachable, for even God cannot fill a cup that is already full! In the book of Proverbs alone the fool is mentioned 76 times. Wow! Think of the mission statement verses that we started with. The second half of the very verse that tells us the beginning of knowledge, tells us the fool's attitude toward this truth.

Proverbs 1:7 – The fear of the Lord is the beginning of knowledge; Fools despise wisdom and instruction.

Proverbs 23:9 – Do not speak in the hearing of a fool, for he will despise the wisdom of your words.

A fool chooses to never learn. A fool will ignore or simply "care less" about remembering the hard lessons from his own life and the lives of others. If the fool could learn, it will always be the hard way. So what is the solution for the fool?

Step #1: Admit that you are a fool.

To start with, try looking into the mirror and saying out loud "I am a fool Lord please help me." They say that the first step to getting help is acknowledging that you have a problem, and the very first person that needs to hear the acknowledgement is you.

Secondly, you have to admit it to another person and let them know that you would like some help.

Proverbs 12:15 – The way of a fool is right in his own eyes, but a wise man is he who listens to counsel.

Write down the name of a person who could help: _____

Step #2: Become teachable.

Advice for the teenager – college graduate

If you are a young man who moved from being naïve straight to being a fool, then admit it to your parent(s), ask for forgiveness and seek their advice. In your life I am sure that you noticed some 'chinks' in your Mom or Dad's armor where you have come to the realization that your parents are not perfect. This should be obvious to you because your parents are sinners just like you, whether redeemed sinners or still in denial. On the other hand, your parents have so much more experience, which just may translate into some important lessons they desire to pass on to you. Some of the most important lessons will be when they were fools themselves. All healthy fathers really do want their sons to be a better person than he is. What will always break your parent's heart is finding out about a mistake you made some other way or from someone else. What will fill your parent's heart is when you come to them and say "Mom/Dad, look, I was a careless fool today so I need to talk, because I need your help…" Here is a four-step process that I highly recommend you commit to memory with the acrostic C.A.L.M.:

(1) Confess your mistakes.

(2) Ask "what do I do?"

(3) Listen to the advice.

(4) Man-up and accept the consequences without playing the victim.

These steps may be hard at times, but please let your parents into your life because there is no other place they would rather be.

Proverbs 4:2 – Hear, O son, the instruction of a *father*, and give attention that you may gain understanding

Proverbs 1:8 – Hear, my son, your *father's* instruction and do not forsake your *mother's* teaching

Advice for the rest of us

There is no other way to become teachable than to "man-up" by having other men actively involved in your life who can and will actually challenge you. When I was a full-time pastor, there was a constant theme in the lives of the men who would come to my office after a major crisis in their lives as a result of being a fool. The theme was that they had zero, and I mean zero godly men in their lives. I would have to start from scratch to get them connected in biblical community. The men who were successful in this area alone didn't merely survive the crisis, they thrived through the crisis and into a healthy godly life. Men, we need godly men in our lives period! Here is by far the best passage in the Bible on this point:

Galatians 6:1-2

Brethren, even if [a]anyone is caught in any trespass, you who are spiritual, restore such a one in a spirit of gentleness; each one looking to yourself, so that you too will not be tempted. [2]Bear one another's burdens, and thereby fulfill the law of Christ.

In your own words write down what this passage means.

_____

_____

_____

Category #3: The Scoffer

This third category of the scoffer or mocker I do not actually have to address, because there is no way this person is reading this book! I will address him though because it is instructive for us to all know so that we can first protect ourselves from arriving here, and second properly respond to the scoffers in our life.

The scoffer can best be described as the critical person who is boastful, argumentative, contentious, haughty, and much too arrogant to even think that he can possibly learn from another. Here are just a few descriptions of this man from the Bible:

Proverbs 21:24 – "Proud," "Haughty," "Scoffer," are his names, who acts with insolent pride.

Proverbs 15:12 – A scoffer does not love one who reproves him, He will not go to the wise.

Proverbs 22:10 – Drive out the scoffer, and contention will go out, even strife and dishonor will cease.

Proverbs 24:9 – The devising of folly is sin, and the scoffer is an abomination to men.

So what is the solution for the scoffer? God breaking him down, and trust me it will be painful, for tough love always is. If you know of a person who fits this description try and keep a relationship but a safe one. Be ready to be there when they may look to you, but do not count on it unless you do this first and most important step— Prayer!

Step #1: Pray for them.

If we have learned anything from the last few wars in the middle east between the United States and its enemies it is this: Win the air war before you send in the ground troops. The same is true in this case. You have to pray for the person in an intercessory way where you begin to feel sorrow for the person being in this state. You have to picture each word as a prayer bomb hitting the target and softening it for when the ground battle begins and the Lord Jesus calls you to active duty. Here is a good way to have intercessory prayer in the life of another.

(1) Place an empty seat next to you and picture the person in that seat.

(2) Ask God to help you see life from their optic. Picture a connected arrow from that person to you. Begin a prayer of discovery. What in his life may have hardened his heart? When he is alone on his bed at night what does he think of? What is his

family situation? Continue to pray in discovery mode so that you begin to feel empathy for this person.

(3) When you have this information, picture another arrow from you to the throne of God. Imagine that you are literally taking his cares and burdens, feeling them, then sending them to a compassionate God.

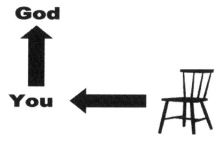

(4) In faith picture God completing the triangle by answering your prayer and hitting his heart with the answer. Something like, "Oh, God please hit his heart and soften it right now wherever he is. Make him sense your work."

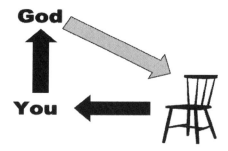

Do this for at least 15 minutes at first, say 5 minutes per step, and then increase it over time. Watch what God does! The first thing that God will do is soften your heart toward him. I had this happen as I prayed for a scoffer in my life. I was really shocked when I started having compassion for this person and feeling sorry for him, especially given our history. You will soon learn that God changes you more than He changes things. This is what intercessory prayer means; it is compassionate prayer on behalf of another, where you are not in his face, but in his shoes.

Step #2: Do not engage in public debate.

Proverbs 9:7-8 – He who corrects a scoffer gets dishonor for himself, and he who reproves a wicked man gets [e]insults for himself. [8]Do not reprove a scoffer, or he will hate you, Reprove a wise man and he will love you.

Matthew 7:6 – "Do not give what is holy to dogs, and do not throw your pearls before swine, or they will trample them under their feet, and turn and tear you to pieces."

Have you ever "cast your pearls before swine"? What do you remember about that experience?

_____

_____

_____

Step #3: Never get to this point yourself

The saddest thing about a scoffer is that he will eventually get into an incredibly stressful anxiety ridden situation and will at that very moment look for wisdom and it will be unavailable to him.

Proverbs 14:6 – A scoffer seeks wisdom and finds none, but knowledge is easy to one who has understanding.

Why do you think this is so? Hint: revisit process of growth.

_____

_____

_____

Prudence As A Lifestyle Not A Drive-thru

"To think is to serve God in the interior court" – Thomas Traherne

We need to pray continually for prudence. Here is a great prayer from the book of Psalms. There is nothing better than praying God's Word back to Him.

Psalm 119:33-40

[33]Teach me, O Lord, the way of Your statutes, And I shall observe it to the end. [34]Give me understanding, that I may observe Your law And keep it with all my heart. [35]Make me walk in the path of Your commandments, For I delight in it. [36]Incline my heart to Your testimonies, And not to dishonest gain. [37]Turn away my eyes from looking at vanity, And revive me in Your ways. [38]Establish Your [m]word to Your servant, [n]As that which produces reverence for You. [39]Turn away my reproach which I dread, For Your ordinances are good. [40]Behold, I long for Your precepts; Revive me through Your righteousness.

We are a fast paced, quick fix, fast food loving culture that has access to more useless information and distractions than any culture in history. We want something now and we can get it with a simple click via an app on our smart phone. If we could gain intelligence by drinking Smart Water or become ethical by drinking Ethos water we no doubt would do it. I admit that I would be all over that idea! The reality is that we cannot pull into the drive-thru line of McVirtue and order a number five with a large Smart Water to help us become wise. There is no degree and no professional certification you could acquire as a "Certified Man of Prudence" that will get you there. Prudence requires work, hard work, but very satisfying work when you see that the great Carpenter Himself is placing hammer to chisel as He shapes you into a man He can use. Every blow by God to your worldview, your life choices, and your very self is done with a life shaping purpose. The purpose is to make you the man of virtue in a culture of vice who is a difference maker not a space taker. There is often pain in the forming process, but He asks that you allow Him to finish His work because there is a beautiful work of art in the making.

Wisdom is acquired throughout your journey by living in such a way that decision-making naturally becomes a process of prudence. Imagine if before making any decisions, you immediately begin by looking back with the property of 'memory' into your rearview mirror to see where you have been. You move further along as you combine that data with where you are. Then you start moving with the property of 'caution' as you look ahead with 'foresight' to where you want to be.

Some of us have acquired some passengers along the way whom God has instructed us to lead and influence. You can think of each child holding a driving permit for life, and they are watching you ,Dad, and picking up driving tips. Taking a look at who is in the sacred place of the passenger seat as a helper suitable and the precious cargo in the back seat makes careless driving even more consequential should you crash. It is what you have loaded into your GPS combined with your willingness to listen to the directions and the wise counsel of brothers who have been there before that will separate the wise man from the foolish man. Christian philosopher JP Moreland in his ground breaking work *Loving God With All of Your Mind* gives the best description of a wise man that I know:

The spiritually mature Christian is a wise person. And a wise person has the skill necessary to lead an exemplary life and to address the issues of the day in a responsible, attractive way that brings honor to God. Wisdom is the fruit of a life of strong study and a developed mind that is receptive to God's Spirit personally and relationally through a network of wise counselors. Wisdom is the application of knowledge gained from studying both God's written Word and the living Word in others who have lived a life worthy of the calling of Christ. If we are going to be wise spiritual people prepared to meet the crises of our age, we must be a studying, learning community that values the life of the mind. Clearly, to become spiritually formed in Christ as a person of wisdom requires that we follow Christ's teaching in this critical area, and it was He who taught us to love the Lord our God with all our minds.[36]

---

[36] J.P. Moreland, *Love Your God With All Your Mind* (Colorado Springs, CO: NavPress, 1997), 39.

"Feeling Led" vs. "Being Led"

"We are much more aware of ourselves than we are of God" – Eugene Peterson

There is a popular modern approach to discovering God's will regarding any number of decisions in life, though popular, is both confusing and troubling. When I was a full-time pastor I would encounter numerous people who would begin a conversation with, "God is telling me to_____." Sometimes what followed was not bad in itself, and at other times what followed was something that I had no doubt God did not say. When it was the latter, the person would challenge me and I would simply go to what God has already said in His word and point out the contradiction between God's Word and this person's liver quiver. As Titus 1:9 instructs, "holding fast the faithful word which is in accordance with the teaching, so that he will be able both to exhort in sound doctrine and to refute those who contradict." So, how do we hear from God and what does that look like in a man's life?

This modern approach to decision making I will call the mystical approach and we will compare it to the biblical model that I will call the prudent approach. Don't misunderstand me, I am not saying that God does not impress things on a man's heart as He sovereignly leads him as to what to do and not do. In fact, I will share a personal example of this supernatural experience below and when I give my testimony in the chapter on temperance. What I am saying is that this is not how God instructs us to live our life day by day by 'punting' decisions to Him and waiting for a feeling as evidence of God's mental dump. This is the unbiblical New Age view of faith disconnected from reason as I discussed earlier.

The graphic on page 101 will illustrate the difference between the unbiblical mystical approach and the biblical prudent approach to making decisions in your life. In fact, there is no Bible verse that teaches the mystical approach—not one! On the other hand, there is the 'yes' prayer of James that I shared earlier:

James 1:5-7

But if any of you lacks wisdom, let him ask of God, who gives to all generously and [a]without reproach, and it will be given to him. [6]But he must ask in faith without any doubting, for the one who doubts is like the surf of the sea, driven and tossed by the wind. [7]For that man ought not to expect that he will receive anything from the Lord.

This is a prayer for wisdom and not a feeling. Add to James 1:5-7 the passage of scripture that speaks specifically to Christians on the topic of discerning God's will. Romans 12:1-2 describes what faith and prudence looks like in a man's life. This approach of faith and prudence will break the chains of uncertainty about your decisions and the carelessness of your decisions.

Read Romans 12:1-2 three times slowly and mark the key words that stand out to you.

Romans 12:1-2

Therefore I urge you, brethren, by the mercies of God, to present your bodies a living and holy sacrifice, [a]acceptable to God, which is your [b]spiritual service of worship. [2]And do not be conformed to this [c]world, but be transformed by the renewing of your mind, so that you may [d]prove what the will of God is, that which is good and [e]acceptable and perfect. [Emphasis mine]

Summarize Romans 12:1-2 in your own words.

_____

_____

_____

_____

_____

The Greek word used for transform in this verse is *metamorphoó* where we get the term metamorphosis. This is a radical change! God is calling us to radical new thinking not baptized old thinking. The Greek word for mind *nooce* means the intellect, or reasoning faculty. The Greek word for will is *theléma* which literally means desires. This is evidence of God calling us to the prudent approach in decision-making using both faith and reason. A reason, by the way, that is in the process of being radically renewed.

I remember as a child growing up in Pittsburgh with five TV

stations, three on VHF and two on UHF. In order to get better reception and to remove the static we would wrap the antennae with aluminum foil. This proved that the problem was in the receiver and not the transmitter. The transmission was clear but became garbled when it hit the receiver. I am not suggesting that you wear an aluminum foil hat to hear God clearly while blocking NSA from reading your mind. What I am suggesting is that we have a problem with our reception when the static of our own desires drown out the voice of God and garbles the picture of His plan.

Merely sitting in the prayer position and waiting for better reception will never work because we have a bad receiver that God wants to bring through a metamorphosis. The only way to fix the receiver is by placing it under the teaching of the word of God personally, through godly counsel, and rubbing shoulders with other men who are on the same journey as you. God knows His plans for you and He desires to reveal them to you. How do you discover God's will?

There are two main approaches shown in the diagram on the next page. There is the mystical approach and the prudent approach. With the mystical approach the man follows his heart in making decisions, and in the prudent approach the man leads his heart. Jeremiah 17:9 teaches that, "The heart is deceitful above all things and beyond cure. Who can understand it?" Men, you cannot know the mind of God or internally discern His voice from your own if you have no idea how God thinks or speaks. God's word provides specifics of how He thinks and how He has actively worked in the lives of several people as examples of hearing His voice. Why do you think that God would preserve for us a library of 66 books that cover 1,500 years of history, and written in three languages? The same Holy Spirit that inspired the Bible is the very same Holy Spirit that dwells within you if you are a Christian. The great reformer Martin Luther once said that, "feelings come and feelings go and feelings are deceiving. My warrant the Word of God none else is worth believing."

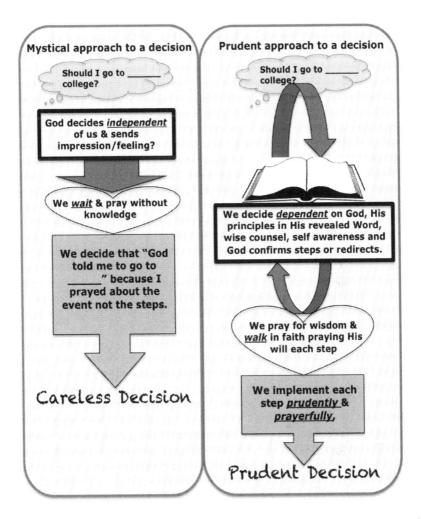

There is another approach to decision making that has started gaining ground lately within Christianity that I will call the passive Father approach. This approach is all reason and no faith as the man views God as a distant Father who is not interested in being involved in the life of His children. This approach makes prayer an empty, rote religious activity that you do, not because God wants to respond, but because He commands you to pray. This view of God as a dead beat Dad not interested in being actively involved in His children's decision-making process is empty and, quite frankly, depressing.

Applying The Prudent Approach

"This is the confidence we have in approaching God: that if we ask anything according to his will, he hears us." – 1 John 5:14

Acts 17:26 – He made from one man every nation of mankind to live on all the face of the earth, having determined their appointed times and the boundaries of their habitation.

When Cheryl and I were looking for a new home, we began to pray and seek God's guidance on what to do. Based on Acts 17:26, we read that God knows exactly where we are going to live and when we will live there. We call this the moving verse, and provide it to any of our friends who are trying to decide whether or not they should move. We know that God does not desire us to be in debt, and so we needed to buy a home that only my salary would support because we had decided that Cheryl would stay home and homeschool our children. All of these served as data points for making a prudent decision.

We found a home in our price range that was out in the country where my wife has always preferred to live. It was a very nice country home with plenty of land but no basement. We were really close to buying this house and we were both excited about it. There was one problem though; I just could not shake my "gut" feeling that it was not right. I prayed and prayed but it would not go away. I hated the thought of disappointing my wife and best friend, but I just had to tell her that I felt the Lord telling me "No." We knew the Lord would want us united on a decision, and in this case He was telling me "No." Of course I wish He would have told her instead, but that was not how He decided to reveal His will.

We took a pause on looking for a house, and a year later in 2001 the housing market in DC was on fire! We found a new home locally in a housing development that was just starting construction. We had the opportunity to hand pick our layout that, of course, included a nice country front porch for Cheryl. We sold our house in a few hours and made enough to cover a 20% down payment. This was great given that if we had sold a year earlier we would have at best broke even.

The following year Cheryl's mother had a severe stroke, and

a year after that we had the basement finished and she moved in so that we could take care of her. Wow! We look back and realized that if we would have bought the home in the country with no basement, we would have had no room for Cheryl's mom to live. God knew the future and we did not. We prayed for direction knowing God's promise in Acts 17:26 and listened when He said "no" even though we had no further information. This is biblical faith in practice when making a prudent decision.

The Calling

"Faith is the art of holding on to things your reason has once accepted in spite of your changing moods." – C.S. Lewis

I remember being in my very first summer module at Southern Evangelical Seminary when the professor asked the class of ~50 students, "Who has read the whole Bible?" Three men including myself raised our hands. Personally, I was shocked! Really. That was ten years ago and I think about it often. Men called into ministry should have worn out Bibles before they hit the seminary door, if they go to seminary at all. How many hands would have gone up if the professor asked, "How many men feel called into ministry?" I bet all fifty. How did they hear that call? How did they interpret what that call means? How can this man distinguish between God's voice and his own, when he has very little of God's voice in his head? What makes him believe that the "call" to ministry means full-time ministry? What made him believe that this call meant seminary right now without any personal relationship developed through the discipline of Bible study? God first and foremost wants *you!* Without you, your gifts will be unfruitful and used in the flesh and not the Spirit.

Acts 4:13 – Now as they observed the confidence of Peter and John and understood that they were uneducated and untrained men, they were amazed, and began to recognize them [a]as having been with Jesus.

I hope that you see the problem here. One of the problems is that God has called everyone into ministry, which is why everyone has a spiritual gift to discover. Every man should sense a call to ministry as he begins to take his faith seriously! You cannot get enough. This, what I term the first call, should be experienced by any man who is growing in his relationship with Christ. I believe that some of the men in the class took this first call and ran with it in a very western way—get the sheepskin! This first call is a Holy discontent felt from seeing God impact you in a very real and personal way, and you want more. Excellent motive! What if one of these men from my seminary class sought wise counsel from you stating that, "I feel God calling me into ministry." What would you say?

I remember listening to a Christian talk show that had a popular and well-respected Christian pastor on taking phone calls. A man called in and stated that he "feels" God calling him into ministry and is trying to figure out what to do. Without any further information the Pastor responded "Go! Apply to seminary and obey God's call." I was floored! That was the most careless and irresponsible piece of advice I have ever heard. A few words of affirmation back and forth and that was it, off he went full speed ahead after he just received careless advice from a seasoned man of God who should have known better. What if he is married and plays back the phone call to his wife. Does she have a chance if she counters? If you are a married man, your very first ministry is to your wife and kids and no other ministry is to take its place—period! The Bible tells us how God Judged Eli's family for his failure as a father,[37] and Samuel's sons were so bad that it led Israel to call for a king in place of God.[38] Your wife and kids are your primary ministry, and if she is not on board then you are probably calling yourself into ministry.

The lesson from all of this is to be patient knowing that the God of the vision is the God of how to get there. And every child of

---

[37] 1Samuel 3:12-13 – At that time I will carry out against Eli everything I spoke against his family—from beginning to end. [13]For I told him that I would judge his family forever because of the sin he knew about; his sons blasphemed God,[a] and he failed to restrain them.

[38] 1Samuel 8:1-5 – And it came about when Samuel was old that he appointed his sons judges over Israel. [2]Now the name of his firstborn was Joel, and the name of his second, Abijah; they were judging in Beersheba. [3]His sons, however, did not walk in his ways, but turned aside after dishonest gain and took bribes and perverted justice. [4]Then all the elders of Israel gathered together and came to Samuel at Ramah; [5]and they said to him, "Behold, you have grown old, and your sons do not walk in your ways. Now appoint a king for us to judge us like all the nations."

God, as any father knows with his own children, is different. Our heavenly Father knows us intimately and He is too creative to have one-size fits all calling. Therefore, it would be careless and not prudent to assume every calling necessarily leads to a seminary door. I wonder how many men have sacrificed their wife and family on the alter of "a calling" that cannot be tested. I wonder how many men blame God for failed marriages because they "obeyed." Men, what we are called to is prudence, and prudence leads us to wise choices based on God's word, godly advice, and a humble spirit laced with a patient approach to seeking God each step along the way. God *actively* leads, and we *actively* follow as I depicted in the diagram on page 101. In essence, we are all called to relational prudence not mystical carelessness. We are responsible for interacting with God so we can properly discern His voice through the static of our own voice or the voices of others. If you are called into full-time or part-time ministry in a formal sense, this second more personal mystical calling will be heard within the process of prudence as you gain the mind of Christ along the way. There is a good reason that wisdom is a property of both the virtue of prudence and the virtue of faith for, "The mind of man plans his way, But the Lord directs his steps." – Proverbs 16:9

A Prudent Approach To God's Word

"Tolerance is the virtue of a man without convictions" – G. K. Chesterton

Every man of virtue needs to be equipped in the Scriptures to properly hear God, for the Scriptures contain the voice of God because it is the Word of God. Praying without reading the Bible is like talking to a stranger whose voice you never heard and asking for advice in your own language. Prayer is primarily answering speech where we respond to God, who must have the first word, then wrestle with Him each time we hear His voice calling us to be more than we are. The primary way God speaks to us is His word where He has chosen to reveal His mind, His heart, and His voice. My children learned to speak my language by first listening to me and speaking the words they learned back to me, but framed by his or her own will and desires. The more time we interact the more they understand their father, and can hear my voice even when I am not around. We must do the same and avoid jumping to the Bible in an emergency "break glass" scenario that will never work. You will never be able to grab a verse and jump immediately into life application. This is the difference between "feeling led" and actually "being led." Without God's word, the feeling could just be indigestion.

There is a method of studying the Bible that every man of virtue should know called the inductive Bible study method.[39] It includes a three step patient listening process of observation, interpretation, and application. These steps allow you to hear God and avoid the danger of *interpolation* in which you insert your voice between the text instead of *interpretation* in which you draw out God's voice from the text. Classically, interpretation means "to draw out", and you are drawing out what God poured in. Theologically speaking, this is called eisegesis verses exegesis. Eisegesis, is inserting your mind and its assumptions into the text, whereas exegesis is discovering God's mind in the text. Observation is answering the question, "What does the text say?" Interpretation answers the question, "What does the text mean?" Finally, application, the step we all jump to too soon, answers the question, "What does the text mean to me?" Or, how does God want me to apply what I learned? Take a look at how this three-step process maps to the virtues prudence and faith:

Bible Study	Prudence	Faith
Observation ⇒	Knowledge ⇒	Content
Interpretation ⇒	Understanding ⇒	Conviction
Application ⇒	Wisdom ⇒	Centrality

Let's put all of this together. The more God's mind reshapes you as you hear Him in the content, the more convictions you will have about what is true and what is false. The more you act on those convictions the more you become absolutely convinced they are true

---

[39] For detailed information on this Bible study method check out Precept Ministries at: http://precept.org/about_inductive_Bible_study

as God's hand becomes evidenced in your life. The more central God is to your life, the deeper the relationship with God will become demonstrating to others that God not only defines your life, but also is central to it. You will not be able to stop talking about Christ, and you will try to convince others that what you believe is true. Getting into God's Word and getting God's Word into you will allow you to discern God's voice from your own.

Hebrews 4:11-13

Therefore let us be diligent to enter that rest, so that no one will fall, through following the same example of disobedience. [12]For the word of God is living and active and sharper than any two-edged sword, and piercing as far as the division of soul and spirit, of both joints and marrow, and able to judge the thoughts and intentions of the heart. [13]And there is no creature hidden from His sight, but all things are open and laid bare to the eyes of Him with whom we have to do.

In what way have you seen or used the mystical approach to decision making instead of the prudent approach? How is it confusing?

_____
_____
_____

Time to get started with a daily discipline of reading God's word. Go to my website and download the 6-Month New Testament Reading Plan and begin growing:

www.MansUltimateChallenge.com/learning-hub

Memory Table: Commit the properties of prudence to memory

Be a man of PRUDENCE and not CARELESSNESS	
Intelligence	Shrewdness
Knowledge	Foresight
Understanding	Reasoning
Wisdom	Discernment
Memory	Teachability
Caution	Circumspection

Adam - my challenge to you is to be a
man of fortitude and not fear.
What is fortitude? Latin "fortis" = strong.
Primarily our response to physical pain and
adversity

- Physical courage

- Emotional courage

- Spiritual courage

Physical Courage
    Though you may be injured or killed
~~fighting a fire~~, ~~arresting a bad guy~~, protecting

5
A MAN OF FORTITUDE
NOT FEAR

"Courage is contagious. When a brave man takes a stand, the spines of others are often stiffened" – Billy Graham

The pillar was the symbol for the virtue of fortitude used by the ancient Greeks given the amount of strength necessary for a pillar to hold up the massive buildings and temples of Greek architecture. The Greeks have been proved correct in selecting this symbol as evidenced by the massive architectures from ancient Greece that are still standing because of the pillars. In some cases the pillars alone are standing even though the roof was destroyed through war or natural disasters. In addition to the pillar the color red was also used, and not just any color red would do to represent this virtue by the ancients—it had to be blood red!

Fortitude is derived from the Latin *fortis* meaning "strong." Therefore fortitude deals primarily with our response to physical pain, and adversity in what we Americans call "guts." Though people

Courage - Adam owning up to mistakes, defense of the weak, doing what's right when no one else is, confronting injustice

Man's Ultimate Challenge

primarily think of physical courage when it comes to fortitude, this virtue encompasses so much more to include the emotional and spiritual courage necessary to stand up for what is right no matter what the cost is to you personally. We see this today when people take a stand for Christ to such a degree that it threatens tight relationships with family, friends, or coworkers. Even more so we see fortitude on display when a Muslim converts to Christianity and his or her own father issues a *fatwa* calling for the death of his very own child.

Fortitude encompasses the properties of valor, courage, magnanimity (generously forgiving a rival when you are in a position of strength), perseverance, patience, bravery, steadfastness, strenuousness, confidence, and honor. With all that fortitude includes as a virtue, you can quickly see how the vice of fear needs to be pushed out as an unwelcome guest in our temple. Fortitude and fear cannot occupy the same space within your heart for one will inevitably drive out the other. Since the vice of fear is more natural due to our fallen state, we need to nurture fortitude by constant practice. Now when I say fear, the type of fear I am referring to is the type that grips your whole being leaving you timid or frozen to the point where the anxiety that accompanies fear begins to fill your whole being with "what ifs" that want to control you.

In the fourteenth century the medieval knights followed the twelve nightly virtues of chivalry as described by the Duke of Burgandy. These knightly virtues are faith, charity, justice, sagacity (discernment), prudence, temperance, resolution (steadfastness), truth, liberality, diligence (strenuousness), hope, and valor. At first blush it looks as if they forgot to include the virtue of fortitude as the other six virtues of faith, hope, charity, justice, temperance, and prudence are listed prominently. That is until you realize the fact that three of the remaining six knightly virtues listed are all properties of fortitude.

Fortitude, then, takes certain strength of the soul that is necessary in the accomplishment of its virtuous ends or purpose. It is fortitude that is required in order to actually carry out the virtues. For instance, faith may provide the reason for a decision, and prudence the wisdom necessary to make the right decision, but it is fortitude that breaks the chains of fear, and activates the will to step forward and implement the decision. Moreover, to execute the decision with the forbearance and endurance needed to continue in the virtuous cause that the virtue of justice informs you are the right thing to do. However, in order to accomplish all of this courageously, the man of fortitude must fear God more than men in such a way as to overcome the fear and intimidation that stands in the way.

The Gift of Anger

"Fear is the path to the dark side. Fear leads to anger. Anger leads to hate. Hate leads to suffering." - Yoda

Often, the emotion needed to break the chains of fear is anger. That's right men, anger! We have totally misunderstood the important role of anger in our metro-sexual culture where men get pedicures and the most prominent pastors speak with the gentle tone of a marriage counselor. Due to the feminization of western civilization, and the church in particular, anger is viewed as an evil that needs to be either medicated or eradicated. Unfortunately, Christianity has been minimized to "being nice." Sure Christians should be considered nice, but that is far from a defining quality and is a tragedy if that is all that the Christian is. A Christian should always be virtuous not nice, and there is a huge difference. There is never a time to not be virtuous, but there are many times you should not be nice. In fact, I would argue that as Christians we don't get angry enough, and when we do get angry it is at the wrong things. In light of this, this chapter is going to focus on understanding anger biblically so that God can redeem our anger enabling us to garner up the courage needed to drive our fear. The most dangerous thing for any man is to have fear driving our anger instead of fortitude driving out fear.

What do you think of when you hear the word anger? Write down some actions or characteristics.

_____

_____

_____

_____

111

Some of us grew up in unhealthy environments where anger was abusive. How can this impact a person's view of anger as only unhealthy?

_____

_____

_____

_____

We are actually commanded to be angry in Ephesians 4:26-27, "Be angry, and yet do not sin; do not let the sun go down on your anger, [27]and do not give the devil [a]an opportunity." We should hate evil because of what it does to the people God loves, and the people we love, and ourselves. Tolerance is lazy, passive, nice, and masks as Biblical Christianity whereas true Christianity is an active love that, when necessary, is a tough love. The classic use of the word tolerance meant to lovingly tolerate persons while challenging the false ideas a person embraced. This use of the word assumed that truth is discoverable, objective, relative to God, and therefore knowable because we are made in His image. This was the measure for the debate. The modern contemporary usage, however, presupposes that truth is relative to the person and unknowable, so hating the false idea but loving the person is viewed as impossible. G.K. Chesterton properly noted that, "tolerance is the virtue of a man without convictions." In the verse below Jesus is angry. His anger is rooted in truth and love for God and people. Is Jesus tolerant (nice) or loving?

John 2:13-16

[13]The Passover of the Jews was near, and Jesus went up to Jerusalem. [14]And He found in the temple those who were selling oxen and sheep and doves, and the money changers seated at their tables. [15]And He made a scourge of cords, and drove them all out of the temple, with the sheep and the oxen; and He poured out the coins of the money changers and overturned their tables; [16]and to those who were selling the doves He said, "Take these things away; stop making My Father's house a [f]place of business."

Here we see Jesus angry, and in His anger He stoked the

courage of fortitude that made Him ready to confront the enemies of God. This type of fortitude was based in an attitude of righteous indignation that hates injustice, immorality, and falsehood. Speaking about Jesus, the book of Hebrews states, "You have loved righteousness and hated lawlessness."[40] I can think of a number of modern day moneychangers of the faith movement where, if Jesus were to show up, He would overturn pulpits and clear out the offering buckets. Yes buckets, five gallon offering paint buckets that fill the false teacher's multi-million dollar robber's den.

One reason for our confusion is the fact that when we think of anger we typically think of an out of control extreme aggressive form of anger; i.e., loud out of control screaming, throwing things, or worse, physically abusing another person. This is, of course, both unbiblical and unmanly. There are three forms of anger, and one is very popular in the "nice" circles of modern conflict avoidant Christianity. Look at these as anger languages, and each of us has a "go to" when we get angry. Although we can and often do express each form, one is as comfortable as an old pair of shoes. Each of these unhealthy expressions of anger has a lie believed instead of a truth embraced.

Below are the three Categories of nonproductive expressions of anger and descriptions of each taken from *The Anger Trap* by Dr. Les Carter. Determine which one best describes you and keep it in mind throughout this section. Often times the anger type matches your personality type. For instance, the extrovert is more than likely to be #1, where the introvert #2 or #3. Again, sometimes, but not always. If three or four descriptions in general fit then this is your anger language. God wants to shape it for His use instead of your abuse. Please note that I include real extremes and marked them with **. These may not be you, but are included both to be exhaustive and to indicate that if this is you, you need to focus on this and maybe get some outside wise counsel.

1. Openly Aggressive Anger – Lie Believed: "You are in my sights so here is a piece of my mind"

- Loud and forceful communication that allows little room for separate ideas

- Being blunt and opinionated
- Becoming involved in bickering and snippy communication
- Complaining and griping or being critical or generally pessimistic

** Using curse words and insulting speech

** Physical expression of intimidation, such as pushing, hitting, or throwing things

- Speaking words of blame and accusation
- Interrupting others in conversation, refusing to listen
- Repeating oneself to emphasize a point; insisting on having the last word
- Giving advice that others do not want
- Reacting to others' thoughts with ready defensiveness, rebutting

(2) Suppression of Anger – Lie believed: "Out of sight out of mind"

** Withdrawal from problems even if it means that problems remain unresolved

- Refusing to expose personal problems or needs
- Being image-conscious to the point of having to appear totally together
- Shying away from controversial or troublesome topics
- Making excuses for others' inappropriate behavior or taking responsibility for making others feel good even when they are wronging you.
- Easily second-guessing your own good judgment

** Playing the role of the people pleaser, trying to keep others happy

- Letting frustration pass without saying anything

- Refusing to let others help, even when you really need it

- Pretending not to have resentment

- Acting out the role of an encouraging or pleasant person, though you do not really feel that way

** Succumbing to the strong will of others, assuming you have no other option

(3) Passive-aggressive Anger – Lie Believed: "You have no idea that you are in my sights, because I will not reveal my mind" **Comes out in "get even" behavior

- Being silent when you know that the other person wants to hear from you

- Making lame excuses for avoiding activities that you do not want to do

- Procrastinating and being chronically forgetful or giving half-hearted efforts

- Saying yes even though you are unlikely to follow through with a request

** Doing tasks in your own manner and at your own time even when you know that it disrupts others (intentionally taking your time, being slow)

- Complaining about people behind their backs, but rarely face-to-face

- Saying whatever the other person wants to hear, and then doing whatever you feel like doing

** Being evasive for the purpose of indicating that you won't be controlled

- Putting off responsibility as you choose playful or lazy options instead

- Repeatedly using the phrase "I don't know" when being asked to explain your choices

** Acting good in front of authority figures or accountability partners, and then acting rebellious when out of their presence

Which one describes your "go to"? (mine is #1) [not sure ask people who are close to you. Trust me they know]

_____

_____

_____

_____

Passive-aggressive anger is a favorite in Christian circles where the man cowardly avoids the conflict and doesn't get mad but gets even. But hey, he or she is usually nice about it. Dr. Carter explains that, "these people manage their anger in a sly, underground way that still indicates a low regard toward others...But they do so with quiet disdain toward the others involved."[41] My favorite Christian Counseling team, Henry Cloud and John Townsend call these people "crazy makers." The aggressive usually reacts and confronts the passive-aggressive and they will say, "I would never do something like that, how can you accuse me." If you ever experienced a "crazy maker" passive-aggressive you know exactly what I mean. What is a shame about them is that you can never resolve the underlying issue because they reply with "what issue, everything is fine." If you are a passive-aggressive you need fortitude in order to have the tough conversation. Pride is rooted in fear and acts vindictively; fortitude is strengthened by humility and confronts courageously.

If a passive-aggressive does not have the fortitude to humbly have the tough conversation then his passive-aggressiveness will bring about a self-fulfilled prophecy of relational contention. His own hurt or insecurity will cause an internal response to an avatar of a person that, to him, has become reality. Thus he ends up fighting with an avatar of a person whom he created and not the real person. So when say an aggressive finally responds as the avatar of this man's own creation would, he cries aloud to those of whom he poisoned with slander, "See I told you that _____ was really like this, poor me who has had to deal with _____." What the passive-aggressive fails to realize is that he brought about a self-fulfilled prophecy by never having the ability to address the real person because the avatar of his

_____

[41] Les Carter, *The Anger Trap* (San Francisco, CA: Jossey-Bass, 2003), 26.

own creation remained in the way. These relationships can never heal until the Holy Spirit of truth deals with actual persons in reality created in His own image and not avatar images of projected reality created by the passive-aggressive. This is a disturbing thing to watch and a terrible to experience! The chains of fear is chasing people away and stunting your growth in Christ.

Proverbs 26:24-26 [passive-aggressive]

He who hates disguises it with his lips, but he lays up deceit in his [l]heart. [25]When [m]he speaks graciously, do not believe him, for there are seven abominations in his heart. [26]Though his hatred covers itself with guile, his wickedness will be revealed before the assembly.

Proverbs 14:17 – "A quick-tempered [aggressive] man acts foolishly, and a man of evil devices [crafty] is hated. [passive-aggressive]"[42]

The suppressive is the second favorite in Christian circles for the same reason as the passive-aggressive is the favorite; namely, on the outside it is nice. On the inside however, it is a cowardly decision of pain avoidance that causes the opposite as pain stacks on top of pain in what is known as a "stacking effect." The chains of fear grip him, just wanting the conflict to go away on its own as the suppressive stuffs it inside over and over again. Reminds me of a quote by Mike Wazowski in the movie Monsters Inc, "Wouldn't it be better if it all just blew away." Like a volcano that blows hot lava as pressure builds over time, so in time, the suppressive is going to blow. Dr. Les Carter notes that in the suppressive, "The anger does not dissolve but is stored (with all of its energy) for release at a later time."[43] And when this man finally blows, lives will be destroyed. If he does not blow, Dr. Carter describes a disturbing alternative as it reveals itself, "in the form of depression, anxiety, or panic attacks."[44] Don't stuff your hurt that is causing anger for a fear of looking bad, or disliking conflict so much that you let yourself have no voice, otherwise you will loose your voice when you finally blow up.

---

[42] Emphasis mine.
[43] Ibid., 22.
[44] Ibid.

The aggressive is the least favorite in modern Christianity for the reason the other two are favorites—it's not nice. Aggressive external anger is what most of us think of when we think of anger. Fear is still at the root and so is hurt and everyone knows it. Unfortunately for the aggressive, "His abusive spirit buried whatever message he needed to convey."[45] Fortitude here is needed so as to have the courage to deal with the hurt, and confront people in a non-explosive loving way. Communicating the hurt without hurting with your words is an art that every man needs to learn.

Proverbs 15:1 – A gentle answer turns away wrath, but a harsh word stirs up anger.

Proverbs 18:18 – A hot-tempered man stirs up strife, but the slow to anger calms a dispute

Proverbs 16:32 – "He who is slow to anger is better than the mighty, And he who rules his spirit, than he who captures a city.'

Proverbs 29:11 – "A fool [a]always loses his temper, But a wise man holds it back."

God wants to redeem your anger for the sake of fortitude so you are not afraid of it, but, instead, able to control it for use when necessary. A man of fortitude needs to be just like Christ, but first in his own temple, his body. There are times when we need to be just like Jesus in the temple when He was angry and it was time to show the unjust their error in a language they understood. The danger for any of us with a fallen-nature is that even righteous indignation can take a turn if it is prolonged, giving the devil an opportunity. Prolonged anger can turn into bitterness as anger begins to control the believer instead of the believer controlling the anger. We must break the chains of the fear of conflict and confront the hurt, seeking forgiveness as we get it wrong along the way, because we will. Choose fortitude over fear, men, so that you can get better and not bitter. As proverbs 14:10 teaches, bitterness hardens the heart for, "Each heart knows its own bitterness, and no one else can share its joy." Think about this verse. Read it again and meditate on it.

Below is the dangerous process of unresolved anger that stacks in the heart.

---

[45] Ibid., 25.

Hurt ⇒ Anger ⇒ Resentment ⇒ Bitterness ⇒ Rage ⇒ Revenge

Romans 12:17-19

Never pay back evil for evil to anyone. [o]Respect what is right in the sight of all men. [18]If possible, so far as it depends on you, be at peace with all men. [19]Never take your own revenge, beloved, but [p]leave room for the wrath of God, for it is written, "Vengeance is Mine, I will repay," says the Lord.

What relationship(s) have been targets of your anger that you need to confront with a spirit of fortitude? Who are you going to ask to hold you accountable to get it done?

_____

_____

_____

_____

Who do you need to seek forgiveness from for being passive-aggressive? Suppressing anger where a person does not realize they hurt you? Being overly aggressive?

_____

_____

_____

_____

Be Brave

""The only thing necessary for the triumph of evil is for good men to do nothing."
– Edmund Burke

In this section I want to address the sin of omission where "being nice" is a grave sin in the life of the people-pleasing passive man. John Chrysostom, the Archbishop of Constantinople from AD 349-407 describes it best, "He who is not angry when he has cause to be, sins. For unreasonable patience is the hotbed of many vices."[46]

---

[46] Kreeft, *Virtue*, 134.

It is the do nothing man that sins when he knows he ought to do something. This man has made an idol out of being nice by avoiding conflict, popularity (being liked), or saving his own skin. James 4:17 addresses the sin of omission, "Therefore, to one who knows the [a]right thing to do and does not do it, to him it is sin." If you want to watch a movie about a man who refused to be passive, I recommend you watch *Machine Gun Preacher*, a true story about a drug dealer and addict who comes to Christ, builds an orphanage in Sudan, and takes up arms to protect the children living there. One word—Awesome!

It has already been demonstrated from the scriptures that anger is misunderstood and itself is not a sin. We also learned that there is more than one expression or language of anger that each of us has as a 'go to' form. Like everything, its misuse can lead toward sin, while anger left unresolved and unaddressed can lead toward a bitter spirit seeking revenge. You could say that a tree of anger stands tall because of its bitter roots. However, getting rightfully angry at the right things and to an appropriate degree is not sin and is actually a healthy motivation in support of the virtue of fortitude. Fortitude needs to always ready to confront and redeemed righteous anger is what every man of virtue needs. In short, anger that is controlled is virtuous; uncontrolled or manipulatively controlled anger is sinful. We will take a look at two excellent examples of men who channeled their anger to make a difference in this world.

Gary Haugen, founder of International Justice Mission,[47] was angry when he saw the injustice of child sex trafficking, modern day slavery, and exploitation of the poor by corrupt governments. The virtue of justice gave him the right motive, charity gave him the empathy, but it is fortitude that gave him the courage to do something about it. Justice and charity without fortitude are just good intentions; you know, that substance that the road to Hell is paved with. This is the proper use of anger as it is motivated by what is right and just, but fueled by the courage needed to do something about it. IJM is working globally making a long-term difference by dealing with these injustices head on. I highly recommend you visit the IJM website for some incredible stories of courage: www.ijm.org.

---

[47] If you want to be equipped to make a difference visit International Justice Mission and do something. www.ijm.org If you want to see the connection between violence and poverty check out Gary Haugen's book: *The Locust Effect: Why the End of Poverty Requires the End of Violence.*

"A true leader has the confidence to stand alone, the courage to make tough decisions, and the compassion to listen to the needs of others. He does not set out to be a leader, but becomes one by the quality of his actions and the integrity of his intent" — Douglas MacArthur

Most people know John Walsh as the dedicated host of America's Most Wanted, the man whose television program has helped take down over 1,050 dangerous fugitives and bring home more than 50 missing children in the past 22 years. I loved watching that program. John Walsh and his wife Revé suffered the most horrendous loss that any parents could endure: the abduction and murder of their six-year-old son, Adam. Ever since that day in 1981, John has dedicated himself to fighting on behalf of not only children, but all victims of violent crime. This is fortitude in action as John Walsh's anger is directed at making a difference not taking personal revenge. President George W. Bush signed a tough law to track and apprehend convicted sex offenders who disappear after their release from prison. It's called "The Adam Walsh Child Protection and Safety Act."

It takes real courage and unselfishness to take a personal tragedy and turn it into a blessing to others. This is a great example of what I call a "so that" ministry. A "so that" ministry is always a ministry we never prayed for, but God uses in a mighty way if we have the fortitude to do things His way. This is fortitude moved by faith trusting that God does not want your revenge but your trust. As Romans 12:19 points out, "Never take your own revenge, beloved, but [p]leave room for the wrath of God, for it is written, 'Vengeance is Mine, I will repay,'" says the Lord.'"

2Corinthians 1:3-5

Blessed be the God and Father of our Lord Jesus Christ, the Father of mercies and God of all comfort, [4]who comforts us in all our affliction *so that* we will be able to comfort those who are in [b]any affliction with the comfort with which we ourselves are comforted by God. [5]For just as the sufferings of Christ are [c]ours in abundance, so also our comfort is abundant through Christ. [Emphasis mine]

After reading 2Corinthians 1:3-5 what do you think your "so that" ministry is? For example: Are you a recovering addict? Have you grown up in an abusive home?

_____
_____
_____
_____

What are you going to do about it? How are you going to demonstrate fortitude?

_____
_____
_____
_____

Being Courageous Daily

"A true soldier fights not because he hates what is in front of him but because he loves what is behind him" – G.K. Chesterton

I remember a student at my seminary whom the professor asked to share his testimony in my ethics class. Brothers, it is a powerful example of fortitude breaking the chains of fear. He grew up in a Muslim family where his father was an Imam in North Africa. He had many siblings given the fact that in Islamic teaching a man can have up to four wives. When he came to Christ and started witnessing to his family, his father responded by issuing a fatwa calling for his death because of his conversion. His mother begged him not to return home, and his father beat his mother when he found out they had spoken. He never did return home, but he made an even bolder move. He went to Egypt to spend the weekend witnessing to his brother who was under his father's authority to kill him. He debated and argued with his brother all weekend and eventually led him to Christ. Unfortunately his brother was murdered shortly thereafter on the orders of his father. Wow! Facing death, displeasing the family, facing physical, spiritual, and emotional isolation because of his love for Jesus Christ. Needless to say we all felt challenged, and frankly I felt like a wimp.

Read the passage below and note the fear and shame that must grip us men when we hear these words:

Matthew 10:32-39

Therefore everyone who [z]confesses Me before men, I will also confess [aa]him before My Father who is in heaven. [33]But whoever [ab]denies Me before men, I will also deny him before My Father who is in heaven. [34]"Do not think that I came to [ac]bring peace on the earth; I did not come to bring peace, but a sword. [35]For I came to set a man against his father, and a daughter against her mother, and a daughter-in-law against her mother-in-law; [36]and a man's enemies will be the members of his household. [37]"He who loves father or mother more than Me is not worthy of Me; and he who loves son or daughter more than Me is not worthy of Me. [38]And he who does not take his cross and follow after Me is not worthy of Me. [39]He who has found his [ad]life will lose it, and he who has lost his [ae]life for My sake will find it.

What are some ways that we can deny Christ before men? (verse 32-33)

_____

_____

_____

_____

What do you think a "denial before men" means based on what Jesus said in verses 32-33?

_____

_____

_____

_____

Have you had family challenges and/or broken relationships in your family because of your faith? In what ways do verses 35-37 challenge you or encourage you?

_____

_____

_____

_____

Now maybe you have a story that is not as dramatic, but have you had an experience, where you had to make a choice to choose Christ over your parents, other family members, or friends? For example, maybe you are from a Hindu family and there are festivals the family invites you to but are full of idolatry. Maybe wedding traditions from your culture would dishonor Christ, or talking to a family member whom you forgave and reconciled with while the rest of the family views this person as the enemy. How did it go? Did you let your fear of the approval of others overtake you? What is the result?

_____

_____

_____

_____

I have a few personal examples where I needed to demonstrate fortitude that are not nearly as dramatic, but maybe you can relate. Early on in my Christian walk I had a few experiences that at first glance, may seem minor but based on where I was on my journey these instances really did fill me with fear. The main reason for this irrational level of fear I experienced is that I am a recovering people-pleaser and co-dependant. If you can relate to me at this point then you will understand how hard it is to demonstrate fortitude in my examples that are more minor to those who do not have this baggage. Praise God he healed me of this! These experiences were the means of my healing that I had to face and demonstrate the power of facing my fears head on filled with the Holy Spirit.

The first example occurred when there was a tragic death of a childhood friend during Halloween from my hometown of Pittsburgh, Pennsylvania. I had moved to the Washington, DC area five years prior and spent many weekends back to visit my friends. I had become a Christian eight months earlier and not a single one of my longtime friends knew about it. Here I was a new Christian revealing myself as a follower of Christ to my friends for the first time. And lucky me, it is following the tragic death of a member of our small friendship circle. Not to mention, I am also in a position of not knowing the spiritual condition of my friend who died and what if they ask me or, even worse, accuse me? Needless to say, I really needed fortitude, because quite frankly, I was feeling very anxious about the whole thing.

I prayed and prayed and prayed constantly the week before, and on the way up to Pittsburgh. I have to say that for the first time in my walk, God gave me a visible sign and I felt God impress upon me a strong sense of peace that it would be ok. I prayed for opportunities to share with my friends and for the grace to respond to any "gut" reaction I may receive. Secondly, I prayed for one particular opportunity and God moved in a powerful way. The day after revealing my newfound faith, I told my friends that I wanted to pray together in front of our friend's casket at the viewing. In fortitude, I stepped forward and stood there for about 10 minutes by myself waiting for my friends to step forward. One by one, every one of them eventually did and I prayed out loud for the very first time. It was an amazing experience that opened tons of doors later that evening to give my testimony and explain to my friends what had happened to me as Christ took center stage in my life.

Write down a moment that you had to demonstrate fortitude.

_____

_____

_____

_____

In a separate more minor everyday incident I was meeting some coworkers of mine for lunch who knew that I had recently become a Christian. I was new to praying over my meals and our lunch arrived. I am ashamed to say that suddenly this wave of fear hit me saying, "Oh no everyone is talking and I need to pray!" I did the lamest head nod prayer that I ever did in my life. In fact my quick head nod to God made me look as if I had caught myself dozing off. Embarrassing! Here, just take my Christian man card now!

One of the benefits of staying in God's word is that the right verse will be "coming soon" when conviction is needed. The following verse was part of my one year Bible reading plan that week and it really hit me hard.

Galatians 1:10 – For am I now seeking the favor of men, or of God? Or am I striving to please men? If I were still trying to please men, I would not be a bond-servant of Christ.

Ouch! I felt convicted and ashamed of myself. Men, I vowed to never let that happen again and I haven't. Now, I just say, "can you hold on for a second", then I pray.

Recall a time where you were ashamed of Christ. How did you handle it? What did you feel?

_____

_____

_____

_____

Memory Table: Commit the properties of fortitude to memory

Be a man of FORTITUDE and not FEAR	
Courage	Valor
Magnanimity (generous in forgiveness)	Perseverance
Patience	Honor
Bravery	Steadfastness
Strenuousness	Confidence

6
A MAN OF JUSTICE
NOT INJUSTICE

"Justice is the love of God and our neighbor which pervades the other virtues"
– Augustine

Properly balanced scales have been the symbol of justice for centuries. The United States built on this idea by adding Lady Justice holding the scales and wearing a blindfold to imply no partiality in judgments. She is to seek the truth, the whole truth, and nothing but the truth. One truth for sure is that at times in our history Lady Justice peeked. Truth is so central to the virtue of justice that if truth were a raw material then the scales of justice would be made out of it. As to the virtue of justice in our lives, we are called to make just and right judgments. What we are placing on the scales to be weighed is right and wrong, good and evil, value and judgment.

The Latin word *aequitas*, where we get the word justice, captures the fact that justice deals primarily with truth in our relationship with others and ourselves. Justice is always individual first bringing an internal harmony to the soul before it can be poured out externally in our relationships with others. A truly just person rejoices in just actions that demonstrate the proper moderation between self-interest and the rights and needs of others. When an injustice is done to another the just person will make every effort to make it right by seeking forgiveness and restoring what was broken as a result of the injustice committed through the practice of restitution.

Justice deals with judging, more specifically, making judgments based on truth alone and without bias or partiality thereby ensuring a right judgment before both God and man. Additionally, a just person assumes the best and gives every person the benefit of the doubt. Furthermore, the practice of justice includes conquering the sin of omission because a man of justice is a person who takes action when he sees an injustice in himself or another. The properties of justice include right and wrong, good and evil, value and judgment, all of which are weighed on the scales of truth.

What causes injustice then? The vice injustice includes the very things that try to tip the balance of the scales such as lies, slander, jealousy, coveting, backbiting, harming another's good name, or both positive and negative racial prejudices. In short, justice deals with judging and is primarily concerned with truth alone as the input, on the other hand, injustice deals with misjudging with lies and prejudice as the primary input.

How does this happen? Well, there is a competing secular view of justice that most of us use as a measure instead of the biblical view of justice that God calls us to. Like all counterfeits, this counterfeit form of justice is close enough to the real that when practiced enough, like a vaccine, it can inoculate you to the truth. This is one example of the many faulty secular views on many topics that is taught by our culture in so many venues that we have caught it like an airborne virus and made it our own. We have to resist the temptation to baptize secular views where man is the measure of truth and not God. The problem with the secular view is best captured in the book of Habakkuk when God referenced the Chaldeans view of justice, "They are dreaded and feared; their justice and [h]authority [i]originate with themselves."[48] For the Christian,

---

[48] Habakkuk 1:7

sociology must submit to theology where God is to be our authority since justice resides in His very nature.

Secular View of Justice   **Biblical View of Justice**

The secular view is built on the sandy shore of atheism as its foundation and Karl Mark as its prophet, whereas the biblical view is built on the rock solid foundation of Jesus Christ. The secular view places God in a box of nonexistence and outside of God is the subjective law of fairness and equitableness. This view goes beyond the justice of equal opportunity by trying to unjustly guarantee equal outcomes. However, the biblical view is built on the premise that because God is just we have the objective virtue of justice that flows from His nature. Based on this view of justice we have commands, principles, and a process on how to execute justice with people within our spheres of influence. In short, justice naturally flows from God because He is just, whereas injustice naturally flows from man because fallen man is unjust. Peter Kreeft provides a thorough explanation of what happens when we make man the measure of justice in place of God:

> Justice, the overall virtue, is the harmony of the soul, as health is the harmony of the body. Justice is not just paying your debts, not just an external relationship between two or more people, but also and first of all the internal relationship within each individual among the parts of the soul. The harmony is hierarchical, not egalitarian. When World follows Man, when within Man Body follows Soul, when within Soul Appetites follow Will and Will follows Reason (Wisdom), we have Justice. When the hierarchy is inverted, we have injustice. Will leading Reason is rationalization and propaganda; Appetites leading Will is greed; Body leading Soul is animalism; World leading Man is unfreedom.[49]

It would do well for us to remember that all of us as sinners

---

[49] Kreeft, *Virtue*, 64.

have a tendency toward injustice. If we didn't then God would not have given us the command to forgive one another 70x7 times! Forgiveness presupposes the existence of the virtue of justice and the reality of injustice. For example, an injustice or sin committed by the person seeking forgiveness and the person offering forgiveness both want to make it right or get to a place of justice because of the injustice the sin brought about. Isn't it fascinating how we are all wired to desire forgiveness and to be forgiven? The fact that we all experience this desire for forgiveness from deep within our being, and want to be forgiven by those whom we have wronged, serve as strong evidence of the virtue of justice and its vice, injustice. The problem usually is that we are prideful and lack the courage to admit that we are wrong and ask for forgiveness. Immediately we see the need for fortitude to overcome unreasonable fears that hinder us in implementing this virtue.

The chain of injustice that needs to be broken in our life if we are going to be men of justice is: Injustice by wrongly judging others. The chains of injustice are made up of a very strong material that can only be cut by one device. The material needing cut are lies and the enemy of lies is truth; thus, truth is the only device that can break these chains. But how do you get to the truth? It is an art not a science that requires a lot of work on your part if you are going to make a right judgment. First, it will require a willingness to trust God and His word as a go to source for truth. Second, it will require that you first and foremost learn to apply His truth to yourself, meaning that you know your blind spots that get in the way of treating others with justice. These two requirements map nicely to the two greatest commandments:

Matthew 22:37-39

You shall love the Lord your God with all your heart, and with all your soul, and with all your mind.' [38]This is the great and [o]foremost commandment. [39]The second is like it, 'you shall love your neighbor as yourself.

Chains of Injustice: Wrongly Judging Others

""Justice is a habit whereby a man renders to each one his due by a constant and perpetual will" – *Thomas Aquinas*

But wait! Doesn't the Bible say "do not judge?" The phrase "the Bible says do not judge," and the way it is presented, is the one Bible myth that causes more trouble between people than any other myth I know. In fact, the very passage a person has in mind, if he has the Bible in mind at all, teaches exactly the opposite! In actuality the whole purpose of the passage is to teach you how to judge, and the principles presented encompass the virtue of justice and it's vice injustice. When you combine this verse with the other verses on judging you end up with a nice framework to judge properly and implement the virtue of justice in your life.

Matthew 7:1-5

[1]"Do not judge so that you will not be judged. [2]For in the way you judge, you will be judged; and [a]by your standard of measure, it will be measured to you. [3]Why do you look at the speck that is in your brother's eye, but do not notice the log that is in your own eye? [4]Or how [b]can you say to your brother, 'Let me take the speck out of your eye,' and behold, the log is in your own eye? [5]You hypocrite, first take the log out of your own eye, and then you will see clearly to take the speck out of your brother's eye."

What do the words "first" and "then" imply that help us draw out the meaning of this passage?

_____

_____

_____

_____

Let's see what the most recognized Bible expert today has to say about this verse in his John MacArthur Bible Commentary:

"As the context reveals, this direction does not prohibit all types of judging. We are to exercise a righteous kind of judgment with careful discernment (John 7:24). Censorious [fault-finding or eager to criticize], hypocritical, self-righteous, or other kinds of unfair judgments are forbidden"[50]

I want to build on this passage by adding another two verses about judging from the mouth of Jesus:

John 7:24 – "Do not judge according to appearance, but [a]judge with righteous judgment."

Luke 12:57 – "And why do you not even on your own initiative judge what is right?"

So it seems that not all judgments are bad when based on objectivity and truth, but that the basis for false judgments based on bias and lies are. When we make ourselves the standard we become unjust, but when we make God the standard we become just in rendering our judgments.

In summary, based on the passages above, we are to judge:

1. Righteously; i.e., make a "right" judgment
2. Not self-righteously
3. Not hypocritically

So, the real question we need to ask is, "What clouds our judgment?" Justice deals with truth in our relations with others. It regulates our actions so that we do not judge rashly because of injustice embedded either within ourselves, or injustice imparted to us from another. There are both internal and external forces of injustice at work that will keep you from discovering truth and leads you to do great harm to yourself and to others. This harm is caused when you emotionally invest in a lie by making a rash unjust judgment with very little data. The Bible warns that, "It is not good for a person to be without knowledge, and he who hurries [b]his footsteps [c]errs."51 Immediately we see that prudence feeds justice by informing you to seek more knowledge, gain understanding, and be wise; thus, avoiding the vice of carelessness leading to an unjust judgment. It is incredibly difficult to recover and see the truth when it finally does arrive because of the emotional investment you make in the lie that blinds you. Here comes truth and then pride takes hold inside of you making you unteachable to the truth and unreachable by the Spirit of truth. Why? Because in our pride we tend to convince ourselves that we cannot be wrong, making humility our enemy at the very moment God requires it to be our friend.

The internal forces of injustice are the most difficult to see because they are "in you" and "feel right" like an old pair of sneakers. It takes discipline, a teachable spirit, and more often than not, another brother in Christ to help you patiently and methodically question every default thought and reaction you make. Christ calls us to take every lofty thing and thought captive, and this is a difficult thing indeed when the "lofty thing" is you.

1Corinthians 10:5 – We are destroying speculations and every lofty thing raised up against the knowledge of God, and we are taking every thought captive to the obedience of Christ

Often when men hear this verse we apply it to unclean thoughts in the area of sexual purity. This verse certainly applies there, but the application is much broader in that every thought means exactly what it says—every thought! The every thought we produce and our enemy uses to deeply wound others through injustice are pride, jealousy, insecurity, conflict avoidance, codependency, confirmation bias, racial prejudices, and misreading people who have a different personality or background from us. In addition, there are external forces of injustice produced by others but processed by our thoughts such as gossip, slander, and backbiting that serve to influence our judgments leading to us committing the grievous sin of harming another's name.

In the rest of this chapter I am going to focus on some of the most common forms of injustice that we both commit and experience. I want to draw our attention here because if we train ourselves to be just in our everyday relationships, then no doubt we will know how to be just and spot injustices in a broader societal context. Our focus will be on these six links of injustice in the chain of judging that need broken in our lives if we are going to be men of justice:

Link-1. Envy/Jealousy

Link-2. Showing partiality and unjust bias

Link-3. A tendency to assume the negative

Link-4. Harming another's name through backbiting and slander

Link-5. Being a "people pleaser" or "codependency"

Link-6. Projection of one's own sin

Before we unpack these six links of injustice in the chain of judging I want you to think of where you make judgments every day several times a day. I want to break down your daily impact zone into the four relational circles shown below. The closer people are to you the more relational impact there is when you are unjust by making an unjust judgment or where a person makes an unjust judgment about you. Relationships are fascinating because they are always bi-directional and multidimensional. In each one of these circles of influence on the diagram you experience a sense of belonging that make it possible for you to make judgments about people and situations. Likewise people in these relational spaces do the same in return. Again, the closer to you a person is the more damage that can and will occur when injustice through making a wrong judgment is done.

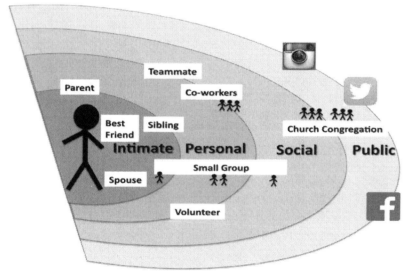

Four Relational Circles

Think about your day. You watched and read a few news stories, you saw a few Instagram pictures, and read a few tweets and Facebook posts. What hot topic in the news did you draw a conclusion on and why? What did you say to yourself about the people who posted on social media? Maybe you are at work and someone comes to you with some "inside" information he or she heard directly, or heard through the grapevine to supposedly help you. What inclined them to share it? Is it totally true? Does it matter? Did you believe it right away? Especially if it was negative, right? What decision are you going to make based on this information? A person in your small group makes a statement and is a little abrupt. What is your judgment about him at that moment?

Name a few judgments you made today, positive or negative. Yes, you made some! Then actively pay attention tomorrow and see where you may be getting it wrong.

_____

_____

_____

Take a look at the four relational circles and take special note of people in your life and write down these names in the spaces on the next page. Also note the strange world of social media where in one news feed you can have people from all four relational spaces together. You would expect people closest to you to properly understand you and your Facebook posts, Instagrams, or tweets without making a rash character judgment right? Maybe you can see the role of judging already and how important it is to get it right. The point is that you can't stop judging and neither can anyone else, for it is what we do daily, hour by hour, minute by minute. The problem is that we often get it wrong and that is why we unjustly judge by, as Matthew 7 puts it, being eager to criticize and fault-finding. We do this to people and people do it to us.

Have you ever been "unfriended" or "blocked" on social media because someone misjudged you due to one of your posts? Think, political, or a misunderstood post based on a rash judgment.

_____

_____

_____

Now let's turn the light inside; How about you? Have you ever "unfriended" someone? Is it possible you misjudged them?

_____

_____

_____

Four Relational Circles Fill-ins

Write down the names of some people who fit in each relational circle. Feel free to add a group that I may have missed in the first picture but you find significant. Do not feel the need to fill in every space, but just write down who comes to mind. You may be like me and find that you need to work on stronger relationships closer in (something us men are not that good at).

Public:_____

_____

_____

Social:_____

_____

_____

Personal:_____

_____

Intimate:_____

Link-1: Envy/Jealousy

"For where jealousy and selfish ambition exist, there is disorder and every evil thing."
– James 3:16

Next to pride, envy or jealousy is the hardest sin to see within ourselves. If we do see it, admitting what we see and are experiencing is indeed jealousy is more difficult than admitting an addiction. Jealousy is unique in that it is the one sin where the sinner experiences no joy while committing it! Think about it. Sin is tempting because it falsely promises to deliver happiness and fulfillment through some pleasure in the moment. But what pleasure is there in the experience of jealousy? I believe that Thomas Aquinas said it best when he defined jealousy as, "sorrow at another's good."

Envy is a powerful force, for it was envy in the hearts of the priests of Israel that led to the crucifixion of the Messiah Jesus. Jesus as God incarnate of course saw the envy in their hearts, but so did the executioner himself Pontius Pilate:

Matthew 27:15-18

Now at the feast the governor was accustomed to release for the [f]people any one prisoner whom they wanted. [16]At that time they were holding a notorious prisoner, called Barabbas. [17]So when the people gathered together, Pilate said to them, "Whom do you want me to release for you? Barabbas, or Jesus who is called Christ?" [18]For he knew that because of envy they had handed Him over.

There is not a single verse in any of the four gospels where it mentions that any of the rulers of Israel saw their own jealousy that was so obvious to others. The book of Proverbs proves true when it asks, "Wrath is fierce and anger is a flood, But who can stand before jealousy?"[52] How about King Saul who chased David his entire life because he was envious of God showing him favor. Saul's jealousy filled him with constant anger ruining his relationship with his wife and his son Jonathan who was David's best friend.[53] I imagine Saul

---

[52] Proverbs 27:4.
[53] 1Samual 18:6-9 – …when David returned from killing the Philistine, that the women came

playing over and over in his head the refrain from the women in the town, "Saul has slain his thousands, and David his ten thousands." I picture Saul grumbling this phrase under his breath adding, "ten thousands and me only thousands, huh I'll show them who is King."

Have you ever experienced envy/jealousy of another person? How did you deal with it? Was it jealousy at good news? Jealousy of a ministry success of a friend who has a similar calling? Maybe you are jealous of a friend's marriage, kids, or area of work where you share the same passion? Explain. (If the answer is no, then you need to really pay attention because I promise you that you have, but you were blind to it and replaced the experience with another word. More than likely a few words of accusation against the person of whom you were envious.)

_____

_____

_____

One of the sure ways to know if an experience may in fact be jealousy is when you hear good news from a family member or friend and your initial reaction is a slight "pause" before you express excitement for them. This may happen when you are removed from their presence physically, or by hanging up the phone, and you feel sorrow at his or her joy—the enemy of jealousy is on the move within your heart. Envy stops you from bragging about your friend or family member's good news to another, or publically on social media. It may even pain you to hit the "like" button, and as for sharing the status in celebration for your friend—forget about it, not going to happen. Brothers this should not be!

I remember when Cheryl and I were trying to get pregnant. We were in a small group with a couple who had a son, and they would pray with us and comfort us as we were into year two and still nothing. During this time they tried to get pregnant again and right away there was success. You can tell that they felt a little awkward giving us the news. I think that both Cheryl and I would tell you that

out of all the cities of Israel, singing and dancing, to meet King Saul, with tambourines, with joy and with [b]musical instruments. 7 The women sang as they [c]played, and said, "Saul has slain his thousands, and David his ten thousands." [8]Then Saul became very angry, for this saying [d]displeased him; and he said, "They have ascribed to David ten thousands, but to me they have ascribed thousands. Now what more can he have but the kingdom?" [9]Saul looked at David with suspicion [kept a jealous eye] from that day on.

we experienced envy at that moment combined with a "why is it so hard for us?" How selfish of us to have a good friend's joy robbed because of envy and dare I say a tinge of accusation against God! I guess I am not so different from Adam after all. On the way home we came to our senses and vowed to ask questions and not rob them of their joy. Jealousy is sneaky.

Over time jealousy unchecked begins a downward spiral of sin as it leads to discontentment, which leads to PMS (Poor Me Syndrome), which leads to a bitter spirit, which leads to quarrels. Discontentment in your heart is telling God His provision is not good enough and you *deserve* more. This is when you start feeling sorry for yourself and envy grows deeper as you want what your brother has. You get bitter as pride informs you that you not only want your brothers joy, but that you are more deserving than he is. Here you will begin to call into question God's justice because He should know how much more deserving you are. This, of course, will lead you to pick fights and quarrels over unrelated things because envy colors your view of your brother.

James 4:1-4

What is the source of quarrels and conflicts among you? [b]Is not the source your pleasures that wage war in your members? [2]You lust and do not have; *so* you commit murder. You are envious and cannot obtain; *so* you fight and quarrel. You do not have because you do not ask. [3]You ask and do not receive, because you ask [c]with wrong motives, so that you may spend *it* [d]on your pleasures.

In what ways does envy specifically cause quarrels?

_____

_____

_____

How does envy reveal itself in your life? How do you recognize it?

_____

_____

_____

If envy is the disease, then what is the cure? There are three antidotes to envy that need to be applied immediately. When you do this daily, it changes your attitude and outlook so that you can appreciate God's unique plan and purpose for you. Here is the formula:

(1) Celebration at another's good

(2) Contentment

(3) Gratitude for God's provision

(1) Celebration at another's good

Celebration at another's good is taking every jealous thought captive by doing the exact opposite of your initial feelings laced reactions. This is leading your heart, not following it for, "The heart is more deceitful than all else and is desperately sick.[54]" Maybe this verse is where we get the saying "green with envy". Don't feel like celebrating, then double the celebration by finding at least two ways to brag publically about how happy you are for your friend. Second, find a special way to let them know you are happy for them. An interesting and unexpecting thing will happen to you—Joy! The envy will be replaced. This is God's way of changing us, and it should be no surprise that faith is the main ingredient in the solution. The solution is obey first (faith) by celebrating your brother and replacing the envy, and your feelings of actual joy for him will follow. Envy is replaced with joy only *after* you celebrate your friend because faith is the fuel that moves you from where you are to where you want to be.

(2) Contentment

Contentment is something that has to be learned, and not just once, but over and over again. This is especially true today in our media heavy culture where advertizing campaigns on TV, radio, Internet adds, billboards, and so forth all have their success dependent on stirring discontentment. Little by little you become dissatisfied to the point where the once new iPhone that has been a blessing is turned into a curse because it is not the latest one that someone else has. I am encouraged by the Scriptures when I see that even the great Apostle Paul had to learn contentment.

Philippians 4:11 – ...for I have *learned* to be [b]content in

---

[54] Jeremiah 17:6.

whatever circumstances I am. [emphasis mine]

(3) Gratitude for God's provision

Celebration replaces the negative thought at the moment while contentment combined with gratitude is the place you want to be so that envy does not have any territory to land. You learn contentment by first learning to praise God in a spirit of thankfulness. When you do this you have to be specific by actually naming what you are thankful for. Do this each and every day and celebrate another whom God has blessed then your new natural response will replace the poison of jealousy. The Bible gives us a list of praiseworthy categories to start with.

Philippians 4:8

[8] Finally, brethren, whatever is true, whatever is honorable, whatever is right, whatever is pure, whatever is [c]lovely, whatever is of good repute, if there is any excellence and if anything worthy of praise, [f]***dwell on these things.*** [emphasis mine]

Are you feeling discontent? Write down five things right now that you are thankful for.

1._____
2._____
3._____
4._____
5._____

Take a moment in prayer to thank God for them and ask His forgiveness for not being grateful for His provision. If you are in a small group pray together.

Link-2: Showing Partiality & Unjust Bias

"These also are sayings of the wise. To show partiality in judgment is not good."
— Proverbs 24:23

We all have a tendency to be partial to certain people over others and this can cloud our judgments leading to injustice. The key is to know what drives your specific tendency toward partiality so you can be aware of it and make a conscious effort to not allow partiality to impact your judgments, "For there is no partiality in God" – Romans 2:11. There are numerous forms of partiality that can cause us to not make "a right judgment" as John 7:24 instructs us to. It can be showing partiality when judging a matter because one person is a friend, family member, your child, spouse, or favorite employee. In these cases you should give the benefit of the doubt to those closest to you, but not partiality when the data is presented.

The tendency to pervert justice by showing partiality to the rich or to the poor will impact all of us in some form or another since God specifically points this out in the Bible.

Leviticus 19:15 – 'You shall do no injustice in judgment; you shall not be partial to the poor nor defer to the great, but you are to judge your neighbor fairly.

I think it is easy for Christians to see partiality toward the rich, especially for those of us who live and work in the Washington D.C. area. Lobbyists make a living trying to get partiality in judgments, and the rich seem to have an ability to buy their way out of prison time. I think most of us can see that "out there" in the world but we must also be aware of the tendency in our churches as the book of James points out:

James 2:1-4

My brethren, do not hold your faith in our glorious Lord Jesus Christ with an attitude of personal favoritism. [2]For if a man comes into your [a]assembly with a gold ring and dressed in [b]fine clothes, and there also comes in a poor man in dirty clothes, [3]and you [c]pay special attention to the one who is wearing the fine clothes, and say, "You sit here in a good place," and you say to the poor man, "You stand over there, or sit down by my footstool," [4]have you not made distinctions among yourselves, and become judges with evil [d]motives?

I believe seeing partiality toward the poor as a bad thing is especially difficult for the modern Christian. A Christian's compassion in seeing the plight of the poor can, and often does, blind him to the point of calling for charity as a replacement for justice instead of a complement to justice. This is unjust as St. Augustine noted, "Charity is no substitute for justice withheld." If a poor man does something wrong both justice and charity have demands, and the man of virtue must make a just judgment in a loving way. Being poor does not give a man a free pass to being unjust as secular/Marxist conflict theory dictates. The modern Christian has had his the heart for the poor twisted through a secular humanist framework of "social justice" and not a biblical framework rooted in God's virtue of justice.

Christian social justice types allow poverty to not only excuse injustice, but it becomes a license, or dare I say "right" to commit injustice. Again, this is Marxism not Christianity. Christians, in particular those trained in the secular seminaries of western civilization, the university, are the most susceptible to unintentionally baptizing this idea from their sociology textbook among other college courses where Karl Marx is king not Jesus. A good example of this particular form of injustice by partiality to the poor is seen in the Israeli-Palestinian conflict. Time and time again Hamas starts lobbing missiles toward Jewish civilian areas in order to murder Jewish civilians. Finally the Israelis respond, and there is outcry for their response that *accidently* kills innocent civilians, but no outcry for the reason a response was needed; namely, the firing of missiles into Israel with the sole purpose and aim of killing civilians. Or, how about excusing the poor in inner city America rioting and destroying businesses, public property, and in some cases other people? Being upset about an injustice, real or perceived, does not excuse injustice as a response from a biblical perspective. This is the classic soft bigotry of low expectations levied on poor people. The extreme of "if poor then innocent" by excuse+right, followed by, if rich then guilty, is unjust. This type of thinking is a result poisonous mental framework of the Karl Marx's conflict theory of the bourgeois verses the proletariat. Atheist Karl Marx by the way is regarded by many as the father of modern sociology, a post Darwin pseudo-science.[55]

---

[55] Some give this title to Auguste Comte who had the view known as "positivism" which is a form of scientism where there is an attempt to define sociology as a science via the scientific method. An obvious failure that is being worked on today in the modern humanist syncretism of the ideas of both Karl Marx and Auguste Comte. Both views are rooted in Atheism and Darwinian evolution regarding the origins humans and their societies. The entire foundation of this modern pseudo-science view is flawed and no Christian can biblically make sociology superior to God by believing, through blind faith, that sociology is "science" and superior to theology. This is the false faith and reason separation in action.

It what ways do we see partiality to the rich today?

_____

_____

_____

It what ways do we see partiality to the poor today in the US or globally?

_____

_____

_____

There is one more form of partiality that leads to injustice in judging matters of truth, and that is the sensitive subject of race. There are two forms of racism worth mentioning that cause injustice through partiality. One I call the negative form of racism that is rooted in hatred of another person because of his or her race, and the second is what I call the positive form of racism rooted in multiculturalism's call to give race and/or cultural heritage primacy in determining one's identity. The negative form of racism is obvious to most of us and has been experienced by a number of us in one form or another. The positive form is not as obvious but also has been experienced by a number of us as well. An example of the negative form of racism occurs when a person *does not* choose to give someone a job because he is of _____ race, so he offers it to another. Whereas the positive form of racism occurs when a person *does choose* to give a person a job because he is of the same race so he unjustly denies the job to the other person. Do you see the sneaky difference? As far as a result, both are forms of unjust bias or partiality against God's standard of justice. Each example unjustly robs a person of the expected justice of an equal opportunity of employment. It just so happens that we either choose to be blind to the positive form of racism or we baptize the positive form with unjust and unbiblical reasoning.

1 Timothy 5:21 – I solemnly charge you in the presence of God and of Christ Jesus and of His chosen angels, to maintain these principles without bias, doing nothing in a spirit of partiality.

James 2:8-9 – If, however, you are fulfilling the [a]royal law according to the Scripture, "You shall love your neighbor as yourself," you are doing well. [9] But if you show partiality, you are committing sin and are convicted by the [b]law as transgressors.

When you give your race or cultural heritage primacy in your identity instead of Christ, then you will baptize the positive racism and walk as unjust before both God and man. A man of virtue walks in disobedience when he chooses to get his identity from a mere physical property such as skin color and not the spiritual quality that is found in Christ. It is, in essence, a form of not only racism, but idolatry as you place the creation above the Creator (Romans 1:21-25). In Christ we are one race, and it is the human race; one color, and it is red, for we are either covered by the blood of Christ or uncovered. You are either covered by the blood of Christ, adopted into His new chosen race and promise of eternity, or you are uncovered, remaining in the old fallen race and the promise of eternal separation from God. When I first see you and you first see me, on the surface we will see the racial properties. Shortly thereafter, neither of us should primarily notice our blackness, brownness, or whiteness, but our Christ-likeness. We should expect those in the world to get their primary identity in the first Adam and the imperfect fallen hyphenated categories rooted in secularism/Marxism and Darwinism. On the other hand, those of us in the Church should get our primary identity in the second Adam— Jesus Christ, and our lives should reflect this reality.

Of course we do not lose our cultural identity in Christ, but our cultural identity must be under the headship of Christ as we submit to Him and make our identity in Christ *primary*. Jesus Christ has called us, His universal Church, to not simply "speak" for His new race of people who are all family by adoption,[56] but to be Ambassadors representing Him within the church and to the world around us. There is one race, the human race, where the image of God rests, and the image of God is never to be minimized to skin pigment. In reality there is only one major pigment called *melanin* that produces every person's skin color. So in a sense we are all shades of brown. In summary, God gave us our cultural background and in Christ these are not to be *erased*, but *embraced* under His headship.

---

[56] John 1:12 – But as many as received Him, to them He gave the right to become children of God, *even* to those who believe in His name.
Ephesians 1:5 –He predestined us to adoption as sons through Jesus Christ to Himself, according to the kind intention of His will.

The issue is primacy! A simple shift such as calling ministries cross-cultural instead of multi-cultural is one way to express this reality of unity in our diversity under the cross of Jesus Christ.

Have you ever experienced negative or positive racism? Explain.

_____

_____

_____

How Faith & Prudence Help The Injustice of Partiality

What is the foundation of a biblical view of the virtue of justice and how does the virtue of prudence play a role? What we are avoiding is carelessness, the vice of prudence. Our unjust biases make us careless, especially if we do not know what they are. And being careless makes us unjust as we make quick judgments about people and situations with very little information (knowledge). In a very significant way the virtue of prudence is the primary guiding force helping us to make a right judgment in the area of partiality and unjust bias.

In chapter four, "Being a Man of Prudence not Carelessness" I include a chart demonstrating how the inductive Bible study method maps to the three levels of faith and three levels of growth in prudence. The purpose of this chart is to demonstrate how the virtues guide us to avoid eisegesis when we study the Bible. As a reminder, **eisegesis** is the practice where your confirmation biases, prejudices, and assumptions are *read into the text* instead of **exegesis** where God's truth is *drawn out of the text*. In fact, to interpret literally means "to draw out" which is exegesis, on the other hand, eisegesis can be said to be the practice of "pouring in."

Bible Study		Prudence		Faith
Observation	⇒	Knowledge	⇒	Content
Interpretation	⇒	Understanding	⇒	Conviction
Application	⇒	Wisdom	⇒	Centrality

As racial tensions flared in our brave new world of smart phone videos, I witnessed Christians on social media and pastors in the Church doing what I call "sociological eisegesis." Since it is true that eisegesis is wrong when reading the Bible then why do we so easily miss our confirmation bias and jump to unjust conclusions when we view another hard to watch two-minute video? The famous saying from the last century of "one picture is worth a thousand words" is reinterpreted in this century to mean that 999 of those words are lies! We can add to this saying that "one video is worth a thousand shares" as lies propagate quickly around the world inciting violence as people make quick careless judgments rooted in the lies of a confirmation bias while truth, the central ingredient of justice, remains wanting.

Watching two minutes of a sixty minute event between a black or white officer in blue and a young black man will predictably lead to sociological eisegesis every time as we insert the video into our own framework of prejudices, assumptions, and biases we attained through experiences and an education rooted in Secular Humanism's Marxist view of sociology. This is careless and leads to unjust accusations and character assassinations of people made in the image of God throughout social media regardless if the confirmation bias is "for" the black or white officer or "for" the black man shot.

It is careless and unjust to engage in sociological eisegesis when partiality is rooted in either negative or positive racism. What is worse is when more information was provided demonstrating the original narrative as false, I saw no public corrections and displays of humility seeking forgiveness for jumping to careless false conclusions that unjustly accused and slandered people. I have come to expect this from the ratings hungry media, but this should never be the case among God's people who should "not judge according to appearance, but judge with righteous judgment" – John 7:24

What is more disturbing to me above all else is hearing strong conservative Bible believing pastors using secular/Marxist sociological language and categories when discussing the topic of race. Everything I heard from these men is no different than what I would hear in a university classroom or on secular media outlets. Think about that for a moment! Shouldn't that fact alone ring an alarm bell when the Church uses the exact same language and sociological assumptions as the world? As the Apostle Paul warns us in Colossians 2:8, "See to it that no one takes you captive through philosophy and empty deception, according to the tradition of men, according to the elementary principles of the world, [a]rather than according to Christ."

Every "conversation about race" started with Marxist assumptions and used secular humanism's language with terms such as "white privilege," a phrase rooted in Marxist conflict theory and its foundation, Darwinian evolution. It is a clear picture of how the bachelor's degree from a secular university took precedence over the master's degree from a biblical seminary. As for the virtue of faith, it is a clear indication of the false faith and reason separation instead of the biblical overlap of faith and reason renewing our minds. The worldview of the culture has been caught by the Church and baptized so that the Church sounds culturally relevant but remains biblically illiterate. Every one of these supposed "conversations" was in reality a monologue not a dialogue built around the wrong assumptions, leading to wrong conclusions, thereby leading to the wrong solutions. So what was missing?

Darwin's original work is titled *On the Origin of Species by Means of Natural Selection, or the Preservation of Favored Races in the Struggle for Life*. Read the title again because I do not want you to miss it. For the record, the phrase "white privilege" is incredibly racist because Darwin believed that different races of people evolved at different times and *rates* placing whites as the most advanced. If that is not racist then I do not know what is! Of course the Darwinian foundation of the belief in this supposed "white privilege" is never discussed, only the implied sociological result in America and Europe. Adolf Hitler didn't miss it as he evoked a genetic cleansing of perceived lesser races to protect and preserve the Aryan race. As the famous evolutionary biologist Stephen Jay Gould wrote, "Biological arguments for racism may have been common before 1859, but they increased by orders of magnitude following the acceptance of evolutionary theory."[57] I repeat, Christians should never import the sociology of the culture into the Church. Our sociology must be rooted in our theology that all people are uniquely

---

[57] S.J. Gould, *Ontogeny and Phylogeny*, Belknap-Harvard Press, Cambridge, Massachusetts, 1977, 127–128.

created in the image of God with both meaning and purpose. These pastors sadly lacked either a biblical worldview or the fortitude necessary to have a real conversation rooted in a biblical sociology. As a result, they baptized a secular monologue rooted in secular/Marxist sociology. Let me explain.

As a reminder, biblical faith is where both faith and reason partially overlap so that we can make wise decisions because God wants us to use both our head and our heart, which is why prudence is so vital. Both faith and prudence share a common property—wisdom. There is a fallacy in logic, how our mind reasons toward what it true so that we can gain wisdom, called 'the reductive fallacy.' The reductive fallacy is known as an oversimplification and exaggeration that occurs whenever the series of actual causes for an event is reduced to merely one oversimplified aspect. In this case, the reductive fallacy for the racially contentious riots where young adults burned down their own city throughout the nation is racism. Thus, a "conversation about race" is an incomplete conversation. Yes there are problems with racism, but there is a larger problem today that is growing throughout the country that should concern the Church; namely, absent fathers due to out of wedlock births.

Biblical sociology must always begin with the marriage and family. The marriage and family is God's foundational societal institution given the fact that it is the only institution created before the Fall. No government in paradise, just the husband and wife becoming one with the goal of producing children. If you are a Christian, especially a pastor, and you never start with or even consider the breakdown of the family in these events, then you are not rooted in biblical sociology. It is time for some Romans 12:2 renewing of the mind to remove the poison of secular/Marxism that cost you or your parents several thousand dollars in college loans. Think for a moment about what you assume as true and where that information came from. Then ask yourself, why do I believe it?

When a father, a young man's first authority in his life, is absent from the home or abusive, then this same man will disrespect and rebel against all authority whether a coach, teacher, or a police officer. The late rapper Tupac Shakur said, "I know for a fact that had I had a father, I'd have some discipline. I'd have more confidence."[58] He also stated, "Your mother cannot calm you down the way a man can, you need a man to teach you how to be a man."[59] Black conservative radio host Larry Elder interviewed Kweisi Mfume, then the president of the NAACP, and asked him: "As between the presence of white racism and the absence of black fathers, which poses the bigger threat to the black community?" Without missing a beat, he said, "The absence of black fathers."[60]

Every man knows that mothers make boys, but fathers make men. As the following chart indicates, the problem of out of wedlock births is a growing crisis in America, while it is epidemic in the black community. If you love the black community like I do, then this should both concern you and motivate you to help our brothers and sisters out in a biblical way. As the enemy slithers in among Christians temping us to commit sociological eisegesis we must have unity around the simple truth—all fathers matter. Minimizing the problem to racism alone is a diversion tactic while the enemy outflanks us by picking off fathers with skilled sniper fire.

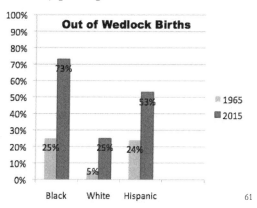

One of the cities that had riots for several days is Baltimore, where only 16 percent of 15 to 17-year-olds have been raised by both their married parents.[62] This places Baltimore among the top five

---

[58] Larry Elder, "Black Fathers Matter" (video, PragerU, June 13, 2016), accessed August 10, 2016, https://www.prageru.com/courses/political-science/black-fathers-matter.

[59] Ibid.

[60] Ibid.

[61] Ibid.

[62] Family Research Council: Marriage and Religion Research Institute, *Violence in Baltimore: Social Science Resources for Journalists and Public Officials*, 2nd ed., May 2015, accessed August 14, 2016, http://downloads.frc.org/EF/EF15E09.pdf.

worst counties in America when measuring intact families. Do you really believe that these facts do not matter and the issues that plague the inner city is simply racism? As a black man himself, Walter E. Williams, a distinguished professor of economics at George Mason University, finds these statistics especially tragic. He writes, "from 1890 to 1940, the black marriage rate was slightly higher than that of whites. Even during slavery, when marriage was forbidden for blacks, most black children lived in biological two-parent families."[63] Dr. Williams pulls no punches as he takes the secular/Marxist sociological assumptions head on:

During the 1960s, devastating nonsense emerged, exemplified by a Johns Hopkins University sociology professor who argued, "It has yet to be shown that the absence of a father was directly responsible for any of the supposed deficiencies of broken homes." The real issue, he went on to say, "is not the lack of male presence but the lack of male income." That suggests marriage and fatherhood can be replaced by a welfare check.

This brings us to the second fact in biblical sociology that we find in the pre-Fall paradise; namely, God gave man a job before He gave him a woman. A job provides a mission and purpose while the family provides meaning and belonging. The secular/Marxist sociological approach denies the value of both. Look at the result! Any "conversation" that leaves out the breakdown of the family as part of the equation when addressing the problems in the inner cities of America is a fear based dereliction of duty on the part of the pastor. As the Bible reminds us, the sin of omission is still a sin: "Therefore, to one who knows the right thing to do and does not do it, to him it is sin." –James 4:17.

God takes the role of a father very seriously and so should we. In 1Samuel 3:13 God judges Eli harshly and holds him accountable for failing at his duty as a father by allowing his sons to act like fools in the community: "For I [God] told him that I would judge his family forever because of the sin he knew about; his sons made themselves contemptible, and he failed to restrain them." Eli was in the home, yet he was a lazy, passive father. Additionally, the

---

[63] Walter E. Williams, "Black Sabotage," Townhall, July 31, 2013, July 31, 2013, accessed August 1, 2016, http://townhall.com/columnists/walterewilliams/2013/07/31/black-selfsabotage-n1651550.

Old Testament ends with a promise to fathers in the family and the New Testament begins with its fulfillment. The very last verse of the Old Testament, before the "silent years" when Israel had no prophet, God announces that the father's heart is the first "hill" He will take when the Messiah comes: 5"Behold, I am going to send you Elijah the prophet before the coming of the great and terrible day of the Lord. 6He will [e]restore the hearts of the fathers to their children and the hearts of the children to their fathers…" – Malachi 4:5-6. This very heart preparation was announced by the angel of the Lord to Zacharias, the father of John the Baptist, "It is he [John] who will go as a forerunner before Him in the spirit and power of Elijah, to turn the hearts of the fathers back to the children…" – Luke 1:17. With this reality of where God's heart is for our role as fathers, men, how can we deny our sacred duty and its impact and witness to the world?

Being men of fortitude and charity, not fear and indifference, demands that the pulpits be filled with biblical sociology in which pastors challenge and encourage the Church to get back to God's design for all people, irrespective of culture, by elevating the marriage and family. Yes, we should address racism in all of its forms expressed by all people, white, black, brown, or yellow because racism is a sin problem not a skin problem. On the other hand, carelessly addressing the topic to "seem relevant" because its in the news, or addressing the topic in isolation of the sociological reality of the breakdown of the family is not only foolish, but sinful. And this makes us men of injustice not justice. Just say "no" to social justice and "yes" to biblical justice while demanding that your church's pulpit honors God above men by doing the same.

I highly recommend the sermon "Race, Culture & Christ"64 from one of my favorite preachers Dr. Tony Evans. If you are in a small group take time to watch the sermon together and combine it with this section of the book for discussion. Dr. Evans tackles the issues discussed in this section regarding black racism, white racism, and Marxist verses biblical sociology. Additionally, I would add the short five-minute video at PragerU65 by Larry Elder titled "Black

64 Dr. Tony Evans," Race Culture & Christ John 4:1-9" (video), posted July 17, 2016, accessed August 11, 2016, https://www.youtube.com/watch?v=KbhNCTJ-dUI.
65 Larry Elder, "Black Fathers Matter" (video, PragerU, June 13, 2016), accessed August 10, 2016, https://www.prageru.com/courses/political-science/black-fathers-matter.

Fathers Matter." Some of the quotes and statistics in this section were taken from this informative video.

In the sermon video by Dr. Tony Evans, what stood out most to you? Why?

_____
_____
_____

Combing the video by Larry Elder "Black Fathers Matter" with the bible what did you learn and how does it change your thinking?

_____
_____
_____

What was your confirmation bias when the riots were occurring? Was it "for" the officer or black man shot? What is your bias based on?

_____
_____
_____

How have you seen or personally experienced the pressure to embrace the primacy of race or culture over the primacy of Christ?

_____
_____
_____

What can you and your church do to support or partner with inner city churches to invest in rebuilding the family?

_____
_____
_____

Link-3: A Tendency To Assume The Negative

"Two negatives make a positive in math not relationships" – Pete Lackey

This link in the chain of wrongly judging others deals with what happens within us as we process information about people around us. First we assume the negative when we hear something harmful such as an accusation against another person that challenges his character. This, of course, finds its link back into backbiting and slander. This is a terrible part of the fallen nature where we are so quick to believe the negative that we demonstrate injustice by not giving our brother the benefit of the doubt. We as the listener are responsible on how we listen when someone is "sharing" with us his offense by another. One of the most practical verses in the Bible that you can apply almost daily deals with this topic.

Proverbs 18:17 – The first [a]to plead his case seems just, Until [b]another comes and examines him.

Proverbs 18:17 – The first to present his case seems right until another comes along and questions him. (NIV)

Take a moment right now to write down Proverbs 18:17 then commit it to memory so that you can apply it daily. Are you a parent, a boss with an open door policy, a family member, a friend? You can apply this verse immediately! I apply this verse constantly. Think about it. You would want to present your side of the story if someone was slandering you, so provide others that same opportunity.

Second, we assume the negative when a harmful experience in the past misinforms us in the present. In many ways, the same life experience that makes us wise can also make us unjustly suspicious of people. I think of an example we addressed earlier on the crisis in the inner city where a police officer from the local precinct, black or white but wearing blue, pulls over a young black male. Both at that moment have a rush of emotions and thoughts as their past experience is brought to bear in the present moment, and how each individual behaves in the first few minutes of contact is critical. Neither person is good or bad, or right or wrong to have those thoughts and emotions. Their experiences are their experiences., and what is needed are more positive experiences and *both* men are responsible for what category of experience that moment adds to.

Aristotle alleged that "old people are very suspicious, for they have often experienced the faults of others."[66] As a middle-aged man, I see this tendency within myself more and more. A common example of this occurs in the workplace where a man has felt slighted by self-promoting leadership so he broad brushes negative judgments on all of management. A new manager comes in that truly does have the best interest of the team above his own, but this man interprets

---

[66] Aquinas, *Summa Theologica* II.60.3.

every good action as bad motives. This new manager does not stand a chance in the heart of the suspicious man.

A just man would be wise to be cautious of people based on his experience, but a foolish and unjust man is always suspicious. People deserve a chance and the benefit of the doubt. This is an excellent application of Jesus' command in Matthew 7:12, "In everything, therefore, treat people the same way you want them to treat you..." I have learned to reset myself and think of each person individually, being mindful of when I am suspicious and not cautious. The best way to discover the difference is by being self-aware when you interpret an action or behavior negatively. Nothing is worse than being falsely accused. Aquinas rightly observes that, "Suspicion, denoted a certain amount of vice, and the further it goes, the more vicious it is."[67]

Link-4: Harming Another's Name Through Backbiting and Slander

"You shall not go about as a slanderer among your people" – Leviticus 19:16

We often talk about gossip and slander but leave out the deadly consequences of it, namely, harming another's name. If you have ever been on the receiving end of slander and found yourself defending your honor, you know how devastating it can be. Often times it is the people whom you thought knew you best, that not only believe the slander but act on it as if it is true. Proverbs 16:28 states that, "A perverse man spreads strife, and a slanderer separates intimate friends." The Hebrew word for perverse, *tahpukah*, literally means "a fraud."

A gossip is a person who shares something shared or observed with others, although it was shared in confidence and meant to be private. A slanderer will take that information or just part of it and attach motives and character judgments to it. Proverbs 20:19 warns us that, "He who goes about as a slanderer reveals secrets, therefore do not associate with a gossip." Unfortunately, we usually find out that a person is a gossip and slanderer the hard way.

---

[67] Ibid.

The passive hearer is just as guilty as the active slanderer. Proverbs 17:4 states, "An evildoer listens to wicked lips; A [a]liar pays attention to a destructive tongue." Many times we can be guilty of just listening to someone share a frustration then make rash false judgments without questioning the person. Sometimes, we just want to be a good friend so we listen and comfort only. We should both actively listen and actively guide. Often times the person does not intend to be speaking ill of another which is where giving someone the benefit of the doubt comes in.

When I was a full-time Pastor at McLean Bible Church I had a man come up to me frustrated with another Pastor who recently took over a ministry area and wanted to institute some changes that this man disagreed with. I listened to him share his frustration with me for about 15 minutes. Finally, I encouraged him because he obviously cared about this ministry and its impact on people's lives. Then I challenged him with a few questions.

Me: "Do you believe that Pastor _____ loves the Lord and cares about this ministry?"

Volunteer: "Yes"

Me: "I know that he does and I can promise you that he certainly cares and wants to do the right thing in the Lord's eyes. Do you trust in God's sovereignty placing _____ above this ministry?"

Volunteer: "Yes"

Me: "Did you speak with _____ about your concerns?"

Volunteer: "Yes"

Me: "Does he know that you spoke to him about your concerns?"

Volunteer: "What!"

Me: "What I mean is did he really understand how important this is to you and your concerns?"

Volunteer: "Yes, I spoke to him after _____ event."

Me: "A hallway conversation on the heels of a big event may not have led him to believe how important your message is. Here is my suggestion. Set up a meeting with him to talk about the ministry and its direction. Then go into the meeting humble and teachable, with a spirit of wanting to help. Provide him any history of the ministry and what worked and did not work. Then offer to be a valuable partner in making it a success."

I prayed with him and off he went. I ran into him a few weeks later and he thanked me for listening and for the advice. He told me that he had a very fruitful meeting and was excited about where the ministry was heading. He said to me at the end, "You know, I shared my frustration with others and you are the only person who challenged me and gave me advice to go back to _____." I said to him, "You know what you have to do now, right?" He looked a little confused. I told him that he now has the responsibility to restore his brother's name by going to each person that he spoke with and ask for forgiveness and update them on what happened. Why?

Proverbs 22:1 – A good name is to be more desired than great riches, favor is better than silver or gold.

So what did this approach accomplish?

For the Pastor:

o Gave the benefit of the doubt to fellow pastor.

o Sowed belief into my fellow pastor.

o I didn't unnecessarily insert myself into the situation.

o I submitted to his authority.

o I honored his good name!

For the volunteer:

o I listened.

o I encouraged him to provide the benefit of the doubt.

o I gave him prudent and not careless advice.

o I encouraged submission to authority.

o In short, I shepherded a sheep who needed a shepherd

The second verse I applied to this situation was the principle found in Matthew 18, a passage of the Bible geared specifically around the virtue of justice. This passage contains the process for church discipline with the desired goal of full restoration of a brother to the church.

Matthew 18:15-20

If your brother sins[k], go and [l]show him his fault [m]in private; if he listens to you, you have won your brother. [16]But if he does not listen to you, take one or two more with you, so that by the mouth of two or three witnesses every [n]fact may be confirmed. [17]If he refuses to listen to them, tell it to the church; and if he refuses to listen even to the church, let him be to you as [o]a Gentile and [p]a tax collector. [18]Truly I say to you, whatever you [q]bind on earth [r]shall have been bound in heaven; and whatever you [s]loose on earth [t]shall have been loosed in heaven. [19]"Again I say to you, that if two of you agree on earth about anything that they may ask, it shall be done for them [u]by My Father who is in heaven. [20]For where two or three have gathered together in My name, I am there in their midst.

Within this passage, the first thing to notice is that verses 19-20 specifically deal with the topic of church discipline and restoration, not prayer in general. This form of justice is so important to the Lord that He promises to be within your midst! Second, this is a reconciliation and restoration process for a brother who *may have* sinned. The process is meant to guarantee that the truth comes out in an objective manner, which is where more people come into play throughout the process. In an ingenious way the biblical process allows for the obvious fact that the accuser may be wrong in his or her accusation; i.e., wrong judgment (v16). This biblical process is not to be confused with a "Performance Management Plan" or other device in the secular workplace that everyone knows is a one-way process to document the accused out the door and into the unemployment line. The Holy Spirit is the Spirit of truth and that is what He works with, truth.

Here is the process:

1. If your brother sinned, go to him in private (v.15)

2. If unsuccessful bring another brother (v.16)[68]

158

3. If accuser is wrong and accusation is false, stop & correct (v.16)

4. If unsuccessful bring it to the assembly (v.17)

5. If unsuccessful remove him so as to remove his influence of others causing them to stumble as well.

This passage did not specifically apply to the situation with the brother complaining about ministry changes given that the situation did not have to do with sin. He may have felt sinned against, but in reality there is no sin. However, the principles of this passage certainly apply. This is why I shepherded him back to the pastor following step one in the process encouraging him to give this pastor the benefit of the doubt. All I heard was this man's issue at this point and I cannot assume I have all of the facts. Furthermore, I have no right inserting myself into the situation without any further information. As you probably expect by now, the Bible has some wisdom to provide in this area.

Proverbs 26:17 – "Like one who takes a dog by the ears is he who passes by and meddles with strife not belonging to him."

I had a similar situation occur where I was the pastor and a man in the congregation approached a friend of mine, and slandered my name because he was unhappy about a boundary I had in my ministry. Unfortunately, this friend took the information, believed it, approached me with an accusation, and tried to setup a "reconciliation" meeting that was organized more like an intervention. I was floored! All of this was done independent of me as my friend never asked me about the situation, and still hasn't years later. Proverbs 18:17 would have been a big help to my friend. Not only because he believed it, but also because he inserted himself in a codependent way (more on this in link-5). What did this unjust approach actually accomplish?

---

[68] This fulfills the requirement of Deuteronomy 19:15 – "A single witness shall not rise up against a man on account of any iniquity or any sin which he has committed; on the evidence of two or three witnesses a matter shall be confirmed." This helps fight against the injustice of slander and false accusation. Again, confirming the goal of getting to the truth. The Holy Spirit is the Spirit of truth and that is what He works with.

For me:

✖ He did not give me the benefit of the doubt.

✖ Sowed unbelief into me.

✖ Unnecessarily inserted himself into the situation.

✖ Did not submit to my authority.

✖ Dishonored my good name!

For the congregant:

✖ He pacified the person & "took up his offense"

✖ He gave a stranger the benefit of the doubt.

✖ He gave careless advice and 'accused me, his brother'.

✖ He encouraged a lack of submission to authority.

✖ He did not even apply the principle of Matthew 18

✖ In short, the congregant needed a shepherd and he got a lawyer

✖ He slandered my name among many people and asked them to "pray for my humility"

Matthew 18 has some fascinating principles you can apply to everyday life including the workplace, at home with family and extended family, and in the neighborhood. The goal is to first do some investigating to see if it applies specifically, or if it applies in principle. As one example, I am a manager in the workplace and I apply the Matthew 18 combined with Proverbs 18 principles frequently. Let's be honest, some people treat the open door policy as a way to work around a colleague and not with a colleague. With that in mind, I always listen, then play the role of a coach and send them back to the fellow employee to work out the issue without unnecessarily stepping in. As a parent I use this when my children come crying about a situation where one of them will say, "he was mean to me." Really? Let me get the kids together and have each of them take turns sharing what happened, ask questions, then teach them how to work it out. Teaching conflict resolution skills early is an imperative for any parent who desires to raise healthy adults.

Link-5. Being a "People-pleaser" or "Codependency"

"Love God, Love Man. That is God's order. The people-pleaser reverses the order with a quiet arrogance that he or she knows how to love better than God who, in His very nature, is love" – Pete Lackey

This section is a tough one so I want to start off right away with a book recommendation. One of the books outside of the Bible that helped me immensely is *Changes That Heal* by Dr. John Townsend. It is in the Kindle store for $3.99 and would be a crime for you not to purchase this book! I would say that codependents and people-pleasers are in ministry positions doing grave damage to people and themselves throughout churches across the country. I am so glad that I chose to partner with God in the healing process before I went into ministry, or I would have never made it. More than likely I would have experienced emotional highs and lows of failure while at the same time blowing up my own family.

Galatians 1:10 – "Am I now trying to win the approval of human beings, or of God? Or am I trying to please people? If I were still trying to please people, I would not be a servant of Christ."

A people-pleaser is a person who has a tendency to pacify people to make them happy. Often this is due to the person having an unhealthy fear of conflict. A co-dependent on the other hand has such a low self-esteem and high need of approval that it makes him overly seek the approval of other people by taking the problem and trying to fix it for them. Codependency is learned in childhood and is particularly common in homes where at least one parent was an addict. The codependency carries on into adulthood as Dr. Shawn Burn, a psychology professor at California Polytechnic State University notes, "These kids are often taught to subvert their own needs to please a difficult parent, and it sets them up for a long-standing pattern of trying to get love and care from a difficult person."

As a recovering co-dependent myself I know how difficult this is to see within yourself. So here we go! First of all a codependent does not know emotionally where he ends and the other person begins. Trust me I know not just through biblical knowledge alone but I know existentially by experience! When I was a codependent I not only had my own relationships, but I took on the added burden of someone else's relationship and "fought for and on the behalf of" the person I was codependent with. For me, as the oldest son in an alcoholic family that experienced divorce, I was codependent with a few people and it was exhausting. Like all codependents my heart was in the right place because I thought that I was helping, but at the end of the day I was causing more damage than I thought because I was getting in God's way by playing God myself. In essence, I was being controlling.

Seriously, I would literally "feel" the wound of the other person through misplaced pity and sense of responsibility and "fight others for them" as if it was me who was injured. I "took on" the "injury" of the other, inserted myself in their place, and caused more relational damage as I tried to fix the damage for them. The problem was that I, with limited knowledge, was playing God whom has unlimited knowledge. In addition, my "knowledge" was often times filled with lies and half-truths as my desire to help was taken advantage of. But God's knowledge is all truth and nobody takes advantage of God! Many of my rescue operations failed even the ones I thought were a success because I am not God and I never let a person feel the consequences of his or her actions. I remember the thought coming to my mind from the Lord one day, "Pete, please stop jumping in and stepping on my nail torn toes! I cannot heal what they cannot feel." It was as if I was reminded that I was putting healing balm on a cancer. Cancer needs removed not covered!

This was an important revelation for me. Think about it for a moment. What makes a person realize the need for Jesus Christ? It is when he or she first realizes that "I am a sinner." Only sinners need saviors! If a person never feels the relational consequences of his sin because someone jumps in to rescue him, he will never feel the real need for a savior. How can a person desire to be justified before God through Jesus Christ when they feel justified before me, a fellow sinner? Having no consequences for sin leaves a person to feel justified in his or her sin and ask: "What sin?" Tough love is tough stuff!

My first opportunity to not be codependent was a difficult test, but I passed and the Lord gave me more and more difficult tests in this area to which I can happily report my victory over codependency. There was a relational cost initially as my family members got angry and accused me of being unloving because I would not jump in to the rescue. God has provided me many opportunities to help others in this area that is epidemic in our culture as the family continues to be torn apart and the children become parental pawns long into adulthood.

As I mentioned earlier, the church is a magnet for the codependent, and a codependent Pastor is a Pastor who will fall and fall hard. They are "people pleasers" and not "God pleasers" and will never know the difference as they "do God's work" taking up the offense of every person with a hurt feeling. This is an absolutely dangerous reversal of what Jesus Himself said was the proper order of the entire Bible: (1) Love God; (2) Love people.

Luke 10:27 – He answered, " 'Love the Lord your God with all your heart and with all your soul and with all your strength and with all your mind'; and, 'Love your neighbor as yourself.' "

If you reverse the order then you are in the dangerous position of arrogantly telling God, "I got this one because I know how to love better that you Lord." Tell this to the codependent Christian worker and he or she will be shocked! I am so grateful that I allowed God into this painful area for healing before I went into ministry. I couldn't imagine feeling overly "responsible" for failed marriages under my care when one or both spouses did not care to reconcile and heal. This is a suicide starter kit! I am glad that God gave me the wisdom to invest in the right people. What I mean is that I will work hard in partnership with the couple who wants to first partner with God and I will not work with the couple who themselves do not care about God or their marriage. That is right, as a Christian Pastor there are people who I will not work with! To borrow from the Bible, I will not make a bad investment with my "two talents." A codependent Christian worker on the other hand will overly care for them, be exhausted, feel frustrated, and like a failure when the divorce goes through as if it was his fault as he questions himself, "If only I…"

Want to test yourself to see if this might be you? Think about a person in whom you are currently in a broken relationship. Now ask yourself, "What sin did he/she commit against *me*?" Having trouble naming it? Why? Now you will know that you are a codependent right away when you cannot name it so you think of secondary consequences such as "well the issues between person1 and person2 affect me!" This is a sure sign that you are codependent with either person1 or person2. How do you know which person? I will give you a hint: It is the not the person with whom you are in a broken or distanced relationship! You, dear brother, are not "affected" but "infected" with codependency and have "taken up the offense" for the other person and improperly inserted yourself where you do not belong. In essence, you are controlling.

You want peace at all costs and are laying that burden on the other person as you protect the "feelings" of another. You broke the relationship and either made things worse or are so controlling that things did not go your way that you harbor a poisonous anger. You cannot carry someone else's sin "offense," and your brother needs you to humbly seek forgiveness for jumping in, inserting yourself, and casting judgment on him while in a position where you do not belong. In summary, it is *you* who took the hurt feelings of the person that you are codependent with, believed it, felt it, and jumped in for them. You are fighting a fight that is not yours to fight.

One of the reasons that it is so difficult to see codependency in yourself, let alone recover from it is that it feels so right! If you are from a damaged family background I can promise you that this is a very real issue for you. The only question is how much of an issue is it?

Are you a people-pleaser or codependent? Not sure, then ask the person who knows you best and love them for the honesty.

_____

_____

_____

Link-6. Projection of one's own sin

I want you to think of the sin that is almost like a spiritual pet peeve. In other words, what drives you crazy when you see it in others?   Is it jealousy, pride, controlling, overly competitive, selfishness, selfish ambition. Write it down here in your own words:

_____

_____

_____

   This link is particularly interesting because of the way you discover that this may be an issue for you. Take what you wrote above and ask yourself if this might be you. Better yet, have you been accused of the very thing that drives you crazy? Long before Sigmund Freud discovered the concept of projection, Thomas Aquinas noted, "A man being evil within himself, and from this very fact, as though conscious of his own wickedness, he is prone to think evil of others."[69]

   I was once counseling a married couple and the wife said to me, "It is just that he is too controlling." I dug for a while to get some examples, and by the second session it hit me, "She is the controlling one." As I listened to her it became clear that she wanted to do things her way and her way only. Furthermore, she wanted to do what she wanted to do and clearly couldn't care less what her husband thought about it. She interpreted his independent view as him controlling her when in reality she was behaving selfishly, "not wanting to be controlled." In short, she rejected his input and didn't care that he thought it inappropriate for his wife to constantly go out drinking with her single friends. As her husband, not wanting her to do it "was controlling." Wow, did she miss it.

   As a test I gave her some homework that was not hard to do, but required her to take my input. You guessed it, she came in the following week and didn't do a single thing. I flipped the page over on my legal pad and showed her what I wrote the week before "prediction, she is the controlling one and projecting that on her husband so she will not do the homework." I went down each of her many examples she provided and demonstrated how in the examples she was projecting her sin onto him and disrespecting/unloving her husband in the process. This is an example of projecting your greatest sin onto others.

   All vehicles have blind spots where you cannot see what is

---

[69] Ibid.

close to you. As you drive along in your journey trying to follow God's map it is your blind spots that will cause you to crash into others. Men, this is a big one. You cannot pray it out, or train it out because it will never occur to you that you need to get it out—it is a blind spot. This is where you need other brothers. Typically it is the brothers that you crash into because of your blind spots that are the key to revealing them and healing them. The problem is that we don't want to hear it because, "It can't be true, I hate _____." It just may be true which is why you project it onto others by accusing them of your own sin.

I have a brother in Christ who hates pride. I know it because not only has he has told me a number of times, but he has accused countless men of having pride issues. What is interesting is the fact that he is one of the most prideful people I know. He has had many men in his life where, for a season, they are really close, then all of the sudden "boom!" The relationship is blown up over him accusing them of being prideful. He simply cannot see it, no matter who approached him with it. The slander prayers soon follow with, you guessed it, "please pray for _____ who is struggling with pride." If he ever looked into his rearview mirror he would notice the carnage behind him.

When you look at the spiritual pet peeve that you wrote down above, is it possible that you have it the most, which is why you have sensitivity to it in others?

_____

_____

_____

_____

We all have blind spots. Think back to some broken relationships in your life. We all have those too. What is the sin in that brother that you believe is the cause of the broken relationships?

_____

_____

_____

_____

Since it is a blind spot, it may be yours and not his. In fact, I bet it is. Go now to that brother!!!! Ask for forgiveness, and reconcile.

Man-up and don't be a man of injustice.

James 5:15 – Therefore, *confess your sins* to one another, and pray for one another so that you may be healed.

With injustice there is always a cost! What is the cost of poor judgment? Your ability to fulfill the greatest commandment. How? Injustice leads to backbiting and slander that damages our relationships and robs your brother of his most precious item—his good name.

God calls us to be men of justice and not injustice. Justice is the virtue that guides us on how we are to carry out the love one another commands in the Bible. It should be clear that this virtue extends to many other areas outside of the topic of judging and the six links in the chains of judging outlined in this chapter. For instance, when selling a home, a car, computer, gaming system, etc. and making sure that you are 100% honest and upfront with all known issues. As another example, how about stealing by plagiarizing papers for school, or downloading illegal music, movies, and software. No matter what the circumstance, we are to choose right over wrong and good over evil so that you can stand clean before both God and man.

Memory Table: Commit the properties of justice to memory

Be a man of JUSTICE and not INJUSTICE	
Right and Wrong	Value and Judgment
Good and Evil	Self-interest and interest of others

7
A MAN OF TEMPERANCE
NOT GLUTTONY

"The loneliest people in the world are those who have exhausted pleasure and come away empty" – Ravi Zacharias

We get the word temperance from the Latin *temperare* which means "to mingle in due proportions or to show restraint." In the New Testament the Greek word *néphalios* is translated as temperate and means "moderate in degree or quality and exercising self- restraint." Temperance is a constant mindfulness and an acute self-awareness so as to avoid the constant temptation for more than what one ought to enjoy. Temperance encompasses the properties or sub-virtues of purity, chastity, moderation, abstention, and most certainly, self-control. In practice, there are times when temperance calls for moderation, deferred gratification, or sometimes total abstention. It is no wonder that the symbol for temperance is a harp suggesting the need for a constant state of contemplation as our fallen nature, left to its own devices, will always scream the gluttonous call of "more!" In the area of temperance we constantly need to be reminded to contemplate our thoughts and desires before we blindly take action because we feel like having "just a little more."

In the New Testament the word *néphalios* is used as a defining virtue to look for when selecting an elder or deacon in the church. In 1Timothy 3:2 we find temperance paired with prudence as particular virtues to look for: "An overseer, then, must be above reproach, the husband of one wife, temperate, prudent, respectable, hospitable, able to teach." Additionally, Titus 2:2 highlights the virtue of temperance along with, faith and charity, as defining qualities of older men: "Older men are to be temperate, dignified, sensible, sound in faith, in love, in perseverance." There is something about this virtue and a man's ability to be successful at implementing it in his life over a long period of time that is to be considered praiseworthy. I believe that 'something' is what we all know by our own experience; namely, that temperance is extremely difficult to be successful at over a long period of time.

Temperance is a virtue that is almost entirely defensive in its implementation and each man in himself must be his own regulator. While fortitude is necessary when times are difficult, temperance is necessary when times are good. With Temperance, pleasure is a virtue, but it is the excess of pleasure that is the vice. Day to day temperance is the virtue necessary in order to protect you from your most deadly personal enemy—yourself! Who else but self has the ability and skill that no other man has to fool you with lies? Temperance in its execution is the righteous habit that enables a man to govern his natural appetite for sensuous pleasures. In short, temperance is bringing under the fruit of self-control the yearning for pleasures and delights that most powerfully attract the human heart. These pleasures are not bad in themselves, but in fact were created by God for our enjoyment as evidenced by the fact that we have pleasure senses that God Himself designed. It doesn't take much contemplation to come to the conclusion that God could have excluded pleasure from His design and made sexual intercourse either bland or painful. God gave us the gift of pleasure, while the Fall of man gave us the curse of demanding an excess of it.

By experience we know that pleasure is part of God's design. At the same time we see addiction from a life of excessive pleasure, which leads us to the vice. The vice of temperance is gluttony; i.e., indulgence, lust, or an inordinate and an excessiveness of pleasure. As fallen men we all have our gluttonous moments, but we must implement the virtue of temperance so that these gluttonous moments do not turn into a gluttonous lifestyle. Hollywood serves as a living memorial to the truth that excessive pleasure brings ruin, not happiness. As you can see from the definition, gluttony primarily has to do with *excessiveness* of pleasure that, in time, leads to the slavery of addiction. It is the promise of freedom, and its immediate experience that seems to deliver on that promise that makes gluttony so dangerous. A man can be gluttonous in his hobbies, sexual appetite, gaming, food, money, and dare I say, a man's smart phone. Gasp! Notice that everything in this list is good in itself. Please don't miss this point men! It is the man's relationship to these things that is either temperate or gluttonous.

With on-line role playing games, escapism has gone to a new level as you make an avatar that looks like you and is in control by you to be whoever you want to be. In fact, the avatar doesn't even have to look like you as you can change your muscle mass, hair color, and many other features with a few clicks of the controller. Whether you play the hero rescuing lives as your avatar saves the day, or the zero ruining lives by having your avatar play dark roles in dark places, again you make the call. As the sophistication of these games plunge you into a world of fantasy forcing moral dilemmas for hours on end and days at a time you literally can lose your true self and struggle even more in the real world. The constant mixing of fantasy and reality in gluttonous binges of the on-line world rewires your brain to the point where the consequences of actions done in fantasy, as one simply re-spawns, get lost in the real world as these same actions ruin people's lives. An inconsequential re-spawn is just not an option in the actual world.

Man is Created to Work

You may be thinking that the chapter on the virtue of temperance is a strange place to add a section on work. Actually it is the perfect place for this topic because it is the idle man who is not operating according to his design and purpose who is the most likely candidate to be a slave to the carnal pleasures. Man is created in the image of God, and like God, man is created to work. As a part of God's original design, man reflects this part of God's image both when he works and when he rests. For you single men, I want you to notice that in the order of creation God gave man a job before He gave him a woman:

Genesis 2:2-3, 15, 18 – By the seventh day God completed His work which He had done, and He rested on the seventh day from all His work which He had done. [3]Then God blessed the seventh day and sanctified it, because in it He rested from all His work which God had created [a]and made... [15]Then the Lord God took the man and put him into the garden of Eden to cultivate [work] it and keep [protect] it.... [18]Then the Lord God said, "It is not good for the man to be alone; I will make him a helper [o]suitable for him."

One curious thing about men over women is the fact that men seek pleasure outlets as an escape when burdened with the stresses of life. This is especially true in regards to the stress of work and its call on a man's heart to protect and provide. As we learned earlier, God cursed man in his work after the Fall making it toilsome and extra difficult. Before the Fall of man, when a man's work was purely good and enjoyable, God still put into His design a need for a day of rest or Sabbath. The day of rest is holy because it is set apart, not because it is to not be fun. What a lie we believe! God created us to have fun and find pleasure in His creation.

There are two common extremes we find in men today that leads us to gluttony, and if we are not careful, eventually addiction and all of the damage that follows. There is the man who is all work and no play. This man works too much and does not take a day of rest weekly so he sets himself up for gluttonous moments of pleasure. He enjoys the work and the sense of accomplishment when a task is finished. I personally love this feeling! It is wonderful to look back when something is finished and take pleasure in the thought of, "Hey, I did that!" Work is good and when we enjoy our work it is both reflecting the image of God and an indication of our pre-Fall state. But it is still work and work is tiresome. The gluttonous formula for this man is simple: excessive work leads to a need for excessive pleasure. God created the Sabbath for our own good and it would benefit men to remember that.

Mark 2:27 – Jesus said to them, "The Sabbath [b]was made [c]for man, and not man [d]for the Sabbath."

What does this verse mean? Read it carefully.

_____

_____

Next, there is the sluggard, a lazy man who does not want to work. This man's idleness leads to a foolish life of all play and no work. There is nothing more damaging to a man than idleness. A lazy and idle man who does not work will always take advantage of God's creation; especially a woman as he looks to a woman for pleasure only. How can he carry out his calling as a man to protect and provide when he denies the very means God uses to carry out this calling? I have come across a lot of men who all of a sudden take great interest in work because they have a new woman in their life. Even though these men have the order wrong of woman first then work, I think that this natural response proves the point that man was created for work and work is the means to protecting and providing.[70] The Bible has a lot to say to the sluggard.

Proverbs 6:9-11 – How long will you lie down, O sluggard? When will you arise from your sleep? [10]"A little sleep, a little slumber, A little folding of the hands to [a]rest"— [11]Your poverty will come in like a [b]vagabond [thief] and your need like [c]an armed man.

Proverbs 13:4 – The soul of the sluggard craves and gets nothing,…

Proverbs 19:15-16 – Laziness casts into a deep sleep, And an idle [a]man will suffer hunger. [16]He who keeps the commandment keeps his soul, But he who [b]is careless of [c]conduct will die.

Proverbs 21:25-26 – The desire of the sluggard puts him to death, For his hands refuse to work; [26]All day long he [a]is craving, While the righteous gives and does not hold back.

---

[70] Here I am not saying that women should not work. What I am saying is that it is a healthy man and not the healthy woman that should feel a sense of duty or moral obligation of making sure the family is protected and provided for. If a wife works as well as the husband that is great! However, what work *means* to each will be different by God's design. It is a healthy woman that will feel the need for security which is the compliment to the healthy man's sense of duty of protecting and providing.

Proverbs 26:14-15 – As the door turns on its hinges, So does the sluggard on his bed. [15]The sluggard buries his hand in the dish; He is weary of bringing it to his mouth again.

You may think that the New Testament would be kinder to the sluggard. That is definitely not the case. Why? Because as this book is seeking to demonstrate, the Holy Spirit is restoring the image of God in us and this restoration process naturally pulls us toward the virtues and away from the vices. The sluggard is in the worst position of all. Chained by every vice that, in time, isolates him from God and others. Finally, over time, it leads him into self-pity, violence, injustice, carelessness, and dead in the pit of despair. Nothing is sadder than a man who has squandered his gifts, his calling, and his purpose. Save the sluggard and you will begin to help a man discover both his gifts and his purpose while at the same time restoring God's image in him.

2 Thessalonians 3:6-12

Now we command you, brethren, in the name of our Lord Jesus Christ, that you [f]*keep away* from every brother who [g]leads an [h]unruly life and not according to the tradition which [i]you received from us. [7]For you yourselves know how you ought to [j]follow our example, because we did not act in an undisciplined manner among you, [8]nor did we eat [k]anyone's bread [l]without paying for it, but with labor and hardship we kept working night and day so that we would not be a burden to any of you; [9]not because we do not have the right to this, but in order to offer ourselves as a model for you, so that you would [m]follow our example. [10]For even when we were with you, we used to give you this order: *if anyone is not willing to work, then he is not to eat*, either. [11]For we hear that some among you are leading an undisciplined life, doing no work at all, but acting like busybodies. [12]Now such persons we command and exhort in the Lord Jesus Christ to work in quiet fashion and eat their own bread. [13]But as for you, brethren, do not grow weary of doing good. [14]If anyone does not obey our [n]instruction [o]in this letter, take special note of that person [p]and *do not associate with him, so that he will be put to shame*. [15]Yet do not regard him as an enemy, but [q]admonish him as a brother. [emphasis mine]

In your own words summarize the key points below.

_____
_____
_____

Pleasure With a Purpose

"Pleasure unbounded by sacredness will leave you emptier than before" – *Ravi Zacharias*

Because temperance deals with pleasure it is typically the vice of this virtue that we have in mind when we think about what is means to be a man of virtue in a culture of vice. I promise you that temperance, like all of the other virtues, will make the Bible come to life as its truth, when applied, is proved to you on a day-to-day basis. Men, keep in mind that God's primary goal for you, following His rescue operation on the cross, is for you to be a man that reflects the image of Christ to the world around you. As demonstrated earlier, God's rules are never arbitrary and pulled out of thin air because God one day decided that He just loves rules. We best function under His care and direction with the virtues that are rooted in His very nature and which He breathed into us. Enjoying what God created plays an important role in our overall healthy functioning as men. In short, pleasure is good. I think C.S. Lewis said it best when he reminds us that, "We might think that God wanted simply obedience to a set of rules: whereas He really wants people of a particular sort."[71] In summary, God wants virtuous men of integrity who are difference makers not space takers.

A gluttonous man misses the fact that too much pleasure is not beneficial when pleasure takes over his life and becomes both the means and the ends of his very existence.[72] In doing so God's true ends are removed and replaced with a gluttonous man's misdirected ends that are, selfish, self-centered and, most of all, lacking in sacredness. Over time it is the true self that is lost as a man becomes

---

[71] C.S. Lewis, *Mere Christianity*, p.77.
[72] We often hear the phrase "the ends do not justify the means." The ends are referring to your goal while the means refers to how you reach that goal. God requires us to use honorable means toward honorable ends. If your end goal is honorable and you achieve that goal in a dishonorable way (means) then both are dishonorable in the sight of God.

possessed by the pleasure of things. Man is meant to bond with God, his wife, and other people made in His image, not things that are less than God, and less than people, and less than himself. When a man bonds to things rather than God and other people it always leads to the addictive chains of both slavery and idolatry. As George MacDonald noted, "A man is a slave to anything that he cannot part with that is less than himself"[73] When pleasure becomes the ends and not merely the means to another sacred good end, then the object of pleasure becomes a false god; an idol made by our very own hands.

In the following section I am going to jump into a number of issues where temperance is called for from a biblical perspective. Two areas in particular I will address are alcohol and sex. I hope to convince you of the biblical worldview that we, unfortunately, will be hard pressed to find in the local church. In both of these areas we will see that applying the virtue of temperance to break the chains of the vice of gluttony demonstrates the powerful truth of God's virtues. I can promise you that some of the answers may surprise you if you are a Baby Boomer, GenX'r or Millennial, with either a strong church background, or very little church. Every generation has imported ideas from both the church and the culture when it comes to sex and alcohol that he believes is biblically sound when in fact it is not. Temperance and its vice of gluttony will once again prove the thesis of this book; namely, the virtues are the practical application of the Bible to everyday life that you have been searching for. The question is, are you going to man-up or be soft?

Sex: Is God a Cosmic Killjoy or Loving Father?

"Surrender to all of our desires leads to...disease, jealousy, lies, concealment and everything that is the reverse of health. For happiness, even in this world, quite a lot of restraint is going to be necessary..." – CS Lewis

God made sexual pleasure for both our enjoyment and, more importantly, as a means to God's more sacred ends. Everything God created has sacredness as an end. A prime example of this is God's design for marriage as a sacred union between a man and a woman.

---

[73] Peter Kreeft, *Back To Virtue*, p.106.

Marriage is unique in that it is the only institution created before the Fall. God, in His magnificent blueprint, designed the physical parts that fit together in such a way that the marriage bond is consummated by a one-flesh sexual union of husband and wife. This sexual union God made pleasurable so as to create a desire for more lovemaking between the husband and wife in order to further their oneness and to produce children. In this particular instance, sexual pleasure is the means God designed into creation for the sacred ends of oneness and procreation. When sexual pleasure is properly placed as the means with oneness as the sacred end, your wife becomes indispensible. On the other hand, when pleasure becomes both the means and the end, your wife is easily replaceable by any woman whether real or virtual. This is the dangerous allure of sexual pleasure for pleasures sake and why marriages today are in crisis. Do you see the difference?

To provide even more evidence in support of God's design for sexual intimacy, our brains are even wired for bonding with the person we have sex with! One fascinating fact is that humans are the only mammals who have sexual intimacy in a very personal way, eyes to eyes, and face to face. It is as if intimacy is meant literally to be pronounced "into-me-see." This fact, along with God's baked in chemical response, is evidence that sex does not just occur in the genital region, but is a whole person experience.[74] There are three powerful chemicals related to human sexuality that help us bond. First there is dopamine that is known as the reward signal. Dopamine rewards us when we do something exciting by flooding our brains with "good feelings." Second there is oxytocin that is the female bonding chemical that is released when a woman is touched in a warm and meaningful way. This creates in her a desire for even more touch leading to sexual intimacy where her brain is flooded with oxytocin. The more oxytocin released, the more a desire for additional intimacy with the man whom she has bonded to. A fascinating detail is that although ocytocin levels skyrocket when a

---

[74] I am a network engineer so I will give you an analogy from my field of expertise. Neurons are data bits that communicate over synapses that serve as network cable. Our brains can be trained for the right things and the wrong things. As patterns of behavior develop over time the synapses regulating those behaviors becomes stronger while at the same time synapses governing infrequent activity weaken over time. For you hunting and fishing types, the river of our choices cuts the channel of our behavioral flow.

woman first falls in love then lowers, it heightens again as the relationship and sexual intimacy continues. Third, there is the male counterpart to oxytocin called vasopressin that is released during intimacy, along with dopamine, which causes a bonding to the woman that he has sexual intimacy with. The American Scientist reports that, "Investigators found that giving a male vasopressin causes him to stay with his mate, whereas blocking this hormone prevents a pair-bond [monogamy] from forming."[75] In summary, dopamine rewards, and vasopressin and oxytocin create an attachment.

All of these design details explain why God calls the husband and the wife to a moral obligation of sexual intimacy in marriage. That's right you read this correctly, it is a moral obligation for the husband and the wife to pursue sexual intimacy with one another so as to increase their marital bond. God calls us to enjoy His gift with our spouse. Sexual intimacy may not be the foundation of a marriage, but it certainly is the glue. This is a far cry from being a cosmic killjoy regarding sexual intimacy. The details of the Bible passages below will prove my point and may even surprise some of you.

Proverbs 5:15-19

Drink water from your own cistern, and [a]fresh water from your own well. [16]Should your springs be dispersed abroad, Streams of water in the streets? [17]Let them be yours alone And not for strangers with you. [18]Let your fountain be blessed, And rejoice in the wife of your youth. [19]As a loving hind and a graceful doe, Let her breasts satisfy you at all times; Be [b]exhilarated always with her love.

Write down the key words from this passage? What does this passage mean? (keep in mind that it is poetical wisdom literature)

Key words: _____

_____

_____

_____

---

[75] Marla V. Broadfoot, "High On Fidelity," The American Scientist On-line, May-June 2002, accessed October, 11 2014, http://www.americanscientist.org/issues/pub/high-on-fidelity.

Song of Solomon 7:6-8, 10

[6]"How beautiful and how delightful you are, [f]My love, with all your charms! [7]"[g]Your stature is like a palm tree, and your breasts are like its clusters. [8]"I said, 'I will climb the palm tree, I will take hold of its fruit stalks.' Oh, may your breasts be like clusters of the vine, [10]"I am my beloved's, and his desire is for me."

Song of Solomon is Biblical poetry written about a husband and wife. Write down what this passage means in your own words. What does it mean to climb the palm tree?

_____

_____

_____

1 Corinthians 7:2-4

But because of immoralities, each man is to have his own wife, and each woman is to have her own husband. [3]The husband must [a]fulfill his duty to his wife, and likewise also the wife to her husband. [4]The wife does not have authority over her own body, but the husband does; and likewise also the husband does not have authority over his own body, but the wife does.

What does the word "duty" signify? (Look it up in a dictionary)

_____

_____

_____

Recently, encouraging studies and news stories provide evidence of the purpose of pleasure in creating oneness in a marriage that is designed to last a lifetime. A recent study revealed that the longer couples are married the more they impact one another emotionally, and they literally grow happy and sad together.[76] One study even suggests that over time a married couple even begin to look alike, which is good news for me and bad news for my wife. This study concludes that, "The longer we are with someone, the more similarities in appearance grow."[77] Finally, there have been a

---

[76] Lifescience, "Couples Grow Old, Happy and Sad Together" December 29, 2010 http://www.livescience.com/11225-couples-grow-happy-sad.html [accessed October 13, 2014]
[77] Lifescience, "Why DO Some Couples Look Alike" February, 14 2006

slew of stories recently of couples married for over fifty years dying within hours of one another. There was a couple from Brazil married 65 years and died 40 minutes apart lying side-by-side.[78] In New York, Ed and Floreen Hale, married 60 years, were holding hands when they died. New York Daily News reported an amazing anomaly, "Doctors and nurses had equally gathered to watch the couple whose bodies were said to be in complete synch on the medical charts."[79] Tom and Naomi Shirley died within 10 minutes of each other. Tom died shortly after his wife not knowing that his bride of 45 years had died merely 10 minutes earlier! This quote from their son is what makes this story my favorite, "'Dad didn't know that she had passed, and she didn't know that he had passed. I don't understand it, but it's beautiful."[80] I think the fact that these stories have been big news stories demonstrates an objective beauty in marital oneness that even the most ardent critic of marriage appreciates.

This good news of God's design and purpose for pleasure becomes bad news when sex is outside of His intended covenantal marital context. The more sexual partners a person has, the more breakup cycles experienced due to the oxytocin and vasopressin bonding meant for oneness. These breakup cycles sever the bond created during intercourse, leaving it damaged for the next sexual relationship. If this continues through a series of relationships, the ability to bond with one's future wife becomes even more difficult. As an illustration, it is as if you place a piece of duct tape on one surface, remove it, add it to another, remove it, then do it again. What happens to the stickiness on the tape needed for a bond? The more it is added and removed the less effective the bond. A casual approach to sex for pleasure only degrades the stickiness or bonding ability that God designed into the sexual process for oneness

http://www.livescience.com/7024-lovers-alike.html [accessed October, 13 2014]
[78] Huffington Post October 9, 2014 "Couple Married 65 Years Dies 40 Minutes Apart, Lying Side-By-Side" http://www.huffingtonpost.com/2014/10/09/couple-dies-minutes-apart_n_5959468.html [accessed October, 13 2014]
[79] New York Daily News, "Elderly New York couple die hours apart holding hands after 60-year vow that he'd never leave her": http://www.nydailynews.com/news/national/elderly-couple-die-hours-holding-hands-60-year-vow-article-1.1622014 [accessed October, 13 2014].
[80] Yahoo News, "Elderly couple die within minutes of each other", March 20, 2014: http://news.yahoo.com/elderly-couple-dies-within-minutes-of-each-other-164002125.html [accessed October, 13 2014]

between the husband and the wife. This explains why the new "hook up" generation is experiencing adultery merely a few years into their marriage. I remember being surprised at the young couples coming into my office with adultery already as an issue.

A serious consideration men, especially teens and younger men, is the fact that even one act of intercourse outside of a marital context causes you to be emotionally attached to the person, and that these attachments can last a lifetime.[81]   If you have had this experience you know all too well the pain of the breakup and the jealous imagining of your girlfriend being with another man.   I believe that the jealous rage cycles we see in men are directly tied to the fact that sex and a pseudo-bond occurred in the relationship minus the marital commitment.   Furthermore, the pseudo-oneness bond due to sex outside of marriage creates situations where a man marries the wrong person because his assessment of the relationship was tainted and unhealthy.

What difference does it make to view sexual pleasure as the means to God's end goal of oneness instead of simply pleasure?

_____

_____

_____

How does this change your view of sexual pleasure?

_____

_____

_____

My Story

For we also once were foolish ourselves, disobedient, deceived, enslaved to various lusts and pleasures - Titus 3:3

Coming to Christ later in life, and taking God's Word seriously from the very beginning, provides me with the unfortunate context of living a life without Him and the wisdom of His word for so long.   When I look back to a time when I was "building my

---

[81] For more information see the book by Dr. Joe S. McIlhaney Jr. and Dr. Freda McKissic Bush called *Hooked: New Science on How Casual Sex is Affecting Our Children.*

testimony" so to speak, I regret so much, while at the same time, I am grateful Christ found me when He did. You should thank God right now if you are a man who grew up in a stable Christian home. Do not make the mistake of thinking, "I do not really have a great testimony." It is far better to have the testimony of God's faithfulness to your Christian heritage than to have the testimony of a man, like me, who was truly lost and now has been found. Your testimony of God's blessing and faithfulness to your own parents is what I am counting on for my own children as my wife and I plant a new tree as first generation Christians.

Deuteronomy 5:9 – "I, the Lord your God, am a jealous God, visiting the iniquity of the fathers on the children, and on the third and the fourth generations of those who hate Me, [10]but showing loving-kindness to thousands, to those who love Me and keep My commandments."

When I came to Christ at 25 years of age, my now wife Cheryl and I were dating, living together, and sleeping together. We eventually got engaged and planned on getting married 18 months later. At the time I was a typical American who always believed that God existed, but He was "out there" somewhere and not relevant to everyday life. I made a joke about born-again Christians that provided an opportunity for a guy from work to witness to me. We talked for two hours and I would say that he answered only about ten percent of my questions. The best answer that he continuously gave was, "That's a good question, but I don't know." Some of you may think that is a terrible answer. For me it was an honest answer and an honest answer is always better than making up some spiritualized nonsensical answer.

On the way home I stumbled across a show called *The Bible Answer Man* and I remember thinking to myself, "Oh no, this will be interesting." I still remember the first two callers that got me hooked on the program. One was an Atheist who was teachable and Hank Hanegreeff spent 15 minutes answering his questions, some of which I had just asked. The next caller was mad at Hank for publically calling out false teachers of the faith movement like Benny Hinn and Kenneth Copeland. Hank began playing sound bites of these men, and challenging this lady noting that, "Every book of the New

Testament deals with calling out false teachers in the church." Huh, I never knew that.

The following weekend, I was helping a friend of mine move and he had on his TV *The One-Year Bible*. I opened it up and the glue made a crackling sound like a bowl of Rice Krispies cereal. I looked at Bob and laughed, joking about the last time he must have read the Bible. I began to reflect on the fact that I commented on the Bible but never actually read it. I liked the format of reading a little of the Bible every day, so I stopped by the local Christian bookstore and picked up a copy. It felt weird walking into that store as I felt like there was a big blinking yellow arrow next to me listing my sins. I began reading through the *One Year Bible* the next morning and wondered if Cheryl would think that I was loosing my mind. Instead, Cheryl told me about her cousins who used to pick her up for church when she was younger. She saw that I was serious about reading it and decided to join me. After six months of reading the Bible and researching how we got the Bible, I gave my life to Christ one morning in our condo. No angel visits, no shining light, just a simple prayer that was serious and from a sincere heart. Little by little my life began to change, and others noticed before I did.

One Saturday morning our daily reading was Hebrews 13:4, "Marriage must be honored by all and the marriage bed kept pure, for God will judge the adulterer and the sexually immoral"[82] Cheryl and I were planning on going on a picnic in the mountains that day and I was ironing my shirt and wrestling with God a bit about the verse.

"but God I love her."

"I plan on marrying her so what is the big deal."

"How has having sex outside of marriage worked out up to this

---

[82] New International Version. This is the version that Cheryl and I were reading at the time so it seems appropriate to use the translation that we were reading. The NASB as a word for word translation is even more explicit: "Marriage is to be held in honor among all, and the marriage bed is to be undefiled; for fornicators and adulterers God will judge." The word translated *sexually immoral or fornicators* is the Greek word *pornia* where we get the modern word pornography. Thus, sexual immorality includes sexual pleasure outside of the bounds of marriage.

point?"

"God you must have a reason for the boundary, but I admit I just don't get it."

As a new believer I had heard Christians say things like "God spoke to me and….." Quite frankly I found it a little weird because I had no idea what they meant. Did God show up? Was the voice audible? What a wacko! For the first time in my life I found out exactly what at least some Christians meant when they said, "God spoke to me." I sensed a phrase impressed upon my mind as I was tossing God all of my questions, "Obey first and your feelings will follow."

I could see Cheryl in the bathroom getting ready so I said to her, "What did you think about the reading this morning?" She was putting her hair in a bow and she paused, then replied, "Yea, we have to talk about that." Whoa! Now I know what the Bible means when it teaches that you are filled with the Holy Spirit and God is everywhere. Through His written word the Holy Spirit spoke to Cheryl and me at the same time, with the same conviction. We were literally and spiritually on the same page.

Cheryl and I spoke that day about what God wanted us to do and the message was obvious because His Word was definitely clear. We decided to obey God and trust that He knows what He is talking about. I want you to see how the virtues are placed into action as we had a decision to make. Prudence or carelessness? God's Word led to a choice of our way and what we think we know or God's way on what we know He knows? Do we care what He says or are we careless demonstrating that we couldn't care less what He says? Fortitude or fear rears its ugly head as we begin to doubt that we can persevere for a year. Gluttony or Temperance comes in as our flesh attempts to persuade us to continue living according to its demands instead. This is tempting of course because pleasure is after all pleasurable! In the end we overcame uncertainty and chose His way that leads us to the implementation of biblical faith.

Notice how the theological virtue of faith calls us to bring the cardinal virtues into alignment against the cardinal vices. The new man restoring the fallen man. Biblical faith is not distant, there is no liver quiver, no spiritualizing, no feeling first. Faith is practical for God's word teaches _____ and we have a choice to either obey God in faith or disobey God in rebellion. What often occurs is a sly relativism of "Did God really say…" Clear choice (prudence) that, in the flesh, is difficult to decide (temperance), and will be difficult to maintain (fortitude). We moved into action (faith) and setup boundaries with each other and would end the nights praying together.

During this time we began attending and getting involved at the church where we decided to get married. I got involved with middle school youth and began feeling a little uneasy about Cheryl and I living together. I know that Cheryl and I were keeping it clean but it seemed difficult for anyone else to believe it and frankly I don't blame them. I was convicted that living together was not a sin in itself, but the proximity enables more opportunities for sin and makes it more difficult to "flee." God's word comes in handy once again, "But among you there must not be even a *hint* of sexual immorality…" – Ephesians 5:3[83] God's word is sly as it first convicted us of the greater sin of sex outside of the bounds of marriage then enabled us to see the sin of a bad example among God's people by living together.[84]

---

[83] New International Version. Emphasis mine.
[84] It is here that some of you may be wondering "isn't sin sin?" Yes and no! Yes regarding justification in that all sin is covered by the blood of Jesus Christ at the cross where the ground is level. But some of us brought more baggage to the cross than others, and those who have been forgiven much more appreciate God's grace much more. This is why Jesus said in Luke 7:47, "For this reason I say to you, her sins, which are many, have been forgiven, for she loved much; but he who is forgiven little, loves little." Just ask anyone who has been forgiven much and they will tell you! In particular we see that sexual sins are greater than other sins due to their impact on God's only institution created before the Fall— marriage! 1Corinthians 6:16-20 states "Or do you not know that the one who joins himself to a prostitute is one body with her? For He says, "The two shall become one flesh." [17]But the one who joins himself to the Lord is one spirit with Him. [18]Flee immorality. *Every other sin that a man commits is outside the body, but the [j]immoral man sins against his own body.* [19]Or do you not know that your body is a [k]temple of the Holy Spirit who is in you, whom you have from [l]God, and that you are not your own? [20]For you have been bought with a price: therefore glorify God in your body." The compare & contrast with sexual sins to every other sin tells us that these are worse (so are the consequences). Additionally, there are degrees of sin with some being worse than others which is why there are degrees of rewards in heaven and degrees of punishment in Hell. This would be a great place to pull out your Bible and study this topic. Here are a few verses about rewards [1Cor 3:8; 15:58, Rev 2:23-26; 11:18; 14:13; 20:11-15; 22:12-13; 1Pet 1:4, 14-17; Rom 2:6; Col 3:24]. Here is one example of a sin being greater than another: John 19:10-11 "So Pilate said to

Cheryl and I decided to start looking for a place to buy together for our future while at the same time serving as a place for me to live until our wedding. God blessed us with a wonderful townhouse in Bristow, Virginia that I moved into January of 1996, five months before our wedding day. I decided to put my bed in the spare bedroom so that we could move into the master bedroom together when we were married. This choice, of course, meant that for financial reasons we had to cut back on some wedding details and were going to have a short honeymoon of local Bed and Breakfasts. Again, a choice. Invest in a fancy wedding *day* and honeymoon or invest in a godly marriage *life*.

So What Did We Learn?

The past is a source of knowledge, and the future is a source of hope. Love of the past implies faith in the future. - Stephen Ambrose

We have been married over 20 years now so what did we learn looking back? For one thing, our friendship grew stronger—a lot stronger. I would have never thought it at the time but Cheryl could easily have become an object to me instead of a whole person. Her body is not mine and my body is not hers until we are married. While we are dating and engaged, we were renters; and renters never treat the property they are renting as good as they treat property they own. This is made clear by 1Corinthians 7:3-4, "The wife does not have authority over her own body, but the husband does; and likewise also the husband does not have authority over his own body, but the wife does." When we would have arguments or disagreements we talked more, because frankly there was nothing else to do.

Secondly, we both believe that God has blessed our marriage because of this early commitment of obedience to Him. There is no other rational explanation of the strong marriage physically, emotionally, and spiritually that we have today, especially with everything in our individual family backgrounds working against us.

Him, "You do not speak to me? Do You not know that I have authority to release you, and I have authority to crucify You?" [11]Jesus answered, "You would have no authority [a]over Me, unless it had been given you from above; for this reason he who delivered Me to you has the *greater sin*." [emphasis mine]

We come from messy backgrounds including the fact that we are both adult children of divorced parents and both of our fathers were alcoholics. Place these two together and statistically it is a miracle if we make it let alone make it while being truly happy and more in love than when we first met.

Thirdly, God has a sense of humor. Cheryl and I taught Preparing For Marriage to several hundred engaged couples at McLean Bible Church for over six years. We are very open about our past mistakes and how God redeemed them when we chose to do it His way. It is not that we are proud about it, quite the opposite. It is our very own "so that" ministry. We just want to encourage couples to take God seriously in this area above all else. God has used our testimony to encourage several couples to make a covenant of purity to God until marriage. Additionally, we have at least two couples every session that decide not to get married. Victory! What a pleasure it is to serve a God who redeems a failure and makes it a victory for His purposes.

What part of our story can you relate to?

_____
_____
_____

I have Failed Now What?

"Therefore repent and return, so that your sins may be wiped away, in order that times of refreshing may come from the presence of the Lord" – Acts 3:19

Life is a journey. As I mentioned earlier, there are three types of vehicles we choose to drive on life's journey. One man jumps into a car with only rearview mirrors and stares at the past wondering why he is not making any forward progress. The second man jumps into a car without rearview mirrors so he has no life context; thus, no idea where he is because he has no idea where he has been. Neither of these men will grow into the man God has called him to be. There is the third vehicle that the man of virtue drives. It has properly placed rearview mirrors and a clear large front window so as to see the road ahead and the past behind him with a little warning, "Objects in the mirror are closer than they appear."

I eventually came to the point in life where I chose the third vehicle, and along the way I picked up a passenger who would be my partner for life. When I picked her up, I tossed her baggage from life onto the luggage rack next to mine. As we loaded the Bible into our GPS, new options to get to our final destination appeared, with the gentle voice of the Holy Spirit saying, "Do a U-turn at the next intersection." There were times when we wanted it our way so we accelerated through the intersections hoping the voice would give us new directions saying "stay straight." But, no, consistently we heard, "make a U-turn at the next intersection." Cheryl and I would look at the map thinking that the way we were going seemed so much shorter than making a U-turn. When we finally yielded and made the U–turn we knew that we were on the right road.

On our journey we picked up a few VIP passengers named Jonah, Sarah, Nathan, and, ok ok, our dog Frodo. They never noticed the luggage rack on the vehicle, and have no idea where we have been on the journey before we picked them up to join us. Cheryl and I both know that a time is coming where we will drop them off and they will have a choice to make of what vehicle to get into and what data to load into their own GPS. And yes, they will each have their own luggage rack with a few bags on top that they themselves picked up on their journey with us as broken, fallen, imperfect parents who themselves needed redeemed. The question at this point is, how do we train them to not make the same mistakes? Are we hypocrites for asking them to maintain a life of purity before marriage when we ourselves have failed on our own journey? Have we lost our authority to speak into this area of their lives? Maybe you have the same questions yourself.

The answer to this question depends on what you see when you look into the rearview mirror and how you processed it, if at all. In the context of the Bible there are two Greek words translated as hypocrite: *hupokrisis* and *hupokrites*. The first word was applied to an actor on the theater stage in Greek Dramas who, of course, while acting pretends to be someone other than himself. As a metaphor then, a hypocrite is a person who plays a part in real life, under a false appearance, pretending to be someone that he or she is not. The second Greek word *hupokrites* is more accusatory stating that the person is acting with the goal of deceit.

So to determine if you are a hypocrite or wise counselor, you have to ask yourself, "Am I pretending to be something that I am not?" When you look back into your life do you put on a mask and pretend you practiced purity when you did not? Or worse, are you prideful and relativistic as you look into the mirror believing that sexual sin was ok for you but not for your kids? Finally, are you walking in truth properly believing that sexual sin was wrong for you and is wrong for your kids? Did you seek forgiveness, repent (a U-turn), and then committed to purity? The first two are hypocrites and the third is not. Cheryl and I choose to not be hypocrites by being open and honest with our story at the appropriate age (no mask). We sought forgiveness and did a U-turn off of our road and onto God's so we can objectively teach our children that it was wrong for us and would be wrong for them.

There are those of you who have a different struggle. You have kept it clean and are still a virgin but question yourself and God's standard as every relational intersection you hear the GPS say, "Please continue straight on the road ahead." Stay straight men! I have never met a virgin enter into marriage with regrets. In fact, a couple that we recently mentored were both virgins and we were excited for them. As this young man went away to hang out with his friends on a bachelor weekend many of the men were proud of him for maintaining his purity all of these years. Some even shared my same regret of, "Way to go man I wish that I could have said the same." I want to say thank you for your example! I always appreciate when I can look at a younger man as an example.

1 Timothy 4:12 – Let no one look down on your youthfulness, but rather in speech, conduct, love, faith and purity, show yourself an example of those who believe.

Some of you reading this book can relate to our story and you may have found yourself in a similar situation. Others of you are single and on the dating scene with a few broken relationships in the rearview mirror, and can relate to the pain of the loss because of the sexual intimacy outside of the marital context as God intended. Well what are you going to do about it? Man-up or be soft?

1 Thessalonians 4:3-5

It is God's will that you should be sanctified [set apart]: that you should avoid sexual immorality; that each of you should learn to control his own body in a way that is holy. It is God's will that you should be sanctified: that you should avoid sexual immorality; that each of you should learn to control his own body in a way that is holy and honorable, not in passionate lust like the heathen, who do not know God.

Then there are those of you reading this book who, due to a divorce, are back on the dating scene and find yourself in the precarious situation of sex outside of marriage. Even worse, maybe some of you are living with your girlfriend and have older kids witnessing you live outside of God's standards. Do you think that it is too late to turn it around? I have personally mentored an older gentleman through this very situation, and what God has done is awesome. All that it took was humility, combined with the courage (fortitude), to make the tough choice. The humility came when he changed his living arrangements within the home per my counsel.[85] and sat down with his kids and explained his choice to change and honor God. In this he asked his kids for forgiveness and instructed them to not follow his bad example of the past but choose the godly example of the present. Well, are you going to man-up or be soft?

Ezekiel 18:14 – Now behold, he has a son who has observed all his father's sins which he committed, and observing does not do likewise.

Where are you on your journey? Do you hear God saying, "Please make a U-turn at the next intersection" or, "Stay straight?" What can you change?

_____

_____

_____

When you look into the rearview mirror what do you see? How have you processed it? What can you celebrate? What are you going to do

[85] Given the children, my advice was prudent suggesting that he needed to stay in the home, and move into another room until they get married. Why not move out? How foolish to have the kids loose an earthly father in the home because the Heavenly Father opened up his.

about it?

_____

_____

_____

As you can clearly see God is not a cosmic killjoy who does not want you to have any fun when it comes to sexual pleasure. Quite the opposite, God is the very source of the pleasure because pleasure was His idea, and the sensations of pleasure are part of His original design. Pleasure has a purpose of not just procreation but oneness. We have to demonstrate faith, prudence, and temperance by trusting God and the guardrails He has in place on the road of life that enables us to be the men of virtue who make a difference in this world. His guardrails are not in place so that we miss the fun on the other side, they are there so that we can enjoy the view without going over of the cliff. The married man honors God with his body by carrying out his marital duty to his wife, whereas the single man honors God with his body by abstention. Both are properties of temperance.

1Corinthians 6:18-20

[18]Flee immorality. Every other sin that a man commits is outside the body, but the [j]immoral man sins against his own body. [19]Or do you not know that your body is a [k]temple of the Holy Spirit who is in you, whom you have from [l]God, and that you are not your own? [20]For you have been bought with a price: therefore glorify God in your body.

I will end this section with a quote from the wonderful book *Sense and Sensuality: Jesus Talks to Oscar Wilde on the Pursuit of Pleasure*. The book is a Socratic dialogue between Jesus and Oscar Wilde as they debate the view of pleasure for pleasures sake, or pleasure in a biblical context.

Jesus: "Every appetite that is abused reconstitutes desire, and it is that altered desire that the enemy of your soul appeals to. Wilde: So my hungers are unnatural? Jesus: They're natural but falsely directed."[86]... "But here's your answer. In seeking pleasure, you

---

[86] Ravi Zacharais, *Sense and Sensuality: Jesus Talks to Oscar Wilde on the Pursuit of Pleasure* (Colorado Springs, CO: Multnomah, 2006), Kindle Electronic Edition: Location 631.

pursued the body and lost the person. You sought the sensation and sacrificed the individual....In pursuing sensuality, you exalt the body and profane the person. It's like emptying a container and throwing it away. Life, then, becomes just a container. Living becomes senseless."[87]

How are you doing in obeying God in this area?

_____

_____

_____

What are you going to change so that you can be a man of temperance?

Single: Temperance means chastity or abstention. (keeping your future marriage bed pure)

Married: Temperance means moderation or limitation of sexual energy to your wife alone. (Hebrews: 13:4 keeping your current marriage bed pure.)

_____

_____

_____

Alcohol: To Drink or Not To Drink

On my first official date with the woman who would become my wife, Cheryl and I discovered we had something in common. Both of our fathers were alcoholics. I joked at that moment, "Both our Dads are alcoholics so we were meant to be together." Many of you reading this book have also experienced the negative impacts of alcohol in your life either due to an alcoholic parent or you yourself as an alcoholic or recovering alcoholic. Outside of this, there are some of you who can point back to a moment of stupidity in your life due to the fact you had a little too much to drink. You find now that you have learned from your mistakes and can enjoy a beer or a glass of wine without too much trouble at all. Then there are those

---

[87] Ibid., Location 695.

of you who have never had a drink in your life and you have no interest in ever having one. Each one of these experiences, along with any teaching that you may have received no doubt informs your current view about alcohol.

There is one area Cheryl and I discovered that we did not have in common. She, though not at all practicing, was a Christian and I was not. I did not find this out until I began reading the Bible as part of my own personal journey seeking God. As noted earlier, I came to Christ after a period of about six months of reading and researching how we got the Bible. After my conversion I took every belief that I ever had and tossed it on the table for a Romans 12:2 biblical examination. One of these areas was the area of alcohol. Is drinking ok or does God forbid it?

At this point in my journey I was involved in a multi-generational men's small group and, as you might expect, I heard a variety of differing views on this topic. Maybe you heard some of these:

"You shouldn't drink alcohol because it harms your witness."

"God created alcohol so enjoy it."

"Jesus turned water into wine as His first miracle so this proves alcohol is ok."

"Wine in biblical times was watered down 2 to 1 and some scholars say as much as 10 parts water one part wine, so it was not wine as we know it today."

"It wasn't wine that Jesus made but grape juice."

"Alcohol is wrong for you because your Dad is an alcoholic so you have the alcoholic gene."

All of the answers above, along with others I cannot remember, are either far too simplistic or seem to be a bias toward one personal view over another. But I was not looking for a personal view, I was looking for the biblical view. Of course with my own background I had a leaning in a particular direction that I had to be mindful of as I dug into God's word for an answer so that I didn't add yet another personal view. As is often the case regarding life's pleasures there is a call for temperance. God has a fence of freedom where we are free to roam, and no crisp clear and direct yes or no "thou shall" or "thou shall not" answer. Some of you despair at this point, "Why not just give us a yes or no God?" But I ask you how are you doing in the areas where God is explicitly clear and direct with the command of "yes" or "no" like the previous section?

So what does the Bible teach regarding the issue of alcohol? The answer is moderation—but... But what? I'll get there. First, we see from the Psalms, the Proverbs, and the first miracle of Jesus that wine is good in itself. Psalm 104:15 states, "And wine which makes man's heart glad, so that he may make his face glisten with oil, and [a]food which sustains man's heart." In context the entire Psalm is about praising God and all of His works. Second, we see in Proverbs 3:10 that as a reward for wisdom God will bless you in abundance including, "Your vats will overflow with new wine." Third, we see that wisdom invites the naïve in to, "Come, eat of my food, and drink of the wine I have mixed." Finally, the wedding at Cana where Jesus performed His first miracle by turning water into wine. Of course, being sinless Jesus would have never turned water into wine causing many people to stumble and sin if wine in itself is bad.

John 2:1-4, 6-10

On the third day there was a wedding in Cana of Galilee, and the mother of Jesus was there; [2]and both Jesus and His disciples were invited to the wedding. [3]When the wine ran out, the mother of Jesus *said to Him, "They have no wine." [6]Now there were six stone water pots set there for the Jewish custom of purification, containing [b]twenty or thirty gallons each. [7]Jesus *said to them, "Fill the water pots with water." So they filled them up to the brim. [8]And He *said to them, "Draw some out now and take it to the [c]headwaiter." So they took it to him. [9]When the headwaiter tasted the water which had become wine, and did not know where it came from (but the servants who had drawn the water knew), the headwaiter *called the bridegroom, [10]and *said to him, "Every man serves the good wine first, and when the people have [d]drunk freely, then he serves the poorer wine; but you have kept the good wine until now."

We learn quite a few things from this passage besides the fact that wine in of itself is not bad but good. First, Jesus did not just simply turn water into wine; according to verse six, He turned 120-180 gallons of water into wine! Second, we learn that although the wine was made from water it was not watered down much at all. How do we know this? According to verse ten the headwaiter could tell by the taste that it was a very high quality wine and not the cheap stuff. If it were watered down ten parts he would never be able to tell the difference.

Here is the "but…" Although wine is good in itself there is a serious warning about the allure of wine and getting drunk. Proverbs 20:1 teaches that, "Wine is a mocker, strong drink a brawler, and whoever [a]is intoxicated by it is not wise." This verse reminds me of a childhood friend of mine whom I nicknamed "beer muscles" because he always wanted to fight when he was drunk. Also, Ephesians 5:18 commands us, "Do not get drunk with wine, [l]for that is dissipation, but be filled with the Spirit." Finally, Proverbs gives us a stark warning about the lying allure of alcohol and its financial consequences:

Proverbs 23:19-21, 30-32

Listen my son and be wise, and direct your heart in the way. Do not be with heavy drinkers of wine, *or* with gluttonous eaters of meat; [21]for the heavy drinker and the glutton will come to poverty, and drowsiness will clothe *one* with rags. Those who linger long over wine, those who go to [a]taste mixed wine. [31]Do not look on the wine when it is red, when it [b]sparkles in the cup, when it goes down smoothly; [32]at the last it bites like a serpent and stings like a viper.

So what is the conclusion of the matter? You have to decide the matter for yourself, as a matter of conscience, whether God wants you to demonstrate temperance through abstention or moderation. And, you have to allow others to come to their own conclusion of the matter, which is why it is called Biblical freedom. Galatians 5:12 instructs us to be careful, "For we were called to freedom, brethren; only do not turn your freedom into an opportunity for the flesh." Moreover, should we choose moderation, in love, we should honor our brother when we are around him and, "Not let what is for you a good thing be spoken of as evil." (Romans 14:16) Why? Because "It is not good to eat meat [sacrificed to idols] or to drink wine, or do anything by which your brother stumbles. The faith you have is your own conviction before God." (Romans 14:21-22) In short, you can choose either moderation or abstention, but do not force your position on another brother. "Whether, then, you eat or drink or whatever you do, do all to the glory of God." (1Corinthians 10:31)

There is another consideration that will lead you purely toward abstention regarding alcohol. If you are a recovering alcoholic then the answer for you must be abstention! Brother, the reality is that you lost this freedom in Christ when addiction took over your life. There was a time when you chose drunkenness with alcohol so much that now instead of you choosing the addiction, the addiction is so strong within you that now it chooses you! If this is you, then you know exactly what I mean.

If you are unsure if you are an alcoholic I have a penetrating question for you to ask yourself: Has anyone ever said to you that they think you have a drinking problem? Brother, I mean anyone, especially those closest to you who have the love and fortitude necessary to say it out loud, directly, to you. If this is the case then you have your answer. The only question remaining is what do you do with the answer whether you like the answer or not. Now take it a step further and try and quit drinking cold turkey for forty days. Why forty? Forty is God's number for testing. When God tests during these forty days another force will be at work as Satan will begin to tempt you. If in your self-talk during this forty-day period you find yourself saying things like, "this is stupid" or, "I have nothing to prove," and you start drinking again; my brother you have a problem. You know my question: Are you going to Man-up or go soft?

Has anyone ever told you that you may have a drinking problem? Who? Write down his or her name and give them a call, and humbly, with a teachable spirit, ask them what they meant. Has God placed someone on your heart who you need to confront regarding this matter? You know the question: What are you going to do about it; Man-up or go soft? **Name:** _____

What Does Temperance With Alcohol Look Like Practically?

When it comes to the topic of alcohol, God builds for us a biblically built fence of freedom to roam in, and where we land within this fence is up to us. Our flesh will pull at us in two directions. Some of us will simply want to abuse God's fence of freedom by removing it and asking others to join in. As an old African proverb states, "One should never remove a fence without first asking why it was put there in the first place." Others will want to move God's fence of freedom into a tight tidy little space where only the teetotaler can comfortably fit. Often times the difference between the man who chooses moderation and the man who chooses abstention is a failure by the teetotaler to recognize that both men are demonstrating the virtue of temperance. As C.S. Lewis notes, "One of the marks of a certain type of bad man is that he cannot give up a thing himself without wanting everyone else to give it up. That is not the Christian way."[88] Below is a diagram I hope will help you understand God's fence of freedom in this area. I added scripture on each fence line you can study on your own in addition to the verses already supplied in this section.

God's Fence of Freedom

---

[88] C.S. Lewis, *Mere Christianity*, p.76.

Temperance & A Call To Prudence

As mentioned above the virtue of temperance includes moderation, abstention, and self-control. In this section it was demonstrated that the practice of each of these properties is considered temperate when it comes to the use of alcohol. It is at this point I want to introduce you to the 80/20 rule when it comes to your freedoms in Christ. The 80% is the vast majority of your life, or your "going in" biblical position within God's fence of freedom where your conscience has led you. The 20% is when your biblical freedom of temperance as moderation is trumped by the virtue of Charity. How will you know when the 20% applies? It is the virtue of prudence that is used to discern when charity trumps your freedoms in Christ. A man of virtue must always seek to be wise with his knowledge of Biblical principles combined with his love of God and his brother for, "Knowledge puffs up but love builds up." (1Crinthians 8:1) It is at this point where the man who chooses abstention has the advantage of not processing much because he has the 100% rule; namely, choosing always to abstain from alcohol. Let me give you an example of a time my wife and I applied the 20% rule.

Cheryl and I had a choice to make when it came to our wedding reception. With alcoholism running rampant throughout our family and a number of family members, my own father included, having great success in recovery, do we serve alcohol at our reception? I mean it is "our day" and we have the freedom in Christ to drink alcohol and neither of us struggles in this area. As prudence and charity would guide us we came to the obvious decision that serving alcohol at our wedding would be a selfish and foolish choice when God would be pleased with an unselfish loving choice. We decided that 1Corinthians 10:31 was a good guide of, "Whether, then, you eat or drink or whatever you do, do all to the glory of God."

There are a few reasons why this decision made good biblical sense. Some a matter of prudence, and others a matter of charity. As for prudence, with all of the major events in our history that alcohol ruined, why in the world would we risk the most important day of our lives being ruined by alcohol? Especially when we are in control of the decision! As for charity, why would we place alcohol in front of people we love who are in a successful recovery, only to risk having them fall off the wagon at our wedding? A day of a witness for Christ would be turned into a day to look back on with dread as a person we love remembers our wedding as nothing more than the day alcohol once again took its grip. Notice the virtues, with agape love [charity] leading the way is what is guiding us, not, "Where is the one verse!"

What is new that you learned from this section?

_____

_____

_____

Application: Is it wise to serve alcohol at your small group? Why or why not? (The answer is not as important as how you get there)

_____

_____

_____

Securing The Border

"Temperance, which is moderation in the sensual desires, also promises purer or more fulfilling pleasures. It is enlightened, mastered, cultivated taste"
– Andre Compte-Sponville

The thesis of this chapter is that pleasure is good, but either too much pleasure, or pleasure outside of God's design, will place you in the chains of gluttony. 1Corinthians 6:12 reminds us that, "All things are lawful for me, but not all things are profitable. All things are lawful for me, but I will not be mastered by anything." Following this theme, CNN carried an article by Dr. Philip Zimbardo and Nikita Duncan entitled, "The Demise of Guys: How video games and porn are ruining a generation." The article poses the question, "Is the overuse of video games and pervasiveness of online porn causing the demise of guys?" The research is in, and the answer is a resounding "YES!" Dr. Zimbardo's TED talk has over two million views demonstrating an increased interest in this topic. As for pornography, temperance calls for *abstention* in a man's life, because it is fundamentally wrong to treat women as commodities and not persons. On the other hand, video games are fun and not bad in themselves so temperance calls for *moderation*.

Both video games and pornography bring a large amount of dopamine rush that is causing a new phenomenon called "arousal addiction." This new addiction found in boys is why Dr. Zimbardo put the two together. Researchers found that, "Young men become hooked on arousal, sacrificing their schoolwork and relationships in the pursuit of getting a tech-based buzz."[89] The concern is that arousal addiction is rewiring the brain and creating, "a generation of risk-averse guys who are unable (and unwilling) to navigate the complexities and risks inherent to real-life relationships, school and employment."[90] Moderation is key men, and for fathers teaching your children moderation when it comes to video games is your responsibility until they leave your home. Temperance avoids extremes and teaches responsibility so that a man can enjoy the pleasures of this life without being mastered by them. In summary, avoid sexual immorality (*pornia*) and demonstrate moderation regarding video games.

How have you seen lack of moderation impact your own life or the life of other men when it comes to video games? What are you going to do about it?

_____

_____

_____

How have you seen lack of abstention impact your own life or the life of other men when it comes to pornography? What are you going to do about it?

_____

_____

_____

---

[89] CNN May 24, 2012 "The Demise of Guys": How video games and porn are ruining a generation" Internet: http://www.cnn.com/2012/05/23/health/living-well/demise-of-guys [accessed August 9, 2016.]
[90] Ibid.

Temperance test: Is this a problem for you? Do a 40 day fast.

One of the things that I have learned from working in the field of network security is that every system has security vulnerabilities. All an attacker needs to do is keep looking. My job on the defensive side is to minimize the attack surface as much as possible by providing layers of security. The Bible teaches that men have a security vulnerability that needs protecting through a layered security approach. This layered approach may protect us from external threats, but often times the most dangerous risk is the insider threat. Our external vulnerabilities are located in the eye-port, which is why pornography is a multibillion-dollar industry with its customers primarily being male. Our flesh is the insider threat that clears the way, by willingly providing an attack surface.

In the chapter on prudence I wrote about the need for a prudent man to not be careless with electronics. This is huge as pornography is not only a click away with computers, but a thumb tap away with smart phones. We know that God created sexual pleasure for a purpose and pornography, in its essence, is misdirected and selfish which is why it is addicting. All addiction increases selfishness in a man, and nothing is more damaging in relationships than selfishness. What we need is a layered security plan in our life so that we have both a good offense and defense. The three-part security plan is to:

1. Identify the threat
2. Secure the border
3. Prevent border crossings.

The wisest man who ever lived left us the Holy Spirit inspired book of Proverbs that he wrote for his son. In chapter four, Solomon gave his son, and all of us, a stark warning and a game plan for maintaining integrity on life's journey:

Proverbs 4:20-27

[20]My son, pay attention to what I say; turn your ear to my words. [21]Do not let them out of your sight, keep them within your heart [22]for they are life to those who find them and health to one's whole body. [23]**Above all else, guard your heart**, for everything you do flows from it. [24]Keep your mouth free of perversity; keep

corrupt talk far from your lips. [25]Let your eyes look straight ahead; fix your gaze directly before you. [26]Give careful thought to the[c] paths for your feet and be steadfast in all your ways. [27]Do not turn to the right or the left; keep your foot from evil.

#1 Identify the threat

What are we protecting when we say the heart? The heart is what makes you who you really are. In Christ we are a new creation and He has given us a new heart with new desires that are in conflict with our old desires.

Biblically the "Heart" is the totality of who we are

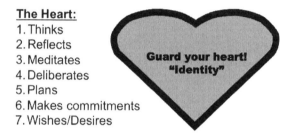

The Heart:
1. Thinks
2. Reflects
3. Meditates
4. Deliberates
5. Plans
6. Makes commitments
7. Wishes/Desires

Guard your heart! "Identity"

We have an enemy on the outside trying to get in, and an enemy within who wants him to come in. This battle requires a battle plan that includes other men who want to help. So, how do we secure the border?

There are two fronts in this battle:

1. The insider threat

2. The outside threat

You cannot win if you do not have good intelligence. Do you know your weaknesses? Your enemy does. When I travel for business, I always bring my Bible and a family picture. When I enter the hotel room, I unplug the TV and setup an area where I place my Bible and family picture. Then I cover the room in prayer. I do not concern myself with my personal laptop because I almost never bring it. If I do bring it, I have Covenant Eyes installed and my wife gets my browsing reports to include Google search terms. If pornography is a big issue for you then you need another man to hold you accountable, not your wife.

#2 Secure the Border

There are two ports that need secured, the mouth-ear port and the eye-port. In Proverbs 4:24 we are instructed to, "Keep your mouth free of perversity; keep corrupt talk far from your lips." The more perverse our mouths the more perverse our heart for, "everything you do flows from it." The eyes are our headlights when we are on the dark roads and they lead us ahead or lead us astray. Our eyes allow entry into our minds where we are designed to record what we see. This is why we can never "unsee" what we have seen because it is recorded and stored for later retrieval. Some of us are blessed with a great memory that can unfortunately turn into a curse if we fill our minds with impure things.

Proverbs 4:25-27

Let your *eyes* look straight ahead; fix your gaze directly before you. [26]Give careful thought to the[c] paths for your feet and be steadfast in all your ways. [27]Do not turn to the right or the left; keep your foot from evil. [Emphasis mine]

The bottom line is that if you want to kill something you go for its source. The Hebrew word for eyes in this verse includes both the physical and mental eye. If I want to kill a weed in my yard I have to get the roots—its source. If I do not it will inevitably come back, and some weeds dig their roots in and come back even stronger! Matthew 6:22-23 reminds us, "The eye is the lamp of the body; so then if your eye is clear, your whole body will be full of light. But if your eye is bad, your whole body will be full of darkness."

We will notice beauty for that is natural. It is what we do that makes the difference. Martin Luther said it best when speaking of lust, "We cannot stop a bird from flying over our head, but we can stop it from building a nest in our hair."

Proverbs 4:20-21 – "My son, pay attention to what I say; turn your ear to my words. [21]Do not let them out of your sight, *keep them* within your heart." [Emphasis mine]

"Keep them" literally means, "To hedge about as with thorns" or, "To protect & attend to." Secure them in place as if building a wall, and that is what we must do. The word of God serves as the bricks and mortar but we must choose to build the wall. Similar to building a brick fence around our home, it can be done a lot quicker with people helping. It is always better having a skilled craftsman lead the team to ensure the quality of the wall.

Who is on your team? Are you trying to do it alone? How is that working out for you? As men we hate asking for help. It is time to man-up, because you need it!

_____

_____

_____

#3 Prevent Border Crossings

Proverbs 4:26 – Give **careful thought** to the[c] paths for your **feet** and be steadfast in all **your ways**. [Emphasis mine]

This is a great verse. To give careful thought means "to roll flat, i.e. prepare (a road)." Our feet mean each step, and "your ways" is referencing your habits. For every step creates a habit and every habit is established as a way of life and becomes natural. So we can only make level paths one step at a time—creating a habit—creating a lifestyle.

How secure is your border regarding pornography?

_____

_____

_____

When you ask for accountability are you serious or faking it?

_____

_____

_____

Temperance Homework: Go to www.covenanteyes.com and download some of their free research on porn and the brain, statistics, and how to get some help. Man-up, and ask a friend to receive your accountability reports. I use Covenant Eyes, and I am glad that I do.

Memory Table: Commit the properties of temperance to memory

Be a man of TEMPERANCE and not GLUTTONY	
Purity	Chastity
Moderation	Abstention
Self-control	

8
A MAN OF CHARITY
NOT INDIFFERENCE

"Greater love [agape] has no one than this than he lay down his life for his friends"
– Jesus

When I use the word charity in referring to this particular theological virtue what I am specifically referencing is that unique form of love that is totally distinctive to Christianity. In today's feelings-driven culture, we have a tendency to overuse the word love to the point where it becomes emptied of its meaning. For example, we say, "I love my wife" then, "I love my new car" knowing we most certainly mean something different when we say "love." Well men you better! Charity has often been used as the English translation of the Greek word love for this very reason, and it is this love used in the New Testament I am referencing.

There are three Greek words in the New Testament translated into the English word love. Because of this, and the fact that in our culture we use the word love to primarily refer to feelings, we miss what God specifically requires of us. The Greek word *philo* that is translated as love is referring to brotherly love and happens to be where we get the name of the city Philadelphia. What is Philadelphia called? The city of brotherly love. *Philo* is a, "you scratch my back and I scratch yours" kind of love you find among friends. The Greek word *eros* that is translated into love is referring specifically to sexual love. This is where we get the English word "erotic" and is the kind of love God references as the unique experience reserved between a husband and a wife. Finally, we come to the Greek word *agape* that is translated into love, and this is the virtue of charity. *Agape* is a sacrificial one-way type of love where I love you and expect absolutely nothing in return.

It is a love that comes into play especially when a person does not feel they deserve love; but they get love anyway. Charity is always one-way! This is the love I am called to regarding my children and my wife. Charity in relationships is a powerful full expression of love when two people *agape* one another. If you were to draw an arrow it would go in one direction from the person demonstrating *agape* to the person receiving *agape*. This is the word used by Jesus Christ in John 15:13 when He said, "Greater love [***agape***] has no one than this than he lay down his life for his friends."

Charity as a virtue is a one-way verb with action moving one-direction with absolutely no expectations of a return on the investment. Charity is a love that flows from God through you to others. It is Charity that is the only virtue included in Jesus' summary of the entire Bible found in the book of Matthew.

Matthew 22:36-40

"Teacher, which is the great commandment in the Law?" [37] And He said to him, "'YOU SHALL **LOVE** THE LORD YOUR GOD WITH ALL YOUR HEART, AND WITH ALL YOUR SOUL, AND WITH ALL YOUR MIND.' [38] This is the great and [c]foremost commandment. [39] The second is like it, 'YOU SHALL **LOVE** YOUR NEIGHBOR AS YOURSELF.' [40] On these two commandments depend the whole Law and the Prophets."

Charity is a sacrificial love that produces in us, over time, a divinely infused habit which inclines our will to cherish God for His own sake above all things, and another for the sake of God who is by nature *agape* love. Thus, charity is an unconditional, voluntary, self-sacrificial love where the good of the beloved is foremost. It requires a proper self-love where you, in full humility, understand that all you have is a gift from God so that you serve Him by serving others. Charity includes the properties of compassion, forgiveness, humility, self-sacrifice, and selflessness. The vice of charity is indifference. Indifference chains you in a state of inaction by producing self-pity, apathy, selfishness, and unforgiveness.

The famous verses in 1 Corinthians 13 that are read at weddings provide a list of what *agape* love looks like in a relationship. We miss the type of love referenced every time we hear these verses because we take our secular culture's superficial definition of love and import that into these verses; thus, we miss the entire point God is making! We then try to run our marriage on this weak "emotional love" then begin to think, "Well, when I stop receiving the things in this list from my spouse it is over!" However, agape love is a giving form of love not a receiving form. Thus you need to measure your *agape* self-sacrificial giving not your superficial emotional receiving.

With this in mind I want you to slowly read 1 Corinthians 13, and I pray that you will never hear these verses the same way again. I will put the Greek word *agape* before love when the virtue charity, the form of divine love, is referenced. In fact, when I perform weddings and first Corinthians is the requested reading, I have the reader read it exactly as I have it below. I do not want love mistaken as a feminine feeling that will make marriage last. Never!

1 Corinthians 13:4-13

[4]*Agape* love is patient, [4]*Agape* love is kind and is not jealous; *Agape* love does not brag and is not arrogant, [5]*Agape* love does not act unbecomingly; *Agape* love does not seek its own, *Agape* love is not provoked, *Agape* love does not take into account a wrong suffered, [6]*Agape* love does not rejoice in unrighteousness, but rejoices with the truth; [7]*Agape* love bears all things, believes all things, hopes all things, and endures all things.

[8]*Agape* love never fails; but if there are gifts of prophecy, they will be done away; if there are tongues, they will cease; if there is knowledge, it will be done away. [9]For we know in part and we

prophesy in part; [10]but when the perfect comes, the partial will be done away. [11]When I was a child, I used to speak like a child, think like a child, reason like a child; when I became a man, I did away with childish things. [12]For now we see in a mirror dimly, but then face to face; now I know in part, but then I will know fully just as I also have been fully known. [13]But now faith, hope, *Agape* love (charity), abide these three; but the greatest of these is *Agape* love.

(reread verse 11) Regarding *agape* love are you a man or a child? Do you expect all love to come your way and only all of your needs to be met? Something to contemplate.

Next, notice that the three theological virtues of faith, hope, and love are listed in verse 13 with the greatest being charity. Why? Because charity is the evidence to God, yourself, and others that you have true biblical faith and real biblical hope. I want to bring into focus three of the actions of *agape* love that every close, meaningful relationship needs to succeed, especially husband-wife and parent-child. If you are single, you can get ahead of the game by practicing this virtue of charity as you begin dating. An even better place to practice charity is with your parents no matter what your age is.

(1) *Agape* **love is patient:** The Greek word for this kind of patience literally means, "To exercise understanding toward persons not circumstances." It is people who need our patience no matter what the circumstances. Marriage is the closest relationship you will have with another person on this earth, so your home needs to be a place of grace. A place where it is safe for family members to vent and show their bad parts to only receive charity in return.

Often in close relationships we commit what is known as the fundamental attribution error. This error occurs when we give ourselves grace on our bad days and not others. For example, I am edgy and irritable with my wife so I attribute this to the fact that I am under stress due to my current circumstances. I expect those close to me to recognize that I am not myself and I could use some grace. However, when my wife is edgy and irritable I attribute it to her character and not her circumstances. I accuse, misjudge her, and offer no grace or benefit of the doubt. This is the fundamental attribution error. My wife needs *agape* love not judgment or accusation! This is a "Love your neighbor as yourself" kind of love.

(2) *Agape* **love does not seek its own:** Charity is a self-giving, self-sacrificial Divine love, which we are to attempt to reflect toward one another. This type of love is supernatural not superficial! For instance, in a marriage, *agape* love calls a husband to never demand his rights from his spouse, instead he is to remember that God demands of him his duties toward his spouse. If this type of love emanated from a man to every person in his life, there is nothing he cannot accomplish. Imagine if in all of our relationships we engaged in a competition of trying to out-serve one another with the only motivation being the benefit of the other. As the moon reflects the sun so we as Christ followers are to reflect the Son.

(3) *Agape* **love does not take into account wrong suffered:** This phrase in the Greek reads, "*Agape* love does not occupy oneself with calculations of continued wrong suffered." Some of us are incredible record keepers, and this is unfortunate. We all have to fight that tendency of the flesh and choose to not remember for the purpose of hurting your spouse, parent, or child by reminding them of their shortcomings. In order to do that store in your heart God's own example of charity toward you: "If you, O Lord, kept a record of sins, O Lord, who could stand?" – Psalm 130:3

What has God erased from your record that you are grateful for?

_____
_____
_____

Pray: Spend some time right now praying and thanking God for each of these and specifically ask Him to help you burn the records that you have stored against another.

Forgiveness

For the virtue of charity we are going to focus on the most misunderstood and difficult act of charity, namely, forgiveness. The reason for this focus is that this is the most difficult area to personally apply the virtue of self-sacrificial love. As a matter of fact, if you fail in this one area alone, walking in a state of grace and charity will be extremely difficult as God haunts you with this unresolved issue that cost Him the cross.

I have seen this picture flying around Facebook this summer that makes the point of forgiveness being misunderstood. On the surface it seems like a great view on one aspect of forgiveness, apologizing to a person you sinned against.

Apologizing
Does not always
mean that you're
wrong and the other
person is right.
It just means that you
value your relationship more
than your ego

This view is completely incorrect and, quite frankly, prideful. When I apologize to my wife I am asking her to forgive me for a wrong I committed against her. I am in fact saying that I was wrong and she is right to be upset about it. I value the truth and the relationship. Apologizing to apologize is either making forgiveness cheap, because you do not think you did anything wrong, or it is exposing you as a people-pleasing conflict avoider. You know, the peace at all costs types.

As I mentioned earlier, my father is an alcoholic and his alcoholism caused much pain and grief in my family growing up. I am the oldest of four boys and I hated my father for it; that is until Christ got a hold of me. It may be surprising, but there is much confusion among Christians on what forgiveness is and is not. I experienced this confusion myself when God was convicting me of the fact that I need to forgive my father. I started to listen to what I would consider good Bible teachers so that I could better understand this important topic. Somehow their sermons on forgiveness just didn't seem right to me. I knew my place as a new Christian so I correctly assumed the problem was me. I had a concordance and a reference study Bible, so I began the task of studying this vital topic.

After much study, I figured out the problem. Many people, including the wonderful pastors I listened to, either combined or confused forgiveness and reconciliation. So when they preach on forgiveness they include reconciliation under the umbrella of forgiveness. Forgiveness is separate and must precede reconciliation. Reconciliation is forgiveness completed. This important distinction is proven with the passage that cleared the fog of confusion for me.

Ephesians 4:31-32 – Get rid of all bitterness, rage, and anger, brawling and slander along with every form of malice. [32]Be kind and compassionate to one another, forgiving each other, just as in Christ God forgave you.

You can see in verse 31 that this list is a result of unforgiveness among people within the church. Through the Holy Spirit the Apostle Paul points believers to the example of Jesus Christ as he calls them to forgive one another. So how did God, in Christ, forgive us?

1.   It was Free!

First and foremost God freely forgave me when I did not deserve it. The important lesson here is that forgiveness is always a gift, and nobody pays for a gift except the one giving it. It is God's agape love that enabled Him to forgive us and pay the price for this forgiveness. When there is forgiveness there is always a cost to the one forgiving. As our example, Jesus forgave us and the cost to Him was crucifixion.

Romans 5:6-8

For while we were still helpless, at the right time Christ died for the ungodly. [7]For one will hardly die for a righteous man; [d]though perhaps for the good man someone would dare even to die. [8]But God demonstrates His own love toward us, in that while we were yet sinners, Christ died for us.

2.   He offered it to me.

He let me know that I was forgiven through His word, the holy Bible.   It was publically on the cross where God demonstrated His forgiveness and just how much it cost Him to forgive me of my sins against Him. Through His letters in the Bible He let me know that I was forgiven, and through the cross He bore the cost of that forgiveness when Jesus Christ paid the penalty for my sins. This is the good news of the gospel.

Hebrews 4:2 – For indeed we have had good news preached to us, just as they also; but the word they heard did not profit them, because it was not united by faith in those who heard.

3. He gave me the choice

Accept or reject? God offered forgiveness to you and me as a gift, but as with all gifts we have to choose to open it. It is here that forgiveness stops and the opportunity for reconciliation begins. Reconciliation is forgiveness completed and occurred when I acknowledged what God said He forgave me for is true. It is "Yes Lord, I am a sinner and I did sin against you. Thanks for forgiving me." Here at this moment I am reconciled to God.

John 1:12 – Yet to all who **received** him, to those who **believed** in his name, he gave the right to become children of God

What if I reject God's offer of forgiveness and say, "I didn't do anything wrong!" Then God still forgave me and the gift sits there wrapped up waiting for me to open it. However I am not reconciled to God, and our relationship is not restored.

1 John 1:10 – "If we claim we have not sinned, we make him out to be a liar and his word has no place in our lives."

As you can see, forgiveness is a gift God offers to every one of us. I opened this gift when I turned around on the road of repentance, asked for forgiveness, and received His gift offer. It was God's environment of charity through forgiveness and acceptance He setup at the cross and offered to me in a letter (the Bible) which enabled me to move toward Him. This is how God forgave you and me as an act of charity and not indifference. He put no hoops for me to jump through or obstacles to avoid. It was charity (*agape* love and grace) because I did not deserve it.

I had to forgive as Christ forgave me, which meant that I had to forgive my Dad and let him know he was forgiven. I took this step when I drove up to Pittsburgh in October of 1995. I wrote my Dad a letter letting him know that I am a Christian and I forgave him for what he did. Forgiveness was letting him off of my hook, and not off of the hook. I placed the letter, along with a One Year Bible, on his doorstep. And, yes, there was a cost to my forgiveness that I had to bear from the whole family. I just couldn't imagine standing before Christ, looking at His wounds and saying, "But Lord you don't understand my wounds." You see, I was the first and only Christian in my family at this point and of course those who have not received forgiveness themselves clearly do not understand it. Add to this the fact that I was the oldest of four boys and we were bound by seeing our father as our common enemy. With a bond like this no wonder I was so angry all of the time!

The uniqueness of Christianity is the fact that you have to receive first before you can give. I have to receive forgiveness for myself before I can give it to others; I have to receive *agape* love before I can give it to others. Every other religious system is a deal of give to get.

2 Corinthians 5:17-20

Therefore, if anyone is in Christ, the new creation has come: [a]The old has gone, the new is here! [18]All this is from God, who reconciled us to himself through Christ and gave us the ministry of reconciliation: [19]that God was reconciling the world to himself in Christ, not counting people's sins against them. And he has committed to us the message of reconciliation. [20]We are therefore Christ's ambassadors, as though God were making his appeal through us. We implore you on Christ's behalf: Be reconciled to God.

Who do you need to forgive? When and how are you going to let them know?

_____

_____

_____

_____

_____

Reconciliation

There is one party involved when there is forgiveness and two parties involved in reconciliation or, what I call forgiveness completed. This same message of forgiveness with an opportunity for reconciliation, we are to practice as men of charity and not indifference. I hope you take this important first step of offering forgiveness to those whom have hurt you. There is no greater act of *agape* love than offering forgiveness to another human being. Don't you feel loved when someone graciously forgives you? Remember, the person sinned against you and you are letting them off of *your book* and not off of *the book.*

I have heard it said that unforgiveness is like drinking poison daily hoping the other person dies. I think this is true. No doubt the bitterness that ensues will block you from becoming a man of charity. Proverbs 14:10 reminds us that, "The heart knows its own bitterness, and a stranger does not share its joy." While Hebrews 12:15 commands, "See to it that no one comes short of the grace of God; that no root of bitterness springing up causes trouble, and by it many be defiled." Being a man who forgives those whom have hurt you so deeply is the example of Christ and the very essence of charity. It is commanded because it is pleasing to God, demonstrates the love of God, is good for you, and good for those around you. Then what is reconciliation and how can I move to this next step? Someone needs to initiate. Men of fortitude and charity garner the courage necessary to do what God requires of Him, while men of fear remain passive and indifferent. Which man are you?

If you are the person who needs to initiate by asking for forgiveness, then do not hesitate. Your current state of indifference to the people you have hurt is wounding them daily and you need to man-up. The first step is a humble heart where you need to admit your mistakes and ask for forgiveness. Do not do the childish "sorry." If the person has truly forgiven you then reconciliation will ensue. Without it reconciliation is impossible. If the person you hurt has forgiven you then it is easier for you to do your part, so what is your excuse? If you are unsure if they have forgiven you then it is by definition more difficult. However, it does not matter to the man of charity who wants to initiate the process by owning his mistakes and not remaining indifferent. There are two types of people who arrive at this step. There is the what I call independent person who will not do his part to seek forgiveness and move toward reconciliation, and then there is the God-dependant person who will do his part, but may have to wait for the other person to forgive and complete the process. The 'independent' is prideful and never does his part by owning his mistakes and asking for forgiveness. He makes excuses, plays the victim, or worse, he makes forgiveness cheap when the cost of his sin was great.

I am always stunned when I meet a man who has never apologized and asked for forgiveness from his family. My goodness, I do this weekly! This often occurs when a person has seriously injured someone and is fearful of the tough conversation. When fear kicks in, fortitude will give you the courage to overcome because a man of virtue must do what is right (justice) not matter what the cost is to him (charity). Humility, godly counsel, and Holy Spirit filled virtues will get you through. This is what makes you God-dependent as you, in faith, believe God for the results because you demonstrated true faith by obedience to what He has called you to do in His word (prudence). Being a God-dependent man activates the grace of God as you, by example, demonstrate how to own your stuff by seeking forgiveness for your part. More importantly, it removes you from the equation so that you do not block the light of Christ. Let me use an illustration. Here is what the person sees when you refuse to act like a man and own your stuff:

Person ⇒ You ⇒ Cross

Imagine the person seeing your face as you block out the grace of God in disobedience keeping the focus on you and your sins against them. Ever had that happen? Now let me meddle a bit and reverse the question: have you ever done that to someone? If you ask a person to forgive you for your sins against him or her, then you are removed from blocking the light of the cross. Now as you ask for forgiveness be specific and do a lot of listening without getting defensive. I do not let my own kids get away with a lame "ah, em, sorry" and our heavenly Father will not let you as an adult get away with it either. The model is "_____ Please forgive me for saying or doing _____." Make no excuses. Now here is what the person sees:

Person ⟹ Cross

The God-dependent who does his part by taking ownership and asking for forgiveness waits patiently, in faith, for God to do His part no matter how long it takes.

If you are the person who needs to initiate by offering forgiveness, like I did with my father, then do not hesitate. Unforgiveness can also block out the power of the cross, but in this case, it is the power of acceptance and forgiveness. When you stand before the Lord upon your death He will be judging you on your part, "As far as it depended on YOU did you live at peace with all men?" Again, I could not imagine staring at His wounds and saying "But Jesus he or she hurt me by _____." Something tells me that my wounds will look extremely small by comparison as I look upon Him who was pierced, beaten, and crucified unjustly without cause for my sins.

There are the deep wounds that we discussed above and there are the day-to-day relationships where we, as sinners, have the tendency to wound one-another. This can be with in-laws, co-workers, siblings, and friends. No matter what, do your part with little to no expectations! I would recommend that you have low or no expectations levied on the other person when you initiate. It is important that the only expectations you have are for yourself before the Lord. For instance, I have personally asked for forgiveness for my reaction, sometimes over-reaction, to a situation only to have it met with complete silence. I had a false expectation that clearly this would be reciprocated and we can move forward with our relationship reconciled and restored. It was not, so I felt angry and upset about it. This is bad on me. I realized my mistake and asked the Lord to forgive me. Be ok with it because you must answer to God for your part.

As a Christian, you have to do your part no matter how hurt you are or what percent you believe that you own. If it is 5% your fault, pray and the number will increase I promise. You have to answer to God and nobody else.

There is always the dangerous temptation to take revenge, which is why verse 17 is before verse 18 in Romans 12.

Romans 12:17 – "Do not repay evil with evil…"

Romans 12:18 – "If possible, so far as it depends on you, be at peace with all men."

Did you notice the words "if possible"? This condition implies that reconciliation and peace is not always possible. Think about it. Remember the Lord has a lot of broken relationships Himself. Ah, surprised? Let me ask you a question: Did Jesus Christ offer forgiveness to the whole world?

Answer: **Yes**

Is the whole world reconciled to Jesus Christ?

Answer: **No**

So if God, through Jesus Christ, cannot force people to be reconciled in relationship with Him then how can you believe that you can force people to be in a reconciled relationship with you? As a matter of fact, a relationship with Jesus Christ will cause incredible dissension and relational turmoil for you as it did for him. Actually, relational turmoil in your closest relational circles is a promise!

Matthew 10:32-38

"Do not think that I came to [ac]bring peace on the earth; I did not come to bring peace, but a sword. [35]For I came to set a man against his father, and a daughter against her mother, and a daughter-in-law against her mother-in-law; [36]and a man's enemies will be the members of his household. [37]"He who loves father or mother more than Me is not worthy of Me; and he who loves son or daughter more than Me is not worthy of Me. [38]And he who does not take his cross and follow after Me is not worthy of Me. [39]He who has found his [ad]life will lose it, and he who has lost his [ae]life for My sake will find it."

Name people that you are currently in relational distress with. What do *you* need to do in order to obey Romans 12:18?

_____

_____

_____

_____

Take these steps, pray, and accept reality:

Step-1: While you wait on the Lord, do not force the issue but be approachable and graceful when you see the person.

Step-2: Make sure you owned your part with clarity and humility.

Step-3: Avoid the temptation to slander or try and force the person about how they need to, "Be reconciled and own their stuff." They know!

Step-4: Remember, you have the responsibility for your relationships not everyone else's. This step is for the codependent I addressed in the chapter on justice and the conflict avoider in the chapter on fortitude:

Proverbs 26:17 – Like one who takes a dog by the ears is he who passes by and meddles with strife not belonging to him.

If you are a third-party "passer by" close to the situation do not assume you know who should do what because you heard one side of the situation. Remember the proverb, "The first to plead his case seems right until another comes along to question him" – Proverbs 18:17

Step #5: Be in community with other godly men who can support you, challenge you, and hold you accountable for your part.

Restitution

Sadly, the idea of restitution is a forgotten concept. This ties into the virtue of justice where a person makes forgiveness cheap with a flippant, "I'm sorry" with no concept of repaying for the wrong committed. For example, you make restitution in physical things by replacing what you broke or returning what you stole. This concept ties nicely into the virtue of justice and is represented in the Old Testament.

Numbers 5:6-8

Speak to the sons of Israel, "When a man or woman commits any of the sins of mankind, acting unfaithfully against the Lord, and that person is guilty, [7]then [a]he shall confess [b]his sins which [c]he has committed, and he shall make restitution in full for his wrong and add to it one-fifth of it, and give it to him whom he has wronged."

I have a recent example of this idea of restitution from a few summers ago. My kids do swim competitively every summer and I feel like a Bedouin as I run around Saturday mornings setting up a canopy in different neighborhoods throughout Prince William County. I had a friend of mine meet me at a pool who offered to help me set up my tent. Well, he accidently broke it. It was clearly a mistake, and I could see it in his face that he felt terrible. Hey, the canopy cost me $80. He apologized, I forgave him, but who pays for the new canopy? As a man of charity I would never ask him to pay for it because he was helping me and it was an accident. Oh well, there is always a cost with forgiveness. Tim would have none of it, and without saying a word a brand new canopy was up the next morning. It was not the same canopy, but an even better one!

Restitution is an easier concept to embrace when it's physical property, but what about relationships? Restitution here is simply demonstrating a desire to rebuild and restore the broken relationship caused by your sin. Just like with physical things, the more expensive the item the more costly the restitution. If you are a parent, adult child, brother, or spouse, and your sin is deep, then restitution will take both time and grace. A lost childhood can never be restored, but it can be redeemed! God redeemed mine, so He can redeem yours if you invite Him to. My Dad and I are reconciled, and we are in the rebuilding process thanks to Jesus Christ. I love him and I am very proud of him being sober for over twenty years!

Here are the three R's of restitution: Restore, Rebuild, Repeat. Once you seek forgiveness and the gift is opened, the relationship is reconciled and forgiveness is completed. You restore the relationship to its original state as far as placement. In the case of a father and a son, you begin to see each other in those roles and behave in such a way appropriate to those roles. Rebuilding is a process of regaining trust by rebuilding the trust bridge between your heart and another's heart. Imagine that the trust bridge is a drawbridge in which you have one side and the other person has the other. Each of you has to choose to let down the trust bridge every day. The more damage done to the bridge the longer it takes to rebuild. Repeat daily, praying that the Lord will weld the bridge shut to where each of you can freely allow every emotion of your true self cross the bridge. Be patient with yourself and the other person.

Each person has a role to play in the rebuilding process by demonstrating charity and not indifference to the relationship. The person who was sinned against and graciously offered forgiveness needs to let down that bridge and carefully allow himself to be vulnerable. This person needs to demonstrate the grace of charity and not indifference as the person forgiven may feel embarrassed and ashamed. He or she may need a hand reaching out demonstrating that the offer of forgiveness was truly genuine. Some, due to shame, find the forgiveness hard to believe and accept. The more shame the person has the more grace he or she will need. The person who has sinned and humbly received forgiveness needs to recognize how precious this gift is and not squander it or take it for granted. He or she must demonstrate the grace of charity at times when the other person does not let down the trust bridge and pulls back a little out of a fear of being hurt again.

From 1 to 10 how good of a forgiver are you?

_____

Have you ever confused forgiveness and reconciliation? Has this kept you from forgiving?

_____
_____
_____
_____

Seeking forgiveness: Whom do you need to *seek* forgiveness from? Do the chains of indifference bind you?

_____

_____

_____

_____

Write down the person and the day that you are committing before the Lord to seeking forgiveness in the next 30 days:

_____

Offering Forgiveness: Write down the day that you are committing before the Lord to formally *offer* forgiveness in the next 30 days:

_____

Train Yourself to Keep Short Accounts

"But solid food is for the mature, who because of practice have their senses trained to discern good and evil." – Hebrews 5:14

The hardest part of forgiveness for most of us comes when we have committed the wrong and need to ask for forgiveness. Quite frankly, we hate admitting that we are wrong and another person is right. It is humbling. In our pride, though, we confuse humbling with humiliating and use it to excuse ourselves from admitting that we are wrong. I believe that this is why that earlier false quote on apologizing was flying around on Facebook. False humility, is pride in a cheap suit.

Early in our marriage my wife and I started something on a whim that turned out to be a very useful tool in training us to keep short accounts with one another. We call it the "I'm right kiss." It is best to explain how the "I'm right kiss" works with an example of when we first used it. Although I cannot remember the specifics, the gist of it is as follows.

Cheryl and I were driving to a friend's house and she

directed, "Honey take the next right." I looked over and replied, "No, it is up there on the left." I drove past her suggested turn and made the left. Well, you guessed it, she was right and I was wrong. She puckered up with a smirk underneath and made me give her a kiss. This became the "I'm right kiss." Whoever is right gets a kiss from whoever is wrong. It is that easy.

Sounds simple, and maybe even silly, but it is quite useful and quite powerful when it really matters. What we are doing with these small gestures of humility is training ourselves to admit when we are wrong when the stakes are low and of little impact. When the stakes are high and really matters, we know, by practice, how to admit when we are wrong. Humility is the main ingredient in forgiveness when you are wrong before the Lord and another person.

We have taught hundreds of engaged couples and marriage coach couples through our Preparing For Marriage class and this is the one tool people have implemented more than anything else. Why? Because it is both easy and practical. We have trained our kids since they were little to use the "I'm right kiss" with one another, and us. I have three kids 17, 15, and 12 and all of them admit when they are wrong and seek forgiveness. That's right, even my teenagers! I attribute it to this simple training tool. The mind is influencing the brain through a small, simple training exercise. Remember, it is the river that cuts the channel.

Luke 7:3-4

Be on your guard! If your brother sins, rebuke him; and if he repents, forgive him. [4]And if he sins against you seven times a day, and returns to you seven times, saying, 'I repent,' [c]forgive him."

When is the last time you asked for forgiveness? Or, do you tend toward "I'm sorry?" Explain the difference

_____

_____

_____

Are you committed to changing your language to God's language of asking for forgiveness and naming it specifically?

____Yes ____No

If you are a parent, when is the last time that you asked your child for forgiveness?

_____

_____

_____

Are you committed to leading in humility by example? This is leadership!

____Yes ____No

What tool are you going to implement to help you grow humility with those who matter most? ("I'm right kiss" or some other tool)

_____

_____

_____

Killing Indifference By Making a Difference

Charity is a daily exercise that a man does in order to kill selfishness in his heart. Indifference in the little things inclines your heart toward indifference in the bigger things. Just like humility and the "I'm right kiss," we need to find small tangible ways to demonstrate charity to strengthen that muscle. Look for ways to daily demonstrate charity in the lives of people by seeing a need then meeting a need. This will help you practice self-sacrifice, which in turn will begin to form compassion in your heart.

Chivalry was not an accident, but daily gracious acts to demonstrate that you are a man of charity who places others above yourself in the small things. I am reminded of a story my friend Jon Roop told me. Jon and his wife, Lori, served as marriage mentors in my Preparing for Marriage class. When Jon was serving in the military he held a door open for a female senior officer. Instead of a thank you, this officer looked at him and quipped, "You are only doing this because I am a women." To which Jon responded, "No, I am doing this because I am a gentleman." Nice! Being a gentleman necessitated acts of charity that reflects the man.

What practical every day steps can you do to replace selfishness with selflessness? If you are married take over that one chore your wife hates and do it well and with a good attitude as an act of charity. Don't talk—do! Do you have a daughter? No matter how old she is, open the door for her, pull out her chair, etc. Sew into her heart qualities to look for by her first "catching" them from her father. Look for ways to serve then serve. It is that simple.

Talk about ideas with some other men and write them down as an action plan and do!

_____
_____
_____
_____

Memory Table: Commit the properties of charity to memory

Be a man of CHARITY and not INDIFFERENCE	
Compassion	Humility
Forgiveness	Self-sacrifice
Selflessness	

9
A MAN OF HOPE
NOT DESPAIR
"It is since Christians have largely ceased to think of the other world that they have become so ineffective in this" – C.S. Lewis

When a Christian uses the word hope, he does not mean a blind optimism or wishful thinking. The modern idea of hope is best understood as wishing for something without any real expectation of knowing whether or not you will obtain what you wish for. This secular modern view of hope is based on fate, chance, serendipity, or good luck. "I hope" has become as empty as "I believe." Since the object of this kind of hope is empty, like wishing on a star, so is the hope itself. This false view of hope not only breeds despair in a man, but feeds uncertainty, the vice of faith. As the great theologian Jiminy Cricket sang to the wooden puppet, Pinocchio, "When you wish upon a star, makes no difference who you are. Anything your heart desires will come to you." But that really isn't true is it? When the blackness of despair comes, any man knows that false hope is no hope at all. However, the theological virtue of hope is based on the reality of God's existence and is rooted in the truth of His word and His promises. As my pastor Lon Solomon says, "Christianity is based on a know-so hope, not a hope-so hope."

The anchor is one of the oldest symbols in Christianity and can be found throughout the catacombs. This symbol for hope is based on Hebrews 6:19, "This hope we have as an anchor of the soul, a hope both sure and steadfast..." The Greek word for anchor in this verse is *agkura* and is a form of the word *agkalé*, which means, "an arm, especially as bent to receive a burden." If you think about what an anchor does, it is suitable for hope to receive and hold our burdens. When a storm breaks on the sea, you drop anchor to hold you steady through the storm so that you do not despair. Likewise, in the storms of life, we need hope to anchor us so that we remain steady and do not despair. This is why the anchor needs to hold onto something solid like a rock. What an amazing visual, for the Bible teaches that the Lord Jesus is our Rock and our hope.

The Greek word for hope in the Bible is *elpis* meaning, "a confidence while waiting with the expectation of obtaining that which is desired." Thus, true hope provides us the capacity for not giving up. The Scholastics taught that hope is the movement of the appetite towards a future good, which though difficult, it is attainable. The properties of hope include freedom, assurance, contentment, peace, longsuffering, perseverance, confidence, and trust. The vice of hope is despair, which includes cynicism, unbelief, helplessness, hopelessness, and doubt. In short, despair is the disease and hope is the cure.

At the Fall we lost hope, and in Christ, hope was restored. Because of the Lord Jesus there is the ultimate hope for eternal life in Heaven as a guarantee because of what He has done on the cross and not what you have done on earth. This is true hope because it is not based on our performance, but is based on the performance of Jesus Christ, who lived a perfect life that we could never live, and offered it to us as a gift. When I die I know that I am going to heaven, and that is my know-so hope rooted in the promise of God because of the payment of my sins by the Lord Jesus on Calvary. Is it arrogant for me as a Christian to say that "I know I am going to heaven"?

Well, it would be arrogant if this confident statement were based on my own supposed good works. However, it is not based on me at all, but is based on Jesus Christ and His perfect life that He lived in my place and offered not only to me, but also to everyone to humbly receive as a gift. Sounds too easy right? This salvation offer is not as easy as some people think due to the requirement of a humble heart, because each of us have to admit that we need a savior. What is more difficult than the humility required to get a man to admit he is wrong and cannot do it himself?

Back To Creation: What is Man Made of?

"Physicians think they do a lot for a patient when they give his disease a name"
—Immanuel Kant.

Before we dive into this vital heavenward virtue, we are going to dig a little deeper into what man is made of. Are we simply a material being or do we have a soul/spirit? There is a long-standing debate as to whether man is merely a material being or a composite of a material body and an immaterial substance known as the soul. Today in philosophy, and in the fairly new field of neuroscience, the debate is known formally as the mind-body problem. Raging since the beginning of time, this debate between scientists of different philosophies and religious systems has an added dimension from the fields of psychology and psychiatry known as the nature-nurture debate. The problem, in short, expresses itself when one is determining the cause of psychological problems, addictions, emotional distress, etc. In other words, what is causing this problem of _____ in a person's life? Does the cause of the problem lie in his body (material) or is the cause of the problem in his soul (immaterial mind/emotions/will)? Is the problem caused by material nature or the relational nurture of the world around him? Christianity then adds to this debate the dimension of spiritual influence. It is the ultimate chicken egg debate that, depending on where one places his faith, has incredible consequences for how you view your problems, help yourself, and provide guidance to others.

In a post-Christian America the philosophy of materialism reigns supreme and gets most of the news coverage. Materialism or naturalism is a philosophy that everything, including emotions, ideas, and the mind itself can be reduced to simply a material substance and material causes. At this point some of you reading are thinking, "I am not much of a science guy, and frankly I am already bored, so what is the big deal?" Well you may not be much of a science guy but this section is critical because you will make decisions based on one approach over another I promise you. In fact, some of you already have. You will be putting blind faith into a medical doctor or a therapist believing that it is the smart, and dare I say, "scientific" thing to do. Moreover, you are a news guy and you will hear false and misleading headlines baptized in the philosophy of materialism gently smuggled into a headline of "Science Discovered that _____" or "Science Confirms that _____."

Almost all psychiatry and psychology today focuses its solutions on a bottom-up, matter-only belief of causation over a top-down, soul-only approach to causation. It is important to note that a scientist or a therapist who believes in the existence of a soul of some form or another is called a "dualist." On the other hand, a therapist who embraces the bottom-up causation for psychological problems is called a materialist. A materialist believes that everything mental is caused by the material because his philosophy (worldview) rather than facts inform him that the brain *is* the mind. So to him, fix the material cause in order to fix the behavior. Whereas a therapist who embraces top-down causation believes that everything mental (soul) causes the material responses that influence behavior because the mind is linked but independent of the brain. So to him, fix the mental cause, fix the behavior. Do you see the difference?

Before I go any further I would like to prove to you that some of the most brilliant scientists in modern times are dualists and believe that the mind or soul is independent but linked to the brain. There is the explicit dualist Charles Sherrington who is considered the father of neuroscience itself! Next we have the dualist Neurosurgeon Wilder Penfield, who is considered the father of modern epilepsy surgery. Then there is Sir John Eccles who is a Nobel Laureate in medicine for his groundbreaking work on the functioning of neuronal synapses. Finally, there is the recent work of UCLA neurologist and neuroscientist Jeffery Swartz who has documented evidence that mental states; i.e., the mind, shows measurable changes in brain function.[91]

Alcoholism is a prime example of a problem and how the approaches to dealing with it differ greatly, depending on the worldview you embrace. Alcoholism is something familiar to most of us, and believing one approach over another has serious implications to your life, to those impacted by the consequences of addiction, and to the addict who is in recovery. Does alcoholism have a genetic cause where one is born with "a disease" (nature) or is the cause of alcoholism the result of one's upbringing where a person learned by example to deal with problems head on, right into a bottle (nurture). The answer you embrace will decide how you handle the problem, and where you believe your responsibility ultimately rests. More importantly, in one view the twelve steps that presuppose personal responsibility make sense, while in the other view they are mere window dressing. Dr. Robert Baron describes the problem and how a new nature-nurture balance in psychology is needed due to the extremes:

> A pure "environmentalism" ruled in psychology; almost everything, most psychologists believed, was shaped by the world around us and our experiences in it. Now, however, the pendulum of scientific *opinion* has swung far back the other way. . . . As is often the case, this shift in scientific opinion has been magnified by the media. Magazines, newspapers, and television programs have jumped on the bandwagon, suggesting that genetic factors are all-powerful and are, in fact, the controlling influence in our lives.[92]

Under the section in his book titled "The Nature-Nurture Controversy in the New Millennium: Adopting a Balanced View of the Role of Genetic Factors in Human Behavior," Dr. Baron outlines the role of a new nature-nurture synthesis:

1. Even if a form of behavior is influenced by genetic factors, this

---

[91] If you would like to read some more information on neuroscience and salient properties of the mind that cannot be reduced to material causes check out this blog post by Dr. Michael Egnor that can be found on my favorite Intelligent Design news site. A site that I check daily! http://www.evolutionnews.org/2009/01/daniel_dennett_call_your_offic015121.html; Internet, [accessed October 20, 2014]

[92] Robert A. Baron., *Essentials of Psychology*, 3d ed.(Needham Heights, Massachusetts: Allyn & Bacon, 2002), 72 [emphasis mine].

doesn't mean that it cannot be modified.

2. Environmental factors almost always play a role, too.

3. We are not simply servants of our genes.

4. Evolution...is not the only view, and to date, has not been "proved" in the same manner as many other scientific theories.

5. Beware of politically driven interpretations of scientific data.

From a biblical perspective this debate is a false dilemma because there exists a third option; namely, it is *both*! Read that sentence again. More specifically, Christianity teaches that the full expression of the problems that plague us is found, not only in our nature and our nurture, but more accurately, in our fallen-nature and our fallen-nurture. Think about the difference for a moment. The nature-nurture models presuppose that man's nature is good (secular humanism/Marxism) whereas the biblical model implies that something is wrong with *both* our nature and our nurture. Man is not simply good, as we all know both biblically and by experience, but he is the good gone bad—he is fallen. This is why we are all born with a tendency toward the vices! More importantly Christianity adds a third element to the debate, our spiritual condition. Are you dead to Christ or alive in Christ? The reason we can be influenced by both fallen-nature and fallen-nurture is because there is more to us than our material substance. There is an immaterial reality that is part of us called a soul that is our true self, which is either connected to God or disconnected. On page 235 is a detailed diagram that I hope helps visualize this concept.

Body only (Secular View)   **Body, Soul/Spirit (Biblical View)**

I would argue that the biblical view shown above is the most scientifically proven fact around, and any true science will never contradict the word of God. The phrase "science says" is misleading in that science doesn't say anything, only the scientists who take the scientific data and run it through the filter of their worldview that presupposes the body-only secular view. The secular therapists will assume they are scientific while missing the fact that their faith is guiding their belief in the body-only approach of only matter matters. His philosophy of materialism or naturalism is smuggled into his approach leaving him blind to his own faith assumptions. We know that there is a non-material part of us the Bible calls the soul because, within ourselves, each of us experiences mental properties such as, consciousness, intention, and purpose. Think for a moment—Are you reading this book because you wanted to or did your chemicals make you do it? This is not as simplistic as it sounds. Really think about it. If there is no mind or soul brothers then free will is merely an illusion. And this is exactly where some of these secular scientists are heading. In summary, human behavior makes the most sense when we explain it in terms of meaning, purpose, desires, beliefs and choices; not chemicals, molecules, volts, wires, and motion.

In our post Christian culture, the real culprits of the materialist philosophical lies we embrace are college textbooks primarily written from this secular materialist confirmation bias. Additionally, the news media has made the secular view of science the authority in areas where this reductionist[93] approach to explanations simply does not belong. As evidenced by the chart on the next page, authoritarian science phrases such as "science tells us we must" and "science tells us we should" have increased significantly in news reporting of science studies since the turn of the century. Look at that hockey stick spike! Is this really an accident? The bottom line, men, is really a matter of faith and where you choose to place it. Is the object of your faith the winds of change of the next "science says…" or in the Bible where the creator's voice of "God says…" can be heard? Look at your approach to problems and you will soon find your answer.

---

[93] In the fields of psychology, psychiatry, and neuroscience the secularist scientist always commits what is known in logic as the reductive fallacy. A reductive fallacy occurs when a person reduces something complex to only one element. For example, reducing something complex such as emotions to merely brain chemicals when there are obviously other factors at work.

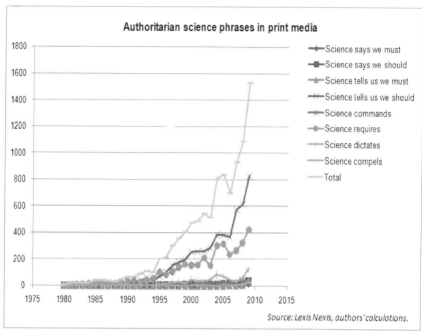

Authoritarian Science Phrases in Media[94]

As demonstrated by my quote from Dr. Baron, the opinion of science is all over the place. What about all of those people who were treated for decades under the model of "all nurture" believing that it was scientific? Or, what about the people now who are being treated under the current winds of science's "all nature" model assuming that medication is the answer to every problem "in our genes" and "in our brain chemicals?" As we know by our experience, the cause can, and often does, flow in *both* directions as our behavior is influenced by the fallen-nature to include our unique personality, and our fallen nurture on how we learned or didn't learn to deal with the issues in life. The results of these influences are expressed in our inclinations toward certain sins and how we feel in different situations. Both of these build on the other and can reveal themselves in troublesome behavior issues on the one hand and/or anxiety and depression on the other.

---

[94] *The American*, on-line Magazine of American Enterprise Institute, July 27, 2010 http://www.american.com/archive/2010/july/science-turns-authoritarian; accessed September 28, 2014.

Fallen Nurture + Fallen Nature

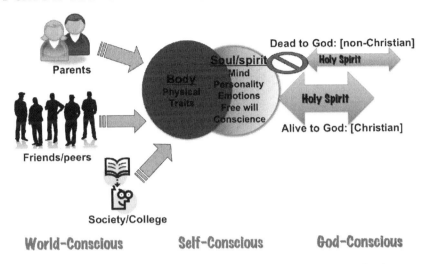

Body, Soul/Spirit Interactions With The World & God

Anxiety, Depression, and Hope

"Beware of despairing about yourself. You are commanded to put your trust in God not yourself" – Augustine

Twenty-first century scientific *opinion* is built on the assumption that we are material beings only; thus, there must by a magic gene for everything. And since the cause is always presumed to be material then the treatment must also be material. As a result, in comes the white magic pill to solve the black magic problem. Additionally, we have the hyper pressure to self-identify with the latest mental "disorder," or "disease" because every gene problem needs a name in order to match the pill solution. Now we can fall into the hopeless trap of identifying with a constant slew of new names of "_____ disorder" that is given to behavior that can change with discipline over medicine, or discipline + medicine temporarily, instead of the medication alone approach. My concern in this shift is that there can be no doubt that we are overmedicating boys and men.

There are two major approaches to solving these issues today. The "Medical Model" that assumes the "body only" view of man is true, and there is the "Counseling model" that assumes the Body/soul view of man is true. Slowly go through this chart below Bob Phillips provides in his wonderful book on anxiety and depression[95]:

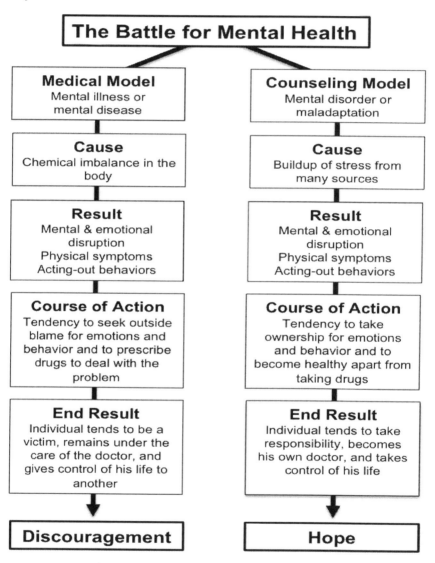

Look at the bottom of the chart again and see the personal implications of the different approaches. One approach leads to

---

[95] Bob Phillips, *Overcoming Anxiety & Depression* (Eugene, Or: Harvest House, 2007), 79.

discouragement and the other approach leads to hope. To put it in the terms of virtues and vices, one approach leads to the vice of despair being expressed in your life while the other approach leads to the virtue of hope being expressed in your life. Do you see the power behind embracing the helpless word disorder? The medical only model takes control away from you, because in this model free will is merely an illusion and does not actually exist. If you take away the power of free will in a person's life then, by definition, you take away a very fundamental feature of the image of God in a person's life. To quickly prove that a free will exists, again, ask yourself if you chose to read this book or if a gene is making you do it. Think about it.

Stay with me here so you understand not only what I am saying, but also what I am not saying. Remember the fallen nature includes the body, so medical treatment for mental challenges that result in chemical upheaval *may* be needed for a time while you work through the fallen-nurture, spiritual, or soul root of the problem. You are not doing yourself any favor trying to work through things when you are not in the healthy mental or emotional state needed to process hard things. This is where medication can help you get to the place where God needs you in order to respond to His Spirit, the counselor's guidance, and your Brothers in Christ. There are long term consequences to short-term feel good fixes if you simply rely on medication to do all of the work. Mental issues are part of the fallen world and of course they need addressed like every other issue that impacts us. But, unlike purely physical diseases behavioral issues [I hate the word disorder because it implies it is unchangeable] need medication and sanctification. Sanctification is behavioral change over time, and yes the medication in most cases will be temporary as sanctification takes hold.

Imagine trying to heal heart disease with medicine only and never changing your eating habits or adding exercise! With the biblical view of man which includes a fallen body avoid the one extreme of being a "no medication ever" brother, and the other extreme of "calling everything a disorder." As Ecclesiastes 7:18 makes clear, "The Man who fears God will avoid all extremes". If you start a medication though, so that you can be in a good place to work these issues you will have to be aware of the dangers of actually "feeling better" because of the medication. Why? Because you have the same fallen nature I do, which means the same tendency to get complacent and lazy. You need the virtue of fortitude to do the hard work of getting to the root issue and pulling out the surrounding weeds. Please do not surrender the battle because now you feel better.

The danger here is choosing to not work through the root cause of your anxiety and depression because the medication makes you "feel" better as it takes away the effect; i.e., the emotional turmoil, or feelings of anxiety or depression. The temptation is to believe that the medicine took away the cause (medical model) when in fact it took away the effect only (counseling model). If you do not do the necessary soul work then you will no doubt find yourself changing medications constantly as the real root issue in your soul will adapt and the emotional turmoil pops up again like the game of whack a weasel. I believe this proves the counseling model because why change medication if the cause is dealt with? What changed? Nothing. The real cause deep within your soul demands to pop through your material being.

Through this soul work you may discover that you are part of the small minority of people who need the medication for a long time or a lifetime, but don't jump there so soon which is a demonstration of carelessness not prudence. Isn't it at least worth a try? How is the current plan working out for you? Only you and the Lord know the answer. I am no expert but I have done a lot of reading that is added to some experience in this area with myself, friends, and people whom I have counseled over the years. For instance, I cured three people in one year of bi-polar "disorder." Want to know how? They didn't have it! In two of the situations the individuals had a major crisis in their life. So of course they experienced "highs and lows" and "bursts of anger" due to the betrayals that blew up their marriage and family life. Their emotional turmoil is normal! The third individual had "extreme highs and lows" because he was addicted to crack cocaine. In each of these instances, the individual went to a psychiatrist who embraced the medical model, received a diagnosis of "bipolar disorder" and were given medication. Think about the lifelong impact of falsely believing something is so deeply wrong with you that you now have a disorder? Again, these are examples and I do not know where you are personally or where people are in your relationship circles of influence.

Reflect: Read the verse below and based on the biblical view of man, circle the parts of a person:

Proverbs 18:14 – The spirit of a man can endure his sickness, But as for a broken spirit who can bear it?

Proverbs 15:13 – A joyful heart makes a cheerful face, But when the heart is sad, the spirit is broken.

1Corinthians 2:11 – For who among men knows the thoughts of a man except the spirit of the man which is in him? Even so the thoughts of God no one knows except the Spirit of God.

Hebrews 4:12 – For the word of God is living and active and sharper than any two-edged sword, and piercing as far as the division of soul and spirit, of both joints and marrow, and able to judge the thoughts and intentions of the heart.

What do the verses imply as far as possible causes of problems a person has?

_____
_____
_____

What do you think about the two models? What can you change in your thinking and approach to mental health issues?

_____
_____
_____

Have you ever heard someone say, "I just know it will get better"? Some people put their trust in their investments, the next promotion, or the things in this life that can quickly disappear. There is truly a feeling of despair when all you have worked for and all you have put your efforts into fail to deliver once it is achieved. The Book of Job reminds us, "So are the paths of all who forget God; and the hope of the godless will perish."[96] Everything we count on, if built on sand apart from God, will eventually fall like a house of cards.[97] We must not cling too tightly to our status, or our dream home for security because they simply will not endure.

A Story of Despair

The world was shocked at the suicide of funny man Robin Williams. Why? He was funny! And we believe that making people smile, is a reflection of a person's own happiness. As someone who has used humor to cover pain all of my life, I can sympathize with this great comedian. The sad thing about Robin Williams was that he was trapped in a cycle of despair that humor, alcohol, and drugs medicated but never eradicated. Anxiety and depression are two forms of despair in this life that even the Christian is not immune to.

Nothing drives me more insane than modern Christianity baptizing positive thinking. This is false hope men. I am sorry, but every day is not a Friday. Christian Philosopher JP Moreland tells of his battle with anxiety and depression in his amazing book *The Lost Virtue of Happiness*:

But my weekly structure of work blinded me to the fact that I wasn't dealing with my mounting inner turmoil and anxiety from all these stressors. When the structure was removed at the end of the school year, everything caught up with me. I crashed and burned. My anxiety grew too great for me to handle, and I descended into a very dark time of deep depression. I began to wake up at two or three o'clock in the morning with a racing heart and an anxious sweat. I couldn't get back to sleep. During the day, I experienced the tightness of anxiety throughout my chest and stomach.[98]

JP Moreland goes on to say that his anxiety and depression lasted seven months and was due to overwork, extended family stressors, and a resurfacing of some early childhood fears. He states that all of this would have lasted longer if he had not reached out for help. That is prudence and humility.

---

[96] Job 8:13.
[97] Matthew 7:25-27.
[98] Moreland, *Happiness*, 155-6.

I have had some friends who are strong, mature believers in the Lord go through the same experiences. Like JP, they sought help from friends, professionally, changing their diet, exercise, and medication to get through the slump of despair. Each of them took a "whole person" approach: body, soul, and spirit. If you have gone through the valley of despair due to anxiety and depression, you know how difficult it can be. It does not make you immature or less of a Christian because you have had these experiences, quite the opposite, it makes you a saved fallen human being. What makes you immature and possibly prideful is doing nothing about it.

I went through what I would term a mild form of depression a few years ago. Within a year, I had left full-time ministry, my mother-in-law who had lived with us for six years had died, I stopped seminary, and I experienced the greatest disappointment from my extended family that I have ever experienced Christmas of that year. It all caught up to me and I just didn't feel right. I felt angry and lost. This is why I call it a mild form because I was lost, confused, and had an undercurrent of anger and sorrow that made me edgy and unpleasant. I reached out to my best friend, who happens to be the man who wrote the forward to this book. There is great power in a godly friend who loves you. I just needed to dump all of this out of my head and receive godly counsel. Galatians 6:2 instructs us to, "Bear one another's burdens, and thereby fulfill the law of Christ."

Psalm 42:4-6

These things I remember and I pour out my soul within me. For I used to go along with the throng *and* [a]lead them in procession to the house of God, With the voice of joy and thanksgiving, a multitude keeping festival. [5]Why are you [b]in despair, O my soul? And *why* have you become disturbed within me? [c]Hope in God, for I shall [d]again praise [e]Him *For* the [f]help of His presence. [6]O my God, my soul is [g]in despair within me;

Have you ever experienced or are you currently experiencing anxiety or depression? (mild or extreme) How did you handle the feeling of despair?

_____

_____

_____

We should not have hope for hope's sake; we must have hope in Jesus Christ our Savior and our Rock. He will give us the strength to go on in life, because we have Him walking with us through it all. There are times when He is walking with us providing His presence through another person which is why Galatians 6:2 is so critical. We are created for relationships; for community. The hope of a Christian is a quiet confidence, a supernatural certainty that breaks the chains of despair as they form. And where do we find this hope? In the pages of Scripture that were written to "give us hope." (Romans 15:4) So anchor your hope in Christ today because He will never disappoint.

Here are a few resources to help you understand anxiety and depression. Nothing gives hope more than prudence as you begin to grow in knowledge and gain a sense of control and understanding of what God may be doing through it all:

Overcoming Anxiety and Depression, by Bob Phillips

The Lost Virtue of Happiness, by J.P. Moreland

Healing Anxiety and Depression, by Daniel G. Amen, M.D.

Eternal Hope in Temporary Suffering

"The frequent attempt to conceal mental pain increases the burden: it's easier to say "My tooth is aching" than "My heart is broken" – C.S. Lewis

Faith and hope are closely linked because both of these theological virtues are made complete in Jesus Christ. In the chapter on faith I shared the story of how we had two years of suffering as my wife was diagnosed with an autoimmune disorder when she got pregnant. Added to this Jonah was born with all kinds of issues that landed him at a tipping point where I prayed the hardest prayer I ever prayed, "Lord, I love that boy please don't take him. If you do I will still love and trust you but I really don't want you to take him." After persevering, looking back I discovered an unexpecting truth–our faith grew. The book of Romans teaches an important truth about growing in Christ that links faith and hope together.

Romans 5:1-5

Therefore, having been justified by faith, [a]we have peace with God through our Lord Jesus Christ, [2]through whom also we have obtained our introduction by faith into this grace in which we stand; and [b]we exult in hope of the glory of God. [3]And not only this, but [c]we also exult in our tribulations, knowing that tribulation brings about perseverance; [4]and perseverance, proven character; and proven character, hope; [5]and hope does not disappoint, because the love of God has been poured out within our hearts through the Holy Spirit who was given to us.

The problem of suffering and evil is a problem for everyone no matter what religious worldview you hold. I believe that Christianity provides the only real answer to this problem through Jesus Christ, God's suffering servant, and through the Holy Spirit referred to by Jesus Christ as the "Comforter" or "Counselor" which He promised would come to all His followers after His resurrection and ascension into Heaven. The Atheist denies that evil exists then conveniently uses "the problem of evil" as a reason to deny God's existence. But, Atheist what is your answer because the problem of evil is a problem for you as well? Answer: What evil so no problem! Thanks, but no thanks, because that is not helpful. Some Eastern religions either deny evil or welcome evil for "balance" while Christianity offers hope in God's sovereignty, justice, love and presence while He walks with us *through* the evil, providing comfort, counsel, and a promise of His divine judgment for evil men who willfully reject Him, and divine mercy for those who willfully accept Him. God is populating the New Heaven and New Earth with those who accept Him from this soon to be Old Earth. God's Son was murdered as prophesied 500 years before the event in Psalm 22:16 that records, "...a band of evildoers has encompassed me; [b]they pierced my hands and my feet." But what about this hope when evil comes knocking?

When the problem of evil becomes up close and personal by taking from us a friend or family member who served the Lord so faithfully, or even a child who had a whole life ahead of them, the question "Why?" becomes a demanding guest in our temple[99]. Now,

---

[99]1Corinthians 3:16.

"Why?" has always been a guest, and at times he behaves like a close family friend providing great counsel and sure answers to some of life's questions right when we need it. But, it is during times of senseless evil that he becomes a demanding guest, even initially drowning out the benevolence of God. How could God be all good, all-powerful, and all knowing when a person made in His image senselessly and violently destroys another image bearer? Why would God allow such evil if He could stop it and how could He allow it if He is all good? I must admit that for me, in my own pride, a disturbing thread that underlies the question, is the belief that though I am finite, with limited power and limited goodness, I know I would have stopped this evil from occurring if I could. It may pain me to say it or even think it, but honestly there it is. Ouch!

Job had asked similar questions of God and received no answer, but yet his hope remained. By implication, it appears God believed that an "answer" is precisely what Job did not need at the moment. Job pondered some more by turning his why questions to his close friends, whose bad counsel and endless words did not seem to help either. What God did give Job were reminders of who He is relative to who Job is. What he needed was faith and hope, anchored in secure facts about God to renew his mind and inform his emotions that were causing even more suffering internally. Job 38 and 39 is where God provides a list of things in creation Job can consider that reveal God's glory and the supremacy of His knowledge and power. These cognitive reminders seemed to Help Job come to the realization that based on what he knows to be true about God he can trust Him even in the things that he does not *now* know or understand.

The Lord Jesus had a similar Job experience with God the Father as the book of Hebrews indicates: "During the days of Jesus' life on earth, He offered up prayers and petitions with loud cries and tears to the One, who could save him from death, and he was heard because of his reverent submission."[100] So Jesus, the only perfectly innocent and pure servant of God, was heard by God, told "no," and His life was taken. The cries and the tears of the Lord Jesus must have been difficult for His all-powerful, all-good Father to hear. As a

---

[100] Hebrews 5:7, NIV. [Emphasis mine].

244

father myself, I imagine that it must have been even more difficult not answering. But, His Father is also eternal and all knowing. He knew the very purpose of His Son's ultimately unjust death was to bring about the ultimately wonderful gift of eternal life to all who believe. An ultimate good (charity), and ultimate justice brought out of an ultimate evil and injustice. Moreover, Christians for over two millennia have personally looked to this Suffering Servant asking God to accept this sacrifice as a payment for his or her sins; thus gaining access to God's kingdom through this door[101] of hope made out of suffering.

Jesus' followers initially did not have any access to this information as evident to their hiding and return to fishing[102] after His death. It was the later resurrection of Jesus that provided them access to additional information that they did not have at the time of their thirty-year-old friend's death. Much later, even more information was provided when the Holy Spirit came and made the purposes of these things known to them.[103] So, in time God began to progressively reveal more and more data to Jesus' disciples and eventually to us in the Bible. What is important to realize is that our all-knowing God is a God who progressively reveals more and more information in His own time according to His purposes and for our good. This is why we need hope and trust in who He is. What's more, God does not remain distant providing a rote answer to suffering in the world but, through His Son Jesus, He existentially *entered into* the unjust suffering of this world!

God gives us something much more important than a full disclosure of all information to answer the "Why" questions, He gives us His presence! Jesus said that it is good that He goes so that the Comforter and Counselor can come[104]. Something tells me He knew that in this fallen world, a Divine Comforter and Counselor is exactly what we would need. It is interesting that in times of despair, like some of us are experiencing, what we need most is the presence of our fellow believers, and what we do not need is "answers" that will not suffice while we are still not home. However, due to God's

---

[101] Luke 13:24.
[102] John 20:26; 21:3.
[103] John 14:26; Acts 1:7; 2Timothy 3:16; 1Peter 1:21.
[104] John 16:7.

progressive revelation given to us in His word, and personally through His Son, we have some important Divine promises the Counselor wants to use to renew our minds and inform our emotions. When we allow lies to play over and over in our minds we become "why" slaves and our emotions become our enemy. On the other hand, when we set our minds on whatever is true[105] we become free, for it is the truth that sets us free.[106]

I don't know about you but I personally love a leader who will consistently go down in the trenches with you. On the other hand, I dislike serving under a leader who will not go but instead he merely looks down at you in the trenches. What an example the Lord Jesus is to us by humbly stepping into this space-time continuum and taking on flesh in order to win every battle in the flesh we cannot win. Then through His suffering on the cross he paid for our sin demonstrating victory in the ultimate battle between good and evil. This victorious identity is how God chooses to see us and how He wants you to see yourself—a victorious warrior. "But wait!" you say, "I am anything but victorious, look at my struggles!" But God says that there is real power in perspective my son.

Proverbs 23:7 – "For as he thinks within himself so he is..."

As I already mentioned, Jesus did not just win and leave us a distant example, but sent us the Holy Spirit in order to help us from the inside out claim our own victories and grow through our failures. He takes our defeats, failures, unjust suffering, and personally comforts us by walking through them with us. But here is the real beauty of His leadership; God uses these very events to mature us through perseverance, and then works through us to comfort and disciple others.

2Corinthians 1:3-4

³Blessed be the God and Father of our Lord Jesus Christ, the Father of mercies and God of all comfort; 4who comforts us in all our affliction so that we may be able to comfort those who are in any affliction with the comfort with which we ourselves are comforted by God. [emphasis added]

---

[105] Philippians 4:8.
[106] John 8:32.

The belief that God is a "God of all comfort" is an essential truth every believer must embrace because life's journey will always pass us through the valley. In the scripture God calls us to do two things with this essential truth taught in these powerful verses. First, God wants us to apply this truth in our own lives by letting Him into the deepest parts of our being to be comforted personally by Him. Second, God wants us to serve others with the same "comfort with which we ourselves are comforted by God." Did you notice the "so that" in verse four? God is comforting us not simply to benefit us, although that is certainly true, but with the intention that we will serve other people out of the same comfort that we have received from the God of compassion. In short, we are called to give it away! Do not miss this. Notice that there is a correlation between the areas of your life that you allow God in to comfort and the type of comfort that you can give away. This is your purpose, this is your calling, this is your personal "so that" ministry. The choice is yours: are you going to be the Dead Sea or a Sea of Galilee?

Our "so that" ministry is the ministry that most of us, if we are honest, never prayed for and that we least expected. Indeed this is our most personal ministry and one that can have the greatest impact for the Kingdom only if we allow God to take hold of it. I call it the ministry that we never prayed for because I do not know anyone who prayed for addiction, prayed for abuse, or prayed for a friend, wife, or child to leave this earth before we think he or she was ready. What you allow God to do with these areas of pain and how far you let Him into the pain will determine if you are a space taker hiding in the foxhole of fear or a difference maker on the battlefield of faith taking the world by storm.

After reading this section, what do you think your "So That" ministry is? What defeat, pain, or suffering in your past does God want to heal and use to minister to others?

_____

_____

_____

What area of defeat or pain have you not allowed God in to comfort you? Man-up and be honest!

_____

_____

_____

When are you going to start? If not now, when?

_____

This is good Leadership! It takes humility to admit our mistakes and it takes a special dose of fortitude to allow God to use them in the lives of other men. I believe that God chooses to use these areas because of the fact that it takes humility, and humility is the key to unlocking God's power in you as Proverbs 15:33 makes clear, "…before honor comes humility." It takes a double dose of fortitude to allow God to use these areas to minister specifically to your children! Men, only God could do something like this! A defeat that haunts you is changed into a victory that moves you. Feeling a little dose of fear? Fortitude is the very virtue that you need to break the chains of fear.

Prayer: Lord Jesus thank you so much for sending me the Comforter when you went to be with the Father; for you knew in this life that is exactly what I would need. Father, I ask your forgiveness for and seek your comfort in _____.
Give me the strength to lead by example and serve your people with the same comfort that I have received from you. Thank you Lord for allowing me to serve You and my brothers with a defeat that you redeemed for as a victory by using _____
to lead and serve my brothers for your kingdom.

Eternal Perspective & Hope
"The *churning inside me never stops; days of suffering confront me*."
—Job 30:27

Do you know that if we lost a loved one who knew the Lord that he or she is the only one alive not contemplating, "Why?" Yes, you heard me—alive! If he or she is a child, the salvation found is secure in none other than God's benevolence.[107] If the child is past an age of accountability, then eternal life began here on earth when he or she received the payment of the Suffering Servant's death on the cross for his or her sins.[108] Because of this, he or she is more alive than any of us here today and that is why when we grieve, we must not grieve like those who have no hope.[109] We are to "encourage one another with these words"[110] knowing that in Christ we do not say "goodbye," but "I will see you later." Yes, we must grieve and receive comfort from God Himself and our fellow believers. Jesus knew that He was going to raise Lazarus from the dead yet still He wept at the loss of His friend.[111] We know that we will have the ultimate reunion with him or her[112] and see the Lord Jesus as clearly as he or she does today—face-to-face.[113]

Have you ever experienced suffering? Did your faith grow or falter—be honest? What role did hope or despair play in the process?

_____

_____

_____

1Thessalonians 4:13-14

[13] But we do not want you to be uninformed, brethren, about those who are asleep, so that you will not grieve as do the rest who have no hope. [14] For if we believe that Jesus died and rose again, even so God will bring with Him those who have fallen asleep [k]in Jesus.

Have you ever lost someone close to you? What do you remember?

_____

_____

_____

---

[107] Isaiah 7:16; 2Samuel 12:23; Psalm 139:14-16; Romans 5:18-19; John 9:41.
[108] John 3:16, 36; 5:24-26; 10:28; 17:2-4; Romans 6:23; 1John 5:11-20; Ephesians 1:11-14; 2:8-10.
[109] 1Thessalonians 4:13.
[110] 1Thessalonians 4:18.
[111] John 11:35.
[112] 1Thessalonians 4:14-17.
[113] 1John 3:2.

In July the Huffington Post had an article by Eleanor Goldberg titled, "Tombstone That Dad Designed For Son Who Had Disabilities Captures Boy's Tenacious Spirit"[114] This tombstone captures hope like no other. Art is powerful when it is used in its proper form of pointing to a reality. Matthew was eleven when he died and he was blind and paralyzed from the neck down from the time of his birth. Eleven years he lived in this condition and his parents took great care of him. Matthew's father said, "Instead of sadness, the statue makes our son Matthew's grave a place of happiness…Many others have found that true also."[115]

What do you think when you look at this picture?

_____

_____

_____

Memory Table: Commit the properties of hope to memory

Be a man of HOPE and not DESPAIR	
Freedom	Assurance
Contentment	Peace
Longsuffering	Perseverance
Trust	Confidence

---

[114] Eleanor Goldberg, "Tombstone That Dad Designed For Son Who Had Disabilities Captures Boy's Tenacious Spirit," *Huffington Post* 31 July 2014. http://www.huffingtonpost.com/2014/07/31/ability-found_n_5638567.html; Internet, accessed November 7, 2014.
[115] Ibid.

Conclusion

"Hope means expectancy when things are otherwise hopeless." – G.K. Chesterton

We began early on in the book with the creation and the Fall that changed our tendencies from the virtues toward the vices. The goal of this book was to introduce you to the only truly virtuous man who ever lived, then died on the cross reconciling our relationship with God and restoring our tendencies toward a virtuous life. In Him we have redemption, reconciliation with God, and a restoration of the image of God through Spirit enabled imitation as we become "men of virtue in a culture of vice." This reality enables us to walk in the Spirit by being men of action who strive toward the virtues. Now it is your turn to pass it on to other men through discipleship or small group. Studying the book again will move you from knowledge to understanding as the concepts presented pierce your heart. Some of the reviews on Amazon reveal this truth as many men share reading the book several times.

If you are a father, you can start with the boy-to-man ceremony using the Man's Ultimate Challenge coins built around the virtues. The coins are available at www.MansUltimateChallenge.org. If you are a man further along in your journey, take this book and work one-on-one in a discipleship or mentoring relationship with another man. If you are involved in your local church then gather some men to go through this book in a small group. I have a Man's Ultimate Challenge summary coin that includes all of the virtues on one coin for you to carry with you as a reminder. Commit to memory all of the properties or sub-virtues of each virtue listed in a table at the end of every chapter. The goal of this is to create 'hooks' in your mind as you process decisions daily in your own life and counsel other men on their journey. There is power in creating a common language among men as we challenge one another to be "men of virtue in a culture of vice."

Until He returns,

Peter P. Lackey, Jr.

APPENDIX A
AN EXERCISE FOR FATHERS & LEADERS

"It is easier to build strong children than repair broken men"
— Frederick Douglas

Symbols have been used throughout history as powerful reminders of something great and significant in history that needs to be remembered. Symbols are also used to symbolize a cause greater than ourselves that we live and fight for. For example, the American flag is a powerful symbol of freedom to those outside of the United States, but inside the United States Old Glory is the banner[116] representing our identity as Americans. To a US service member this flag and what it symbolizes is a cause worth fighting and dying for.

Sometimes a symbol that is meant to be derogatory to a particular group of people is embraced by that group as a motivation or clarion call for others to embrace their cause. This is the case for the cross, a symbol of shame that now Christians embrace as a symbol of God's love and acceptance. A more recent example of this occurred this past summer and involved the 14th letter of the Arabic alphabet pronounced "noon":

---

[116] One of the names of God is Jehovah Nissi and means The LORD is My Banner and is taken from Exodus 17:15 – And Moses built an alter, and named it The LORD is my Banner.

The terrorist group ISIS began marking Christians that they brutally murdered with this symbol that stands for Nasara or Nazarenes. Twitter was trending for several days with #WeAreN as Christians around the world began adding this symbol to their social media accounts as a show of solidarity for these persecuted brothers and sisters in Christ. The important point men is that symbols are always used to point beyond themselves to its substance or true significance.

Symbols are everywhere around us, on buildings, money, family items, etc.. Make a list of 10 symbols below.

1._____
2._____
3._____
4._____
5._____
6._____
7._____
8._____
9._____
10._____

Write down the name of some symbols from your own life that are meaningful to you and explain why.

_____
_____
_____

What do you remember when you see them?

_____
_____
_____

God has also used symbols in the lives of His people since the creation of the world. He gave Christians two powerful symbols to help a forgetful people remember the significance of the cross. He gave us baptism as an *event to remember*; an external symbol that serves as a reminder that we are identified with Christ when we accepted Him into our lives as our Lord and Savior. When we are dipped into the water during baptism, it symbolizes the death to our old self connected to the burial of Jesus, and when we come up out of the water, we are raised a new self identified with Jesus Christ's resurrection. Furthermore, this is a public declaration to the world that you are not your own, you were bought at a price,[117] and that price, Jesus on the cross, was the price of your adoption as a son of the living God. Additionally, God also gave us communion as *a continual reminder* of the body that was broken for us, and the blood that was shed for us as a covering for our sins.

Celtic Trinity Knot

If you already have a virtue summary coin with all 7 virtue symbols or if you have a set of Man's Ultimate Challenge coins,[118] you will notice that on the back of each challenge coin[119] an ancient Trinity knot. This is our unit symbol that serves to remind us that in God we find our true identity, and that we are not alone since many other men serve the same King under His banner. A unit symbol is just that, a symbol that represents a unit of men serving together and fighting the same cause, for the same purpose, and under the authority of the same banner.

In Exodus 17 Moses records how the Lord God fought the Amalekites on behalf of the Israelites against seemingly impossible odds. To commemorate this victory he built an alter and named it Jehovah Nissi which is translated "The Lord our Banner." We are to remember that God is our Banner and He fights on our behalf when

---

[117] Or do you not know that your body is a [a]temple of the Holy Spirit who is in you, whom you have from [b]God, and that you are not your own? 20For you have been bought with a price: therefore glorify God in your body. – 1 Corinthians 6:19-20

[118] You can purchase a set or a summary coin at www.MansUltimateChallenge.com

[119] To find out the fascinating military history of the challenge coin see my article at www.MansUltimateChallenge.com/backstory.

our hands are lifted up toward Him in total surrender to His authority. God is our unit commander and He has a very special role for you to play. And just like every unit commander He assigns His soldiers different tasks based on their gifts, talents, and role the Commander decides He uniquely needs him to fill.

It is critical that you get this point: there are no one-man units in existence in any military now, in the past, or will there be in the future. Why? Because we are not destined to fight any battle alone! Every battle is part of the same war with the same enemy and it dishonors God when we reject this reality. The word of God explains the power of a unit and contrasts that to the powerlessness of a man fighting alone:

Ecclesiastes 4:9,10-12

[10]Two are better than one because they have a good return for their labor. [11]For if either of them falls, the one will lift up his companion. But woe to the one who falls when there is not another to lift him up. [12]And if one can overpower him who is alone, two can resist him. A cord of three *strands* is not quickly torn apart.

This unit symbol not only reminds us that we are part of a unit, but in the case of Christianity it also informs us that we serve a God who is not a distant and detached Leader. Hebrews 4:15-16 states, [15]"For we do not have a high priest who cannot sympathize with our weaknesses, but One who has been tempted in all things as *we are, yet* without sin."

There are a few things that you will find in common on every one of the seven individual challenge coins. On the front you will find the Latin phrase *Semper Paratus* which is translated into English as "always ready." This phrase is to remind us that we are to always be ready for battle because being a man of virtue is a battle that is continuous, daily, and even every hour. 1 Peter 5:8 calls us to, "Be of sober spirit, be on the alert. Your adversary the devil prowls about like a roaring lion, seeking someone to devour."[120] Our duty is to not

---

[120] The Greek word used in this verse for adversary is *antifikos*, which references an opponent in a lawsuit. Satan will take the law of God, which is good in itself, and accuse you

be the "someone" whom gets devoured, and the only way that happens is when we choose to fight alongside other men and never alone.

Our military unit symbol is found on the back of each challenge coin and is the ancient Trinity knot. This unit symbol was chosen because we belong to the one true triune God who has His seal of ownership on us.[121] Christianity is unique in this claim of the one God whom exists not alone but in eternal relationship with each person of the Godhead: Father, Son, and Holy Spirit. For you men who love math, remember that this is not 1+1+1 but, mathematically, the Trinity is expressed as 1x1x1. In fact the very first time that aloneness ever existed in all of eternity was when God created Adam.

As God ended each day of creation He announced that "it was good" but after the creation of the very first man God announced that, "it was *very* good."[122] As man begins to explore his domain that his Creator gave him, he quickly comes to the conclusion that he is different from the other living things that God created. So, God announces in Genesis 2:18, "that it is *not good* for man to be alone." [123] Only another person who is also made in the image of God could cure this aloneness. Isn't it interesting that "going green," eating organic, and giving animals names only revealed this difference to Adam existentially?[124] But what are we doing today in our post-Christian western civilization? When people give up on human relationships today they try this failed formula and try to cure

by constantly reminding you of your failures and shortcomings. Never allow this to be a focus because your sin nature is why you needed a Savior! Remember God's grace when you feel accused and give thanks and praise to God for loving you, saving you, and most of all using you as a force for good in a world that rejects His gift.

[121] 2Corinthians 1:21-22 – Now He who established us with you in Christ and anointed us is God, who also set His *seal of ownership* in us and Gave us the Spirit in our hearts as a pledge. [emphasis added]
Ephesians 1:13 – In Him, you also, after hearing the message of truth the gospel of your salvation-having also believed you were *sealed* in Him with the Holy Spirit of promise, [emphasis added]
Ephesians 4:30 – And do not grieve the Holy Spirit of God, by whom you were *sealed* for the day of redemption. [emphasis added]

[122] Genesis 1:2-31.

[123] [emphasis added].

[124] This is a fancy way of saying that Adam learned this difference by experience in his existence along side these animals.

the experience of aloneness by becoming one with the earth and giving their pets human names.[125] God created us for more and we need other people in our lives, but not just any human being in this post-Fall world.

There is a band of brothers both locally and around the world whom all have this unit seal of ownership engraved on their hearts. This is encouraging because we are not alone in this battle and we are called to lead. In his book *The Leadership Engine: Building Leaders at Every Level* Noel Tichy recalls a story about a Navy SEAL who knows leadership because he shows leadership!

Recently in Cornodo, California, Rear Admiral Ray Smith, a Navy SEAL since the Vietnam War, visited a class of SEALs graduating from Basic Underwater Demolition SEAL Training. Only 20% of the candidates who enter this elite six-month program survive its great physical and mental demands to graduate. Throughout the day, Smith, in his fifties, participated in the same physical training as the SEAL candidates who were all in their twenties. At the end of the day, he met alone with the graduates. Speaking as a successful leader who had been exactly where they were, he laid out for them his teachable point of view on the leadership duties of becoming a SEAL, the conduct, honor and teamwork required, and the need for them to develop other leaders.[126]

Do you think these men listened to this leader at the end of the day? What an example this 50 year old Navy SEAL was to the young future leaders in their 20's! We have to look at every single man that we invest in as a future leader. There are two important leadership qualities that this Navy SEAL taught us that I want to highlight.

---

[125] Sadly, the father of the modern animal rights movement is Peter Singer, a utilitarian bioethics professor at Princeton University. In fact, he even has a slanderous politically correct term "specism" that he uses for those of us that believe that the human species is significantly different and deserving of more rights than other animals.
[126] Noel Tichy with Eli Cohen, *The Leadership Engine: Building Leaders at Every Level* (Dallas, TX: Pritchett, 1998), 2.

(1) Good Leaders Serve in The Trenches:

John 13:3-4

Jesus knew that the Father had put all things under his power, and that he had come from God and was returning to God; *⁴so he got up from the meal, took off his outer clothing, and wrapped a towel around his waist.* [emphasis mine]

A servant-leader knows that he learns the most by never being afraid to get into the trenches with his unit. The leader learns this lesson when he ponders the question, "Am I really humble enough to get my hands dirty and serve?" When answered correctly the leader **goes** and gains a sense of appreciation and empathy for what his team goes through on a day-to-day basis. In short, the leader is in touch with his team's reality and everyone who he serves knows it. One of my favorite leadership sayings is, "he who thinks he is leading and has no one following is merely taking a walk." It is much easier to lead when your hands and feet have the same stains as the men in your unit.

As a follower of Christ, we do all have the same stain—sin. As we learned in the previous chapters this can either negatively influence your leadership or positively influence your leadership; it all depends on your fuel. Is the Spirit or the flesh fueling you? When someone shares in your unit, do you stand above the trench and *look* and wonder how he got there? Or, do you *go* down into the trench with the cry of, "Me too! For I am as stained as you are, so let's get out of this together." As you can see the first response is fueled by the pride of the 'flesh' while the second response is fueled by the humility of the 'Spirit.' This leads us to the second leadership quality this Navy SEAL taught us.

(2) Good Leaders Step Down to Stay Up:

John 1:1-2; 14

In the beginning was the Word, and the Word was with God, and the Word was God. ²He was with God in the beginning…¹⁴*The Word became flesh and made his dwelling among us…* [emphasis mine]

A reachable leader is easily accessible to those whom he leads. No leader can influence his unit by maintaining a long distance relationship, for this is no relationship at all. God the Son gave this example as He left His heavenly throne and made Himself available to us in the flesh. If God in His position of ultimate authority can leave His throne and make Himself available[127], then should we not leave our "throne" and make ourselves available? This can be as simple as a father stepping down into the world of his son that has totally different interests than him so as to be an influence. For example, this is the father who is a complete sports nut and played certain sports his whole life who has a son God gave him that could care less about sports because God placed music and the arts in his heart. This father must step down into the world of the arts in order to stay up in the heart of his son as a man of influence. Or, you love music, the arts, and intellectual activity but God gives you a son who is a complete jock! Now what? Well Dad time to step down into the world of sports in order to stay up as a man of influence.

This "stepping down" can feel awkward as men sometimes and it has absolutely nothing to do with not wanting to step down and serve but with a sense of inadequacy. Nothing feels worse to a man than the feeling of cluelessness and having no idea what you are talking about. I know; amen! As you would expect God has an answer for this as well:

2Corinthians 3:5 – Not that we are adequate in ourselves to consider anything as coming from ourselves, but our adequacy is from God

Describe a time where you felt inadequate? Did you allow God in to help? How did He help?

---

[127] Philippians 2:4-7 – do not merely look out for your own personal interests, but also for the interests of others. 5Have this attitude in yourselves which was also in Christ Jesus 6who although He existed in the form of God did not regard equality with God a thing to be grasped, 7but emptied Himself, taking the form of a bond-servant, and being made in the likeness of men.

The Apostles were twelve ordinary men that God used to do extraordinary things. Yet these men went up against the most educated men in the ancient world who were educated into ignorance. C.S. Lewis notes that, "Anyone who is honestly trying to be a Christian will soon find his intelligence sharpened: one of the reasons why it needs no special education to be a Christian is that Christianity is an education itself."[128] God can never fill a cup that is already full!

Acts 4:13 – As they observed the confidence of Peter and John, and understood that *they were uneducated and untrained men*, they were marveling and began to recognize them as having been with Jesus.

Ah, we are back to identity! In a culture that worships the sheepskin[129] instead of the Shepherd, this is a hard saying indeed. We find yet another identity thief in your college alma mater if this is where you rest your sense of self-worth. I am as ordinary as they come and so are most of us no matter what our background. The secret is to be teachable so that you are reachable by God. I do this by praying for wisdom over everything that I want to learn and then thanking God for His promise to provide. I have had to get many certifications for work and I am 33 for 33 in passing tests by praying over every book I have to study. Yes, I have to do the work, but I partner with He who knows all things and gave me the job in the first place. I already had you practice this verse in Chapter 2 but the application is not limited to only Bible study so memorize this verse and use it in faith often. Notice that the virtue of faith is what breaks the chains of the vice of uncertainty.

James 1:5-7

But if any of you lacks wisdom let him ask God who gives to all men generously and without reproach and it will be given to him. [6]But let him ask in faith without any doubting for the one who doubts is like the surf of the sea driven and tossed by the wind.

---

[128] Lewis, C.S., *Mere Christianity*, (New York, NY: Touchstone, 1996), 75.
[129] Originally college degrees were printed on thin sheepskin instead of paper.

⁷For let not that man expect that he will receive anything from the Lord

Why is this especially difficult for men? It is because of the way we are wired as men who typically connect around a common interest or activity whereas women find any excuse to connect. Can you imagine a household of men getting together to look at baskets? A common interest or activity usually serves as a natural bridge point to begin building a healthy relationship with another man, especially a son. Well, men, we have a duty to build a bridge where one does not exist in order to get from where we are to where he is. It would be just like God to force a father to humble himself, while at the same time call him to enter into another creative part of His being and His creation. God wants to show you more of Himself through a son that reflects another aspect of God.

Semper Paratus Exercise

"Friendship is born at that moment when one person says to another "What? You too? I thought I was the only one" –C.S. Lewis

This exercise can be used as an individual study where you identify your interests and seek other men with those same interests or if you are discipling your son, you can either work together or ask him the questions below. If you are in a small group doing this study then try to step into your brother's world and you invite your brother into yours. Watch how much closer you become as you take this step and live life shoulder to shoulder. The key is discovering the connect points.

Proverbs 18:24 – A man of too many friends comes to ruin, But there is a friend who sticks closer than a brother.

1.   If working alone fill out one side. If you are a Dad, identify your interests below on the left and have your son identify his interests on the right. And yes gaming counts as an interest ☺ Write your name above your list.

Name: _____   **Name:** _____

_____   _____

_____   _____

_____   _____

2. Draw a line and connect existing bridge points of similar interests that you notice above (if any).

For Example:

_____Art_____ <----------> _____Art_____

_____Football_____ <---------->_____Football_____

3. Where there exist no natural bridge points for connecting, each person write down the most important interest below under your name:

Name: _____   **Name:** _____

_____   _____

_____   _____

_____   _____

4. Read the verses below and discuss what it means:

Proverbs 15:22 – Without consultation plans are frustrated, but with many counselors they succeed.

Proverbs 1:5 – A wise man will hear and increase in learning, And a man of understanding will acquire wise counsel

5. Unit Consultation: Time to apply the verse.

Dad, ask your son, "What advice do you have for me so that I can build a connection bridge to you in the area that is most important to you? Who do you recommend that I talk to get more information? Is there a website or a book that I can purchase? Write down the advice below.

_____

_____

_____

_____

_____

_____

_____

_____

_____

_____

_____

_____

6: TAKE ACTION AND START BUILDING THAT BRIDGE!

APPENDIX B
THE CANON: HOW WE GOT THE BIBLE

"For we did not follow cleverly devised tales when we made known to you the power and coming of our Lord Jesus Christ, but we were eyewitnesses of His majesty" – 2Peter 1:16

The 66 Books of the Bible are known as the 'canon' of scripture. The word 'canon' comes from a Greek word that means 'measuring stick.' Hence, the Bible is the measurer for what is truth and what is error. When the church formally recognized which books belonged in the canon, there were five primary tests that were applied to the books. While reading the questions below you will see that the church discovered what books belong in the canon. They didn't arbitrarily determine or pick which books belonged in the canon from a bunch of books. The thought by some that some books were thrown out because their ideas "lost the battle" falsely presupposes that all of the other so called gospels were equally valid, historically accurate, and thus worthy of consideration. Just because another story exists does not make it immediately valid, especially if the "gospel" is known to have been written hundreds of years after the historical events of Jesus' life. An example from our lifetime is the conspiracy story that the World Trade Center towers were destroyed by the US and not Islamic terrorists. The existence of this 'story' does not make it equal with known facts. Now imagine if this conspiracy story comes up 100-200 years from 9/11/2001 and this is what we have with the "Gnostic gospels."

From looking at the information provided above and reading the questions below you will in fact notice that the books were already determined for them. God determined the canonicity of the scripture by determining who would deliver His message. The messenger of God's message was confirmed to the people of God by miracles (Hebrews 2:2-4). Below is the test of canonicity formulated into 5 questions:

1. **Was the book written or backed by a prophet or apostle of God?**

2. **Is the book authoritative?**

3. **Does the book tell the truth about God and doctrine as it is already known by previous revelation?**

4. **Did the book come with the power of God?**

5. **Was the book accepted by the people of God?**

There were a number of ways for immediate contemporaries to confirm whether someone was a prophet of God. Some were confirmed supernaturally (Exodus 3–4; Acts 2:22; 2 Corinthians 12:12; Heb. 2:3–4). Sometimes this came as immediate confirmation of their authority over nature or the accuracy of their predictive prophecy. Indeed, false prophets were weeded out if their predictions did not come true (Deuteronomy 18:20–22). Alleged revelations that contradicted previously revealed truths were rejected as well (Deuteronomy 13:1–3).

Evidence that each prophet's contemporaries authenticated and added his books to a growing canon comes through citations from subsequent writings. Moses' writings are cited through the Old Testament, beginning with his immediate successor Joshua and continuing to be cited by kings and prophets (Joshua 1:7; 1 Kings 2:3; 2 Kings 14:6 ; 2 Chronicles 17:9; Ezra 3:2, 6:18, 7:6-11; Nehemiah 1:7-9, 13:1; Jeremiah 8:8; Malachi 4:4). Later prophets cite earlier ones (e.g., Jeremiah 26:18; Ezekiel 14:14, 20; Daniel 9:2; Jonah 2:2–9; Micah 4:1–3).

The Old Testament speaks of how the people of God knew what prophets fulfilled the biblical tests for God's representatives, and they legitimized them by accepting the writings as from God. For example, Moses' books were accepted immediately and stored in a holy place (Deuteronomy 31:26). Joshua's writing was immediately accepted and preserved along with Moses' Law (Joshua 24:26). Samuel added to the collection (1 Samuel 10:25). Daniel already had a copy of his prophetic contemporary Jeremiah (Daniel 9:2) and the law (Daniel 9:11, 13). Let's take a look at the New Testament.

New Testament Timeline:

- Jesus dies on the cross around AD 30 – 33. Nobody knows the date specifically because there is no number 0 that transitions the time BC and AD.

- Paul's Epistles written between AD 48 – 60

- Gospels written between AD 60 – 90

In his groundbreaking work on early Christian artifacts Larry Hurtado discovered that in the Leuven Database of Ancient Books [LDAB] 73% of all codices listed are Christian and of the 5% total of second century Christian manuscripts listed, an amazing 71% are codices. Codices are the early versions of a bound book form similar to books today. Christians overwhelmingly preferred the codex to the roll papyrus that was typically used but why? Hurtado concludes that "by the end of the second century (and perhaps earlier) Christians were seeking to place in one codex multiple texts, especially texts that they wished to link in common regard and usage as scripture." This is important because of how the New Testament was being formed as the church gathered the writings from the Apostles who were selected by Jesus Himself as His witnesses. Now take this newly discovered information from 2006 and add it to what we already know from history.

A brief history of the New Testament up until the death of the Apostles:

- Paul's letters collected into what was called the "Pauline Corpus." This collection contained all 13 Epistles and was passed around the different churches.

- The order in the Pauline corpus was the same as it is today, ordered by length.

-       The 4 Gospels stayed local and were gathered together and began to circulate as a fourfold record in the early second century (~100 AD)

In the New Testament the pattern established in the Old Testament continues. For example, the Bible speaks of sharing the Scripture with other churches (Colossians 4:16; 1 Thessalonians 5:27).   Also, Jesus promised his Apostles to communicate the scripture through them (John 14:26; 1:13). While the Apostles were writing they recognized this and identified the Holy Spirit as the source of the information, not themselves. (2 Timothy 3:16; 2 Peter 1:20-21; 1 Thessalonians 2:13) Additionally, the Apostles recognize one another's writing as coming from God. For example, Paul quotes Luke in 1 Timothy 5:17-18 [an exact quote from the Greek text] and Peter calls Paul's letters scripture in 2 Peter 3:15-16, also Peter quotes Matthew (2Peter 1:17), and finally Jude (4–12) cites 2 Peter. Interestingly Paul also hints that there may be letters in existence that are falsely attributed to the apostles. (2Thessalonians 2:2)

APPENDIX C
JESUS OUTSIDE THE BIBLE

"'The reader may rest assured that nothing has been found [by archaeologists] to disturb a reasonable faith, and nothing has been discovered which can disprove a single theological doctrine. We no longer trouble ourselves with attempts to 'harmonize' religion and science, or to 'prove' the Bible. The Bible can stand for itself." – Dr. William F. Albright, eminent archeologist who confirmed the authenticity of the Dead Sea Scrolls following their discovery"

Flavious Josephus (37-97 AD): Famous Jewish historian

"Now there was about this time Jesus, a wise man, if it be lawful to call him a man; for he was a doer of wonderful works, a teacher of such men as receive the truth with pleasure. He drew over to him both many Jews and many of the Gentiles. He was Christ. And when Pilate, at the suggestion of the principle men among us, had condemned him to the cross, those that loved him at first did not forsake him; for he appeared to them alive again the third day, as the divine prophets had foretold these and ten thousand other wonderful things concerning him. And the tribe of Christians, so named from him, are not extinct at this day." – Antiquities Book 18, Chapter 3 (3).

In addition he spoke of James the brother of Jesus who was called the Christ. –Antiquities Book 20, Chapter 9 (1).

Thallus (52 AD): Historian of Trojan Wars (Quoted by Julius Africanus)

In the 3rd book of Histories explains away the darkness after the crucifixion as an eclipse of the sun – "reasonably as it seems to me"

"On the whole world there pressed a most fearful darkness; and the rocks were rent by an earthquake, and many places in Judea and other districts were thrown down." This darkness Thallus, in the third book of his History, calls, as appears to me without reason, an eclipse of the sun.

Interestingly enough Julius Africanus objected to Thallus' rationalization concerning the darkness that fell over the land during the time of the crucifixion because an eclipse could not take place during the time of the full moon as was the case during the Jewish Passover season. As you can see, naturalistic interpretations of miraculous events are not new to college classes, History Channel, or other TV specials.

Question: If there are historical documents that explain away these events what does this say about the historicity of the events? Answer: They happened!!! Check it out.

Matthew 27:45-52 -Now from the sixth hour darkness fell upon all the land until the ninth hour. About the ninth hour Jesus cried out with a loud voice, saying, "ELI, ELI, LAMA SABACHTHANI?" that is, "MY GOD, MY GOD, WHY HAVE YOU FORSAKEN ME?" And some of those who were standing there, when they heard it, began saying, "This man is calling for Elijah." Immediately one of them ran, and taking a sponge, he filled it with sour wine and put it on a reed, and gave Him a drink. But the rest of them said, " Let us see whether Elijah will come to save Him." And Jesus cried out again with a loud voice, and yielded up His spirit. And behold, the veil of the temple was torn in two from top to bottom; and the earth shook and the rocks were split.

Mara bar Serapion (73AD)

He writes to his son about acting with wisdom to endure tyranny and gives examples of how the wise triumph over their oppressors . [What advantage did] the Jews gain by killing their wise king, because their kingdom was taken away at that very time? God justly repaid the Jews. They, desolate and driven from their own kingdom, are scattered through every nation. Yet their wise king [is not dead, for he lives in the] new laws he laid down. (paraphrased)

Phlegan (80 AD): Freed slave of Emperor Hadrian

"Jesus while alive was of no assistance to himself, but that He arose after death, and exhibited the marks of His punishment, and showed how His hands had been pierced by nails."

"The eclipse in the time of Tiberius Caesar, in whose reign Jesus appears to have been crucified, and the great earthquakes which then took place…"

Cornelius Tacitus (115 AD): A Famous Roman Historian who lived AD 55 - 120

"Consequently, to get rid of the report, Nero fastened the guilt and inflicted the most exquisite tortures on a class hated for their abominations, called Christians by the populace. Christus, from whom the name had its origin, suffered the extreme penalty during the reign of Tiberius at the hands of one of our procurators, Pontius Pilatus, and a most mischievous superstition, thus checked for the moment, again broke out not only in Judea, the first source of the evil, but even in Rome…"

From the above quote we can see an inference to the resurrection of Jesus Christ!

Good Resources:

Associates for Biblical Research: www.Biblearchaeology.org

Baker Encyclopedia of Christian Apologetics By: Dr. Norman Geisler

Jesus Outside the New Testament By: Robert Van Horst

APPENDIX D
PREPARING A CALL TO MANHOOD CEREMONY

"Be on the alert, stand firm in the faith, act like men, be strong."
1 Corinthians 16:13

I am a Christian apologetics geek who loves theology and philosophy, and there has been asleep inside of me an artistic side I inherited from my father. My son Jonah has this same artistic side along with a love of learning that I have. When this idea came to me for a meaningful, up to date, and timeless tool to use for Jonah's rite of passage ceremony I could not stop researching and designing. Amazing how God awakened this creativity and combined it with my love of theology and philosophy.

Man's Ultimate Challenge may have started as a ready made tool for fathers and mentors to use in the lives of younger men, but it grew into a tool that equips these same men for their own journey. Man's Ultimate Challenge uses US military challenge coins that I designed around the virtues and vices. Every symbol, color, and number has meaning traced all of the way back to antiquity. This book is meant to challenge men to:

1. be men of **Fortitude** and not **Fear**
2. be men of **Prudence** and not **Carelessness**
3. be men of **Temperance** and not **Gluttony**
4. be men of **Justice** and not **Injustice**

5. be men of **Faith** and not **Uncertainty**

6. be men of **Hope** and not **Despair**

7. be men of **Charity** and not **Indifference**

These virtues sit at the core of a man and give a man a meaningful target to shoot at! I want to place a powerful tool in the hands of men who are sick of the sin management approach to their walk with Christ and replace it with a hope filled call to live in Christ. I know men want to have Christ impact their lives in a meaningful way and then pass it on by making a significant difference in the lives of other men. This is especially true if you have sons, are a coach, teacher, pastor, or mentor! Most men want to do something, and some men feel an internal sense of duty that they "ought" to do something, but they have two problems: (1) What do I do? (2) How do I do it? The purpose of Man's Ultimate Challenge is to solve these 'what' and 'how' problems!

(For Fathers, Grandfathers, and Mentors)

At an event you organize, Man's Ultimate Challenge uses the military tradition of challenge coins as an event to remember to turn that "man" switch on that is at the center of all men. There are seven virtues and vices with a Challenge Coin for each one. A fascinating fact is that in the Bible seven is God's number for covenant and completeness. In some way I see these seven virtues as our "covenant of obedience to God" as a living sacrifice to Him who made us complete in Him. Each challenge coin has a symbol and a color that has been used for 2,000 years throughout history to represent the virtues in writings, on statues, shields, family crests, and code of arms.

Now don't miss this next point! There are many opportunities to challenge a man at any age and stage outside of a teenage "rite of passage" event that I mentioned. The key is to find a key transitional life stage to "flick the man switch." Here are some examples:

1. A Manhood Challenge after high school graduation and before college as your son steps out on his own for the very first time.

2. A Manhood Challenge upon graduation from college as your son steps out into the real world for the very first time.

3. A Manhood Challenge before marriage as your son steps out into this critical life stage where he will really need to man-up! (I had a friend do this and it was powerful!)

4. A Manhood Challenge as a mentor to a young man in your life as a man of influence such as a formal mentor, coach, grandfather, uncle, etc.

5. Discipleship challenge on what a Godly man looks like for new believers. (I came to Christ at 25 and if my first men's group would have done this I would have not only felt challenge to "man-up" but I would have been in tears)

In short, any major transition point in a man's life! It is NEVER too late to challenge a man who needs to be challenged!

How Does A Manhood Ceremony Work?

Before the ceremony: First of all you need to purchase a set of Man's Ultimate Challenge coins (see Figure-2) that are designed by me and made in the United States by a United States Marine. Second, you need to prepare at least one month before the Rite of Passage Ceremony or other challenge event. Where can you buy a set of coins? They are available at www.MansUltimateChallenge.com

Figure-2: 7 Individual Virtue Coins + 1 Summary Coin

Step #1: With the virtues and vices in mind, prayerfully select **7** men (one for each virtue) that best exemplify that virtue or have learned much from the grip of the corresponding vice. If you do not have 7 men then be creative. For example, you can have one man do the three theological virtues of faith, hope, and charity and link them together.

Avoid the temptation to include someone out of obligation! This day is about honoring your son, so be a God-pleaser rather than a people-pleaser. Leader, your challenge will not be one of the seven virtues but will focus on the source of his identity; i.e., from God and not others, which is, where the Trinity knot on the back of all seven coins comes in. More on that later.

Step #2: Select a place and time for the event. You can have this ceremony anywhere but make it a surprise! We had breakfast at an old-fashioned restaurant in a private room with a nice thick round table to symbolize that Jonah is now equal with us as a man. Some men have done it outside at a meaningful family place or during a man weekend. No matter where you choose to do the event the goal is to make him know that today is different and special. My son said to me on the day of his challenge, "Dad, I feel special today."

Step #3: Mail or hand deliver to the men who will be a part of the "Man's Ultimate Challenge" rite of passage ceremony these four things:

1. The challenge coin corresponding to the virtue that is his personal challenge to your son. The document you will send them has a picture that will suffice for their preparation. However, in order to ensure the coins make it to the event and provide them to the men as they arrive. You make the call.

2. The letter below with instructions. Personalize the letter template below and add any other details such as event location information, directions, dress code if any, etc.

Letter Template for example if a Father is challenging his son

Thanks for agreeing to speak into the life of _____

during his transition to manhood ceremony (or other title). _____ has his body transitioning by God's good design, but your job is to challenge him to transition his heart and soul because that is not automatic!

Attached is a document that explains what we are doing for him. This document has everything that you will need to include the details behind every symbol on each coin. We will be challenging him on the seven virtues. To better understand the virtues, I recommend looking at the vice because, as we all know, that feels "natural" to our fallen nature. I would like you to challenge my son on the virtue of _____. You are to talk about the front of your challenge coin but not the back, as that will be my job at the end as part of my challenging him on his identity. Your challenge is your challenge and no topic is off the table!! It just needs to be connected with the virtue and it's symbol and should be:

(a) Personal from you to him, for example:

- Have you seen some property of the virtue in him that you can use to encourage him?

- Is there someone in your life who modeled the virtue to you?

- Have you failed by allowing the corresponding "vice" of the virtue to grab hold of you? How did that teach you to value the virtue?

- Why is this virtue important to try to master now as a teenager or a young man in Christ? How will the choices he makes impact or shape the rest of his life?

- Do you have a personal story that he can take with him?

(b) Scriptural

- Is there a Bible verse that ties into your example that is meaningful to you and why? How have you seen this truth play out in real life?

In addition, please write out your challenge so that I can collect them for him to hold onto after the event. I will use this book and study the virtues with him throughout the year and I would love to refer to YOU and YOUR challenge to him when we get to your virtue.

You do not have to use any scripture or quotes that I provide on the slides. This is YOUR challenge to _____.

3. Either send the men a copy of this book or attach the document Mans Ultimate Challenge Event Virtue Details that can be found on my website www.MansUltimateChallenge.com. This document contains all of the details behind the virtue, sub-virtues, the corresponding vice, and the symbols represented on each coin. This is great background information and gives all men the same starting point. This book contains even more information and a deep study for personal growth and reflection for each man.

4. Give them a time limit! Have the men write down the challenge. Preferably one page but no more than two pages because every man has to take his turn! The reason for writing this down is twofold:

(a) Every man can have a focus so that he does not go over his allotted time. (figure 8 men total x 7 minutes = 56 minutes)

(b) Your son will have this personal challenge to keep with him forever. Dad, make a copy for yourself!

***Warning above: Inform each man that he is to speak about his specific virtue and vice along with ANYTHING on the front of the challenge coin, but not the back of the coin.

During the Rite of Passage Challenge Ceremony:

Step #4: Explain to your son why you are all gathered. Make it a big deal! Also, give a brief explanation of what a challenge coin is with a brief history that can be found on my website at: www.MansUltimateChallenge.com/backstory

Step #5: Have each man present his challenge coin and begin (5-7 minutes each)

The order of who goes before you does not matter. To start the challenge each man places his coin on the table or through a handshake as is the classical method. As the coin is presented, each man begins with the phrase "_____ my challenge to you is to be a man of (name the virtue) and not (name the vice)." For example, "Jonah, my challenge to you is to be a man of FAITH and not UNCERTAINTY."

Step #6: YOU, the leader, will challenge your son (or man who you are disciplining/mentoring) on where he must get his identity and sense of belonging—God! This is represented by the Trinity knot unit symbol on the back of ALL 7 challenge coins. A man of virtue must get his identity form God and not from his degree, job, team, or club that he belongs to. These may be important but must never be central to who one really is as a man. On the more negative side of identity, we must never allow our true identity to be stolen. There are identity thieves everywhere that want to rob us of our true selves by calling us to label ourselves by our sin, temptations, failures, or the color of our skin. MultiCULTuralism wants us to place ourselves into separate little cults by making our primary identity the color of our skin, which a man of God must never do.

Have your son flip over every coin and present him the Summary Coin (has all 7 virtue symbols on it)

What is great about this program is that this is not "canned" because every man will take the truths of these virtues and personalize it with their own life story. My job is to provide the truth as taught in the sacred scriptures and throughout antiquity, your job is to apply it. The coins can be purchased through my website at www.MansUltimateChallenge.com and come shipped with details about the coins, virtues and meaning behind the symbols. These details, along with this step-by-step "how to" can also be accessed through the website.

You have the book, you have the coin, and you need the challenge. Are you ready?

Galatians 5:15-16 — Therefore be careful how you walk, not as unwise men but as wise, making the most of your time, because the days are evil"

BIBLIOGRAPHY

Aquinas, Thomas. Summa Theologica.

Baron, Robert A. Essentials of Psychology, 3d ed. Needham Heights, Massachusetts: Allyn & Bacon, 2002.

Carter, Les. The Anger Trap. San Francisco, CA: Jossey-Bass, 2003.

Geisler, Norman. Systematic Theology Volume three. Bloomington, MN: Bethany House, 2004.

Kreeft, Peter. Back to Virtue. San Francisco, CA: Ignatius Press, 1992.

Lewis, C.S. Mere Christianity. New York, NY: HarperCollins, 1952/2001.

MacArthur, John. The MacArthur Bible Commentary. Nashville, TN: Thomas Nelson, 2005.

Moreland, J.P. & Craig, William Lane. Philosophical Foundations for a Christian Worldview. Downers Grove, IL: InterVarsity Press, 2003.

Moreland, J. P. The Lost Virtue of Happiness: Discovering the Disciplines of the Good Life. Colorado Springs, CO: NavPress, 2006.

Moreland, J.P. Love Your God With All Your Mind. Colorado Springs, CO: NavPress, 1997.

Phillips, Bob. Overcoming Anxiety & Depression. Eugene, Or: Harvest House, 2007.

Sire, James W. The Universe Next Door 4th ed. Downers Grove IL: InterVarsity Press, 2004.

Warren, Rick. The Purpose Driven Life: What On Earth AM I Here For? Exp. Ed. Grand Rapids, Mi: Zondervan, 2012.

Zacharias, Ravi. Sense and Sensualtiy: Jesus Talks to Oscar Wilde on the Pursuit of Pleasure. Colorado Springs, CO: Multnomah, 2006.

ABOUT THE AUTHOR

Since accepting Christ in 1995, Pete Lackey has dedicated his life answering questions that serve as true barriers to the knowledge of Jesus Christ. He has built an impressive research library over the years to equip himself and others with topics spanning philosophy, science, various world religions, and the mysterious worlds of the cult and the occult. His specific specialty is comparing and contrasting different belief systems with the Christian worldview in order to demonstrate why Christianity is true. Pete has taught on these topics in numerous venues around the Washington D.C. metropolitan area.

Pete attended Southern Evangelical Seminary and served on staff at McLean Bible Church for seven years as the Director of Marriage & Family and as the Director of Preparing for Marriage where he taught with his wife of over 18 years. Both he and his wife as adult children of divorced parents bring a unique passion and perspective on the importance of a strong marriage built around a Christian worldview.

Pete has been part of the McLean Bible Church family for over 18 years and has earned the reputation as the man to come to when it comes to questions of the faith. With his library, passion, and experience answering questions, he will either have the answer or know where to go to get the answer to your questions. Moreover, he skillfully knows how to get to the real question behind the question. Pete believes that only the Christian worldview provides truly satisfying answers to the deep questions of every human heart; questions of origins, meaning, destiny, and purpose.

Pete Lackey is the Founder of "Man's Ultimate Challenge" a ministry that equips Fathers with a powerful up-to-date rite-of-passage tool to strategically call his son into authentic manhood. He lives with his wife and three children in Northern Virginia.

Made in the USA
Charleston, SC
23 October 2016